SYRIANUS

On Aristotle

Metaphysics 13-14

SYRIANUS
On Aristotle
Metaphysics 13-14

Translated by
John Dillon and Dominic O'Meara

Duckworth

Ancient Commentators on Aristotle
General Editor: Richard Sorabji

First published in 2006 by
Gerald Duckworth & Co. Ltd.
90-93 Cowcross Street, London EC1M 6BF
Tel: 020 7490 7300
Fax: 020 7490 0080
inquiries@duckworth-publishers.co.uk
www.ducknet.co.uk

A catalogue record for this book is available
from the British Library

ISBN 0 7156 3574 3
EAN 9780715635742

Acknowledgements

The present translations have been made possible by generous and imaginative funding from the following sources: the National Endowment for the Humanities, Division of Research Programs, an independent federal agency of the USA; the Leverhulme Trust; the British Academy; the Jowett Copyright Trustees; the Royal Society (UK); Centro Internazionale A. Beltrame di Storia dello Spazio e del Tempo (Padua); Mario Mignucci; Liverpool University; the Leventis Foundation; the Arts and Humanities Research Council; Gresham College; the Esmée Fairbairn Charitable Trust; the Henry Brown Trust; Mr and Mrs N. Egon; the Netherlands Organisation for Scientific Research (NWO/GW). The editor wishes to thank Edward Hussey, Terrence Irwin, Ian Mueller, John Cleary, and Lloyd Gerson for their comments, Michael Griffin for preparing the volume for press, and Deborah Blake at Duckworth, who has been the publisher responsible for every volume since the first.

Typeset by Ray Davies
Printed in Great Britain by
Biddles Ltd, King's Lynn, Norfolk

Contents

Conventions

[...] Square brackets enclose words or phrases that have been added to the translation or the lemmata for purposes of clarity, as well as those portions of the lemmata which are not quoted by Syrianus.

<...> Angle brackets enclose conjectures relating to the Greek text, i.e. additions to the transmitted text deriving from parallel sources and editorial conjecture, and transposition of words or phrases. Accompanying notes provide further details.

(...) Round brackets, besides being used for ordinary parentheses, contain transliterated Greek words and Bekker pages references to the Aristotelian text.

{...} Braces contain words which the editors regard as added later to the text that Syrianus wrote.

Introduction

1. Life and works

Of the life of Syrianus few details are preserved to us.[1] We can deduce from a surviving fragment of Damascius' *Philosophical History* (§56 Athanassiadi) that he was from Alexandria,[2] and since he died in or around 437 at an advanced age, we may assume a birth-date of approximately 375 AD. Son of a certain Philoxenus, he, no doubt after studies in rhetoric and the other 'preliminary sciences' in Alexandria (of which he exhibits many traces throughout his surviving works), made his way to Athens, and became a pupil, and ultimately the designated successor, of the distinguished Neoplatonist philosopher Plutarchus, son of Nestorius, head of the Athenian Academy in the early decades of the fifth century. We may imagine him making this move at some time around the turn of the century – even as his most famous pupil, Proclus, did some thirty years later.

Damascius, in a possibly idealising vein, describes him (§47 Athanassiadi) as 'tall and good-looking, and possessing a health and strength which lacked no general or particular natural qualities'. We acquire a sort of snap-shot of him (though very much at second-hand) in late middle age from Marinus (*VP* 11-12), when Proclus arrives in Athens in 431. Proclus finds his way to Syrianus' house, which is also the seat of the school, situated just to the south of the Acropolis, not far from the Theatre of Dionysus. Syrianus is at home, in the company of his senior assistant Lachares, and they receive the young Proclus, initially with some caution, as one could not be certain, in those troublous times for Hellenes, where a new visitor's religious allegiances might lie. They were greatly reassured, however, to observe Proclus, as he left them, saluting the Moon, and agreed that he should be accepted into the school.

At this stage, Syrianus had already virtually assumed control of the school, as Plutarchus was by now very old and doing very little teaching (though he did take on the young Proclus, to read Aristotle's *De Anima*, and the *Phaedo*), but within a year or so Plutarchus died, and Syrianus formally succeeded him. He himself, however, only lasted in the post another five years or so, dying not long after 437 AD. At any rate, Proclus, who is reported by Marinus (*VP* 13) to have produced his *Timaeus Commentary* 'in his twenty-eighth year', that is to say, 438 or 440 (depending on whether[1] we assume him to have been born in 410 or 412), speaks of his Master in the past tense (while also freely acknowledging how much his exegesis owes to his instruction). We also have the story in Marinus, no doubt relayed from Proclus himself, that Syrianus, in his old age, offered Proclus and his fellow-student Domninus a choice of a seminar on the Chaldaean Oracles or the Orphic Poems, but, while the two of them were still haggling over this agonising choice, the old man died.

It is remarkable, in view of the relative shortness of the period of their association, how deeply Syrianus influenced Proclus, both spiritually and intellectually.[3] Syrianus was buried in a tomb on the slopes of Lycabettus, and, nearly fifty years later, in 485, when Proclus came to die, he asked to be buried in the same tomb (Marinus, *VP* 36).

Was Syrianus married? Marinus gives no indication that he was. Damascius speaks of his pupil Hermeias marrying his relative (*prosêkousa genei tôi megalôi Syrianôi*) Aedesia, which proves nothing; but the Syrianus who composes the *Commentary on Hermogenes* dedicates it to his 'son' Alexander.[4] This has caused some confusion, leading certain scholars to doubt whether the *Commentary on Hermogenes* is by 'our' Syrianus at all, but there is no serious linguistic or doctrinal reason to doubt this (though there is in truth very little philosophy evident in the work), so that we must either accept that Syrianus was indeed married, or resolve to take the 'sonship' of Alexander in some metaphorical sense – a favourite pupil, perhaps.

This brings us, at any rate, to the question of Syrianus' *oeuvre*. Unlike his famous pupil Proclus, Syrianus was not a prolific writer. He is credited in the *Suda* (s.v.) with a number of works:

A *Commentary on Homer*, 7 books
On the Republic of Plato, 4 books
On the Theology of Orpheus, 2 books
On the Gods in Homer
Concordance of Orpheus, Pythagoras and Plato
On the [*Chaldaean*] *Oracles*, 10 books
– and certain other works of commentary (*kai alla tina exêgêtika*).

Under this latter rubric we may perhaps include, besides the present work, and a short commentary on Aristotle's *Categories* attested to by Simplicius,[5] commentaries at least on Plato's *Timaeus* and *Parmenides*, since there is ample evidence of exegesis by him of both those dialogues in the commentaries of Proclus,[6] but there remains the disquieting possibility that Syrianus' views, as reported by Proclus, were merely orally delivered.[7] However, we do have evidence of a work of commentary on the *Republic*, which certainly formed the basis for Proclus' views on that dialogue,[8] so we may probably credit him with written commentaries on these important dialogues also.[9] It must also be said, however, that works with the same titles as those listed here are also credited by the *Suda* to

Proclus, in the entry under his name, so there remains the possibility that all of the above works were at least edited by Proclus, perhaps only from Syrianus' lectures.

At all events, it is evident to one who makes the effort to translate him that composition did not come easily to Syrianus. His writing is a good deal more crabbed than that of Proclus, and it is on occasion not easy to grasp his meaning – and this despite his (presumed) familiarity with rhetorical theory. However, a certain liveliness is injected into the text by the degree of polemic against Aristotle in which he indulges, at least in his commentary on these two books, a topic to which section 4 of this Introduction is devoted – though this too can pose its own problems of translation, as one strives to strike the right note.

As regards the *Metaphysics* itself, it seems that, while Syrianus doubtless commented orally on the whole work in the course of taking his students through the works of Aristotle, he confined his written comments to certain books in which he had a particular interest, or rather, perhaps, which he deemed to require special attention from a Platonist. His particular reasons for choosing Books 3 and 4 may most properly be treated in the introduction to the translation of those books, but in the case of Books 13 and 14, the stimulus is plainly their strongly polemical nature. Aristotle is, after all, in these books, striking at the core of the Pythagorean-Platonic world-view, and Syrianus, admiring though he is of Aristotle's intellectual power,[10] and committed as he is in general to the doctrine of the 'harmony of Plato and Aristotle',[11] is not going to let him get away with this.[12]

2. Syrianus' philosophy of mathematics

Syrianus' treatment of mathematical number is different from his treatment of divine number.[13] It has been very well described by Ian Mueller, 'Syrianus and the concept of mathematical number', in G. Bechtle, D. O'Meara, eds, *La philosophie des mathématiques de l'antiquité tardive*, Fribourg 1998, 71-83, and the following summary supplied by Richard Sorabji is based on Mueller's article.

Euclid had defined mathematical number as a multiplicity of units, *Elements* 7, def. 2. But Syrianus makes these units or 'monads' merely the *matter* or *substratum* of number, on which we have to impose, as form, the triad, pentad, heptad, ennead, etc., that we carry in our souls (133,4-5; 10-12). Only so can the units compose three, five, seven or nine; they are not number otherwise (152,8-10). There is only one triad, just as we nowadays think there is only one number, three. In an ennead, there are not three triads, but the one triad taken three times (134,5-20; 135,16-136,17). Addition, division and multiplication apply to the substratum only (133,4-15; 134,5-20). This answers some of the problems that Socrates expressed about addition and division in *Phaedo* 96E6-97B3, before resorting to the theory of Forms as a solution. Because the triad, etc., are innate in our souls, arithmetical knowledge is innate in all humans (133,14).

The triad or pentad in our soul is itself a unit which owes its unity to having proceeded in its turn from a still higher unit outside the soul in the intelligible world (132,8-14; 135,16-32).

The five units or 'monads' that compose five owe their multiplicity to what Plato called the indefinite dyad (132, 8-14). This indefinite dyad is also in our souls (132,14-20), and it is a kind of matter, dianoetic matter, or the matter of thought (133,14-15).

Within our souls there are two kinds of mathematical number (88,7-9; 123,19-20. One is the monadic number made up of units, the other is the substantial *logos*, the essential concept of a given number, which corresponds to form.

Different again from his treatment of mathematical number is Syrianus' treatment of geometrical entities.[14] He rejects the view of Aristotle that geometrical figures are *abstracted* (*aphairein*) by us from perceptible figures in the sensible world. In order to think of a triangle, Aristotle supposes that we make use of triangular objects in the sensible world, but ignore their irrelevant features. Geometrical triangles exist potentially within physical objects, but they need to be actualised by our mental processes. In order to think of a geometrical figure, we have to ignore far more than we do when thinking of a physical object: we have to ignore the matter in which it is embedded, e.g. *Physics* 2.2, *Metaphysics* 6.1. The figures come to be located within the sensible forms which in perception we receive, *On the Soul* 3.8, 432a4-6, and we think them within images (*phantasmata*), *On the Soul* 3.7, 431b2, so that the intellect is the place of these forms, in which it receives them, *On the Soul* 3.4, 429a15; a27. The most graphic description of the thought process is given in *On Memory* 1, 449b30-450a7. We put before the mind's eye an image of a triangle, but ignore its irrelevant features.

Syrianus has a telling line of objection. He complains that we do not see every shape, and that the shapes we do see are not precise. If it be replied that they could be made precise, he has a very good answer: how would we know what changes to make except through our possessing precise concepts recollected in Plato's way from before birth (95,29-38)? The same question could have been asked about how we know which features of our image to ignore. Syrianus' questions were to be repeated by Proclus, Simplicius and Olympiodorus. Aristotle could have cited as the source of precision the active intellect which in *On the Soul* 3.5 he regards as thinking uninterruptedly within us. But this would be to abandon his whole enterprise of giving an empirical account of how we can think of geometrical figures.

Syrianus' rival view is that our minds contain geometrical *logoi* or concepts gained from pre-natal acquaintance with the Platonic Forms. It is these Platonic concepts that can, because of their accuracy, be used to correct the inexact Aristotelian form residing in sensibles, 95,29-36. These concepts are not spread out, but we project (*proballesthai*) them onto the screen of the imagination where they come to be spread out. The geometrical figures in the imagination are said, 91,29-34, to be parasitic (*parhuphistasthai*) on the concepts in the mind. Geometers, in his view, would prefer to study the undivided concepts themselves, but through weakness are forced to study the concepts in their images. This theory too is repeated by Proclus and ps.-Simplicius (= Priscian?). But at *in DA* 233,12 and 277,1-6, ps.-Simplicius ascribes the theory of projection in mathematics to the Pythagoreans. So although Porphyry already uses the term 'projection', it may have been introduced into *geometry* by Iamblichus, who sought to integrate Pythagorean philosophy with Platonic. Syrianus at 186,17-19 ascribes to Plato the simpler idea that the objects of geometry reside in the imagination, but not the idea of projection.

It is fortunately not necessary for the understanding of Syrianus' philosophical position in this commentary to enter into a full exposition of the complexities of his metaphysics in its most developed form, as discernible from references in such works as Proclus' commentaries on the *Timaeus* and the *Parmenides*, and his *Platonic Theology*, since Syrianus does not choose to unveil any more of it here than is appropriate to the defence of the mathematical doctrines of the ancient Platonists and Pythagoreans, which he discerns as being under attack from Aristotle in these two books.[15]

For the purpose of dealing with Aristotle, Syrianus is content to expound a system (which he loyally fathers upon 'the Pythagoreans', or 'the men of old', but which owes its origins to much more recent sources, notably Iamblichus)[16] involving a supreme One (implicitly, but not explicitly, above Being), which presides over a pair of principles, Limit (*peras*), or the Monad (*monas*), and Unlimitedness (*apeiria*), or the Indefinite Dyad (*aoristos duas*). In terms of Iamblichean metaphysics, this pair would constitute the lowest level of the henadic realm, and their product, the so-called *mikton* ('mixed entity'), or *hênômenon* ('the Unified'), can be taken as the sum-total of the henads, or archetypes of the Forms, which constitute the contents of the realm of Intellect.

Here, however, since Syrianus is primarily concerned with the nature of Number, it is the Form-numbers which are presented as the first products of the union of the Monad and Dyad. There is a significant passage at p. 112,14ff. (Kroll), where, in the process of confuting Aristotle's malevolent jibes, he expounds the Pythagorean doctrine at some length:

Now these men claimed that, after the single first principle of all things, which they were pleased to term the Good and the supraessential One, there were two principles of everything, the Monad and the Dyad of infinite potency (*apeirodunamos*), and they apportioned these principles at each level of being in the mode proper to each. For there is an element analogous to the Good in each realm of being, and likewise entities assimilated to the primary Monad and Dyad.

Then, after some criticism of Aristotle, he continues with his exposition (112,31ff.):

> We say, then, that the nature of principles is quite distinct from that of Forms, even if some connection of an homonymous nature should supervene in their regard, or rather, not in respect of them themselves (for how could anything supervene upon the most divine of beings?), but in respect of our treatment of them. For a start, the Dyad *qua* principle is the author for all things of generative power and procession and multiplicity (*plêthos*) and multiplication (*pollaplasiasmos*), and rouses up all things and stirs them to the generation of and forethought for and care of what is secondary to them, and further fills all the divine and intellective and psychic and natural and sensible realms (*diakosmoi*) with the numbers proper to them; and it does not grant that anything whatever is ungenerated of those things which are of a nature to come into existence. The Essential Dyad, for example, confers its own form on all things, whether souls or natures or bodies; so that if the whole world is divided in two, or only the heavens, or the reason-principles of the soul, or, prior to the reason-principles, the circles (for these are the first participants to be affected by the division into two), or some particular living thing that has two eyes or hands or feet, or some other physical attribute, possesses throughout all of itself, along with its own Form, also the Dyad, we will say that this feature is present to them from no other ultimate cause than the Essential Dyad, which is on the one hand first among all the biform entities among the Forms and their cause, but is not for this reason the archetypal Dyad, by which both it and the whole of Intellect is generated. And we say the same about the Monad; for there is a distinction between the archetypal Monad which, together with the Dyad, is the cause of existence to all things, bestowing upon everything self-identity and stability and coherence and eternal life, and the Essential Monad which holds first place of honour among the Forms, by participation in which all things which have been given form enjoy unity and are held together by the principle of coherence (*hexis*) proper to them.

The Dyad, then, is responsible for all multiplicity and individuation in the universe, beginning with the succession of natural numbers, while the Monad imposes Form and individuating qualities on things.

The first product, however, of this pair of principles, as has been said, is the sequence of Form-numbers, which are in one way infinite, but in another may be consummated in the Decad, as comprising all the basic relationships and ratios between numbers, out of which all others may be constructed. We find a significant passage on this at p. 150,4ff.:

> That every type of proportion (*analogia*) should be exhibited within

the Decad is obvious enough; for arithmetical proportion occurs in the natural progression of numbers, while geometrical is to be seen in 1, 2, 4, and 1, 3, 9, and the harmonic in 2, 3, 6 and 3, 4, 6. All things, then, he (sc. Aristotle) says, they attributed to the first principles, that is to say to the Monad and the Dyad, Rest and Good to the Monad, Motion and Evil to the Dyad. They could indeed give the title of first principles also to the two columns of opposites (*sustoikhiai*) in the numbers up to ten, and very aptly so, since even among real beings some depend on the first principles alone, the single One and the pair following upon it, while others have taken on also a formal cause. Why this should be, though, is a rather long story.

The core of the Decad, in turn, is the so-called *tetraktus*, the sequence of the first four numbers, the total of which in fact makes up the Decad. The first four numbers may also be viewed as the archetypes, and generative causes, of the four geometrical elements, point, line, plane and solid, as he reminds us just below (150,27ff.). And so a universe begins to take shape.

We do not need to pursue that process any further on this occasion, since Syrianus is not here concerned with the generation of the Soul or of the physical world, but we do need to say something more about the distinctions that Syrianus would make between various levels of number, since that can be a cause of some confusion, and does involve certain difficulties of translation.

First of all we have, as has been seen, a supreme One, which may also be termed the Good, and then a pair of Monad and Dyad. These, despite Aristotle's efforts to muddy the waters, are not to be regarded as numbers at all, but rather 'principles' (*arkhai*). Their immediate products, however, are, not 'ordinary', monadic or unitary numbers, which are addible to one another (*sumblêtoi*), and composed of undifferentiated units (*monadikoi*), but rather the Form-numbers, which must be regarded rather as 'what it is to be Two, or Three, or Seven', are not addible (*asumblêtoi*), and are not composed of undifferentiated units that can be added to or subtracted from them. Such intelligible numbers, which are also Forms, are creative principles in the universe, and are themselves real essences.

It is this sort of number that attracts a good deal of Aristotle's fire in Books 13 and 14, and it is, correspondingly, Syrianus' concern to defend its existence, and indeed necessity, and to distinguish it from ordinary numbers, which he accepts as inherent in physical things, and supervenient on them – 'later-born' (*husterogeneis*), as he terms them. For Aristotle, however, these are the only meaningful type of number. In consequence, we are faced, for much of the commentary, not with any meeting of minds, but rather with a sensation of ships passing in the night, hooting at one another obscurely and menacingly through the murk. Aristotle, on his part, is not concerned to give a scholarly or fair-minded account of the Platonist position, because he regards it as inherently absurd, and worthy only of demolition by any device of satire or rhetorical distortion he can muster. Syrianus, in response, adopts a tone of lofty condescension in face of Aristotle's inability or unwillingness to comprehend the higher reaches of Pythagorean mathematical theory, and devotes a good deal of the commentary to trying to set him right on these questions. The result is a highly anomalous Neoplatonic commentary, the nature of which we will explore somewhat further in the fourth section of this Introduction. First, however, we must deal with another troublesome question.

3. Syrianus, Alexander and ps.-Alexander

A conspicuous feature of Syrianus' commentary on Books 13 and 14 is the numerous parallels, often *verbatim*, though on occasion exhibiting a degree of summarising,[17] between Syrianus and the extant commentary on Books 6-14 of the *Metaphysics* that has come down to us in the manuscripts under the name of Alexander of Aphrodisias, but which is universally agreed not to be from his hand. Over the identity of the author, and the relations between him and Syrianus, controversy has long raged, a controversy on which, unfortunately, no unassailable conclusions have been reached, but on which no editor or translator of Syrianus' work can avoid taking some note.

In particular, in recent times a lively contest has been joined on this topic between Leonardo Tarán[18] and Concetta Luna,[19] the former maintaining that Syrianus is dependent on ps.-Alexander, who must therefore be an author of the period between Alexander himself and Syrianus, and thus, most probably, of the fourth century AD; while Luna supports the view of many previous scholars, and most notably Karl Praechter,[20] that the author is none other than Michael of Ephesus, the early twelfth century Byzantine commentator and member of the intellectual circle of Anna Comnena.[21]

The question is of some importance to decide, since, as Luna herself points out (op. cit., p. 1), Syrianus makes considerable use of some source, whatever that may be, for what may be termed the non-controversial parts of his exegesis of Aristotle's text in Books 13 and 14, normally at the beginning of his comment on a given lemma. Of 3023 lines of his commentary on Book 13 in the Berlin edition, there are 247 lines in common with ps.-Alexander, while for the commentary on Book 14 the figures are 97 lines out of 1040 (one eleventh and one sixteenth of the whole respectively). In face of this phenomenon, a number of alternative solutions can be advanced:

(1) Syrianus is dependent on ps.-Alexander.
(2) Ps.-Alexander is dependent on Syrianus.
(3) Both Syrianus and ps.-Alexander depend on a common source.

Tarán's claim is, as stated above, that Syrianus is dependent on ps.-Alexander. His chief argument for this is that both Syrianus and the author commit a number of errors in the interpretation of Aristotle's text that could not be imputed to the real Alexander, and that Syrianus must be relying on ps.-Alexander rather than the other way about. To take one notable example, at p. 777,11-21 of his commentary (which corresponds to p. 154,5-13 of Syrianus' commentary), commenting on *Met.* 13, 1085a9-14, ps.-Alexander imputes to Plato the doctrine connecting the numbers 2, 3 and 4 with line, plane and solid respectively, and that according to which it is the Forms, by participation in the One, that produce the magnitudes to another, unidentified, Platonist, whereas earlier, in a comment on *Met.* 3, 1001b19-25, the real Alexander, at p. 228,10-28, has (correctly) identified the former of these doctrines with Xenocrates and the latter with Plato. This, and a few other less striking passages, lead Tarán to conclude (1) that ps.-Alexander, *without access to the genuine commentary of Alexander on Books 6-14*, composed his own commentary, which he then dishonestly attributed to Alexander; and (2) that Syrianus, coming upon this forged commentary, made use of it in place of the genuine commentary, which must not have been any longer available in his day.

In response to this, Luna (pp. 39-42) suggests that, since Alexander's attribution of the two doctrines may have been somewhat obscured by his adducing also of the evidence of the *Peri Philosophias*, and the question was not in any case of great importance to Syrianus, the latter may simply have got them round the wrong way. Luna, however, can the more easily suppose this because she has convinced herself that ps.-Alexander, whom she identifies, very plausibly, on the basis of numerous linguistic concordances,[22] with Michael of Ephesus, is actually making use of Syrianus, rather than of Alexander himself. This assumption, however, though not impossible – if Syrianus is available to us (through a fourteenth-century MS), he was in principle available also to Michael – I find implausible and unnecessary.

Two arguments in favour of this theory which she adduces seem less than compelling. The first concerns the alleged utilisation by Michael of a passage of Syrianus in which the latter quotes Iamblichus, in the fifth book of his *Summary of Pythagorean Doctrines*,[23] on the subject of the void, and in particular on the question of there being a *paradeigma tou kenou* among the numbers, or indeed anywhere among real beings. This Iamblichus denies, and Syrianus' agrees with him. Michael, on the other hand, as Luna admits (pp. 5-6), while using the expression, asserts that there is such a paradigm of void among the numbers (771,22ff.). The flaw in the argument, however, is that there is no reason to suppose that this turn of phrase was in any way distinctive of Iamblichus. Syrianus employs it independently of adducing the authority of Iamblichus in support of the doctrine, so that the actual phrase may perfectly well have been used by Alexander as well, whence Michael can have derived it. The same applies to a parallel passage mentioning the Orphic poems (Syr. *in Met.* 182,9-28/ ps.-Alex. 821,5-21): there is really no reason why Alexander could not be familiar with an Orphic cosmogony.[24]

As against these alleged dependences, we have the overwhelming fact that Michael lacks entirely any trace of Syrianus' distinctive polemical purpose and material (for which see the next section). His only purpose is to elucidate Aristotle, without a trace of the righteous Platonic/Pythagorean indignation that animates Syrianus. In order to do that, he quite shamelessly borrows from the commentary of Alexander, which was available to him, as it had been six centuries previously to Syrianus, but not to us; and he borrowed so successfully that, at some later stage in the tradition – some time after his composition of the commentary in the late eleventh or early twelfth century, but some time before the transcription of the earliest extant MS, A (Par. gr. 1876), of the thirteenth century – the commentary supplanted that of Alexander, and was attributed to him (apart from the stray scholion mentioned above, n. 18).

There is one other curious little piece of evidence bearing on this that has been used in favour of the attribution to Michael, but in which Leonardo Tarán quite rightly detects a flaw. The flaw does not, however, I think, point to the conclusion which he would draw from it. There is a passage in one of Michael's works, his commentary on the *Parva Naturalia*,[25] which runs as follows:

> The treatises *On the Parts of Animals* and *On the Gait of Animals*, and further those *On Memory and Recollection*, *On the Movement of Animals*, and *On the Generation of Animals*, and *On Shortness and Length of Life*, and along with these that *On Old Age and Youth*, I have now elucidated to the best of my ability. I urge those who may come upon these, if they gain any benefit from them, to give hearty thanks; if they do not gain any such benefit, then at least no harm will accrue to them from them. *I have also written a commentary on the Metaphysics from Book Z through to N.* And now, if God grants me the opportunity, I will make a new start, and enter upon the elucidation of the treatise *On Colours*.

Tarán's claim, and I agree with him in this, is that the sentence in italics is glaringly intrusive within the passage as a whole. Michael is running through his commentaries on Aristotle's biological and psychological (broadly, 'scientific') works, and promising (at least) one more to round off the collection; he is not concerned here to list *all* his Aristotelian commentaries. A mention of a commentary on the *Metaphysics* is not required by the context. So this sentence has been added by an assiduous scribe or scholarly reader, who knew that Michael had written a commentary on at least part of the *Metaphysics*, and – missing the point of his present remarks – wonders why he has not mentioned it here; so he helpfully adds it in. Tarán, as I say, is quite right to discern the intrusive nature of the sentence, but unjustified, I feel, in trying to argue from that that the testimony is worthless. On the contrary, I would regard it as remaining most valuable, even if not emanating directly from the horse's mouth.

A further interesting piece of evidence, not dealt with by Tarán, is the fact that in one manuscript, the *Parisinus graecus* 1853, a scholiast, in three places (ff. 260^r, 272^r, 301bis^r), identifies comments by ps.-Alexander as belonging to *ho Ephesios*, referring plainly to Michael.

So we do, then, have some evidence that Michael wrote a commentary on these books, and that what we have before us is it. Despite the attribution to Alexander in most manuscripts, it seems that a tradition persisted among scribes and scholars that Michael was the true author. Problems certainly remain, however. Why, one may ask, did he choose to write a commentary at all, especially if, as we assume, he did have access to that of Alexander? He may be compressing his original somewhat,[26] but he is still composing a copious commentary – if anything, it is Syrianus who is the more compendious, in many cases where they can be compared.[27] He may also, particularly in Book 12, be modifying some comments of Alexander which would be offensive to Christian orthodoxy. It would require a more detailed study of the work than can be given to it here to provide even a tentative answer to these questions.[28]

But further, why did the real commentary of Alexander give way to that of Michael? And if Michael is here committing a conscious forgery, and putting Alexander's name to his work, how comes it that a later reader knows that the commentary is his?[29] Tarán's claim that Alexander's commentary was lost, and thus not available to ps.-Alexander, is only tenable on the assumption that ps.-Alexander precedes Syrianus, and that Syrianus is dependent on him, and I regard that as a rather desperate hypothesis. As it is, I can only raise these interesting questions, and leave them to later scholars to solve. Their solution, at any rate, is not essential to the appreciation of the present work.

4. Syrianus as a polemicist[30]

We may turn now to a notable feature of this commentary that is not so dependent on conjecture. The great majority of the Neoplatonic commentators on Aristotle, notably Ammonius, Simplicius, and John Philoponus (though the latter not infrequently is developing his own, unorthodox Christian agenda in opposition to Aristotle), may be classed as sympathetic or constructive critics. They find themselves able to maintain the pious fiction, part of the Neoplatonist consensus since at least Porphyry,[31] that Aristotle is essentially in agreement with Plato, differing from him only on peripheral matters or in degrees of emphasis.

For considerable stretches of Aristotle's *oeuvre*, such a position is defensible, at least with a generous infusion of goodwill,[32] but there are some passages in face of which any attempt at a benign synthesis must break down, and one of these is certainly Books 13 and 14 of the *Metaphysics*, where Aristotle is indulging in more or less unremitting polemic against his former colleagues in the Academy. When, therefore, Syrianus resolved to embark on a commentary on these two books,[33] he approached

them in a belligerent spirit quite different from that of the later Alexandrian commentators, though by no means inappropriate to the
subject-matter.

What I would like to dwell on here is not so much the substantive
philosophical positions taken up by Syrianus in the commentary – these
are dealt with in section 2 above – as the rhetorical strategies which he
adopts in responding to Aristotle's own polemical sallies. The commentary
on Books 13 and 14, in Syrianus' view (81,20-2), is divided into three major
topics: (1) whether the objects of the mathematical sciences exist (covering
the first three chapters of Book 13); (2) whether the Forms exist, and, if
so, how many there are (covering the rest of Book 13);[34] and (3) whether
these are the first principles of beings (constituting the subject of Book 14).
I will select examples from each of these sections to illustrate my theme.[35]

Syrianus, we may note, begins his commentary with a ringing tribute
to Aristotle's excellence as a philosopher, in which he declares his great
admiration for his many contributions to knowledge, but at the same time
makes it clear that he is not prepared to let him get away with any biased
or ill-informed criticism of Pythagorean and Platonic doctrine. We need
not doubt that Syrianus' expression of admiration for Aristotle is sincerely
meant, but it also undoubtedly serves a rhetorical purpose, as a foil to
what is to follow, since these are more or less the last kind words that we
are going to hear about Aristotle for the rest of the commentary. Indeed,
straightaway things begin to go downhill.

In what directly follows, Syrianus sets out a good deal of his proposed
strategy in dealing with Aristotle. Plato and the Pythagoreans are infalli-
bly correct. That is the principle from which we start. When Aristotle
directs criticisms at their doctrines, therefore, he is either misunderstanding their position, and attacking some straw man, or he is 'imposing his
own hypotheses', generating a contradiction by using terms in his own
sense, not in the sense employed by the Pythagoreans and Platonists.
Syrianus' strategy, then, in general is to attack Aristotle from higher
ground, simply expounding to him, and to us, the correct Platonist doctrine. Elsewhere, though, he goes toe-to-toe with him, swapping sarcasm
for sarcasm. There are, however, other occasions also when he seeks to
confute Aristotle from his own mouth, quoting Aristotle against Aristotle.
I will select examples of all three procedures in turn, as they each possess
their own interest.

It should be borne in mind in all this that Syrianus, though primarily a
philosopher, is also thoroughly proficient in the arts of rhetoric. His only
other surviving work, in fact,[36] is a commentary on the two handbooks of
Hermogenes, *Peri ideôn* and *Peri staseôn*, in the course of which he reveals
a comprehensive and intimate knowledge of all the wiles of the rhetori-
cian. We must not therefore be surprised if we find him using various
rhetorical devices throughout this commentary.

We may take our start from a passage where Aristotle is accused of
misrepresenting Platonic-Pythagorean doctrine. Aristotle starts out in

Book 13, as we recall, by raising the question of the mode of existence of the objects of the mathematical sciences. In the course of ch. 1, at 1076a33-6, he propounds the following division: 'If the objects of mathematics exist, they must necessarily exist either in perceptible things, as some say, or separate from perceptible things (there are some too who say this); or, if neither one nor the other, either they do not exist at all, or they exist in some other way.'

This division, of course, is intended to expose the contradictions of the Platonist position, a fact to which Syrianus is very much alert. His comment on this is as follows (84,10ff.):

Now he is right in employing this division, except in so far as he has postulated that there are some who have left mathematical objects as inherent in perceptible things, and he has very well discerned and expressed the conclusion to his hypothesis; for if they are neither separate nor inseparable from perceptible things, either they do not exist at all, or they acquire whatever degree of existence they possess in some other way – that is, they are generated in us by abstraction (*aphairesis*), which is in fact his own view. He attacks both the position that they are inseparable from perceptible things and that they have a separate existence, in order that they may not exist in any way at all, like the notorious 'thingummybob' (*skindapsos*), or precisely his own position may prevail, that they are derived from perceptible things by abstraction.

Syrianus then turns to the beginning of ch. 2, 1076a38-b13, where Aristotle demonstrates to his own satisfaction that the objects of mathematics cannot be in sensible things, because (a) it is impossible for two solids (*sterea*) to occupy the same space at the same time, and (b) on this same theory all other potentialities and characteristics would exist in sensible things, and none of them would exist separately. To this Syrianus responds as follows (84,20ff.):

Whether he constructs a strong or a weak argument in this passage is nothing to the point; for neither any of the Pythagoreans nor Plato himself nor any of the Platonists of his time postulated that geometrical figures and volumes inhered in perceptible objects; if Severus, or some other of those who commented on Plato in later times, basing themselves on the teachings of Aristotle himself, have made illegitimate use of mathematical entities in their explanation of physical causes, that has nothing to do with the ancients, whose doctrines he is here attempting to refute; so that I will direct no response to him on this question from the perspective of such sources.

So, as far as Syrianus is concerned, Aristotle is attacking straw men, and does not deserve a response. His reference to the second century AD

Platonist Severus is most interesting, but its rhetorical purpose is to suggest that if Severus came up with a theory like this, it is only because he is himself influenced by Aristotle.[37]

In any case, continues Syrianus, it is not true that two 'solid' (in the sense of three-dimensional) bodies cannot occupy the same space. To buttress this assertion, he adduces (84,32ff.), rather interestingly, the example of extension (*diastêma*) in general, which permeates the whole physical universe,

> neither cutting up other things nor itself cut up as it is divided along with the air and the rest of bodies, but extends throughout the cosmos steadfast, firm, unmoved, and exempt from any alteration, providing a place and receptacle and bound and circumscription and everything of that sort to the sum-total of the visible cosmos.

One aspect of this that is interesting is that he does not absolutely claim this doctrine of *diastêma* as an extended, but not physically resistant, body as main-line Platonism, but refers it rather (84,31ff.) to 'those who postulate this theory', so the question presents itself as to who these persons might be. It becomes plain as the text proceeds that this 'extension' is closely connected with the World Soul, and may in fact be taken as its 'pneumatic vehicle'. At any rate, he speaks of it (85,7ff.) as 'possessing its substance (*skhein tên hupostasin*) in co-operation with the will and intellection of the cosmic Soul, Soul making it spherical through its vision of Intellect'. It is plain that this is Soul's vehicle for its direction of the physical cosmos. Its interpenetration with the cosmos is compared a little further down (19-22) to the light of various lamps pervading a room. This use of light as an analogy is of considerable significance.

In this connection, Wilhelm Kroll (in a note in the apparatus ad loc.) has acutely drawn attention to a passage of Proclus' *Commentary on the Republic* (2,196,22ff.) – a work heavily dependent on Syrianus, as Anne Sheppard has amply demonstrated[38] – in which he reports the identification (which he attributes originally to Porphyry, but endorses himself), of the pillar of light seen by the souls in the Myth of Er during their perambulations (*Rep.* 10, 616B) with the *okhêma* of the cosmic Soul, which is to be taken as 'a body prior to the body of the cosmos, immediately attached to the Soul of the Universe'.

Kroll is very probably correct here to make the connection. I dwell on this curious piece of Neoplatonic lore in the present context just to illustrate one strategy which Syrianus employs in his confutation of Aristotle: the exposition of 'true' Platonic/Pythagorean doctrine in order to demonstrate Aristotle's inadequate grasp of the 'realities'. Against Aristotle, this strategy has to be accounted entirely futile, since Aristotle would have had nothing but contempt for these Pythagorean 'realities' (especially such an entity as a cosmic pneumatic vehicle!), had they been expounded to him;

but we may be grateful for the various insights into the development of later Platonist doctrine afforded to us by Syrianus' expositions.

Another characteristic passage occurs rather later, at 160,23ff., on 13, 1086a29-35, where Aristotle is taking one of his many digs both at Speusippus (though Syrianus does not recognise this; he thinks rather of the Pythagoreans), and at Plato himself: 'The people who posit only numbers, and mathematical numbers at that, may be considered later; but as for those who speak of the Forms, we can observe at the same time their way of thinking and the difficulties which befall them. For they not only treat of the Forms as universal substances,[39] but also as separable and as particulars; but it has already been argued that this is not possible.' Syrianus responds as follows:

> It is not surprising that they seem to you to say this, since you postulate that individuals are the only substances.[40] They, on the other hand, rising to an almost incomprehensible superiority over your sort of substances, postulate as substances the Forms, and declare that they actually embrace universals and in a unitary mode comprehend at a higher level the causes of both universals and individuals, being neither universals in the manner of the reason-principles on the level of soul nor individuals and mathematically one in accordance with the appearances of the lowest level of images in Matter.

Once again, the point is that Aristotle is simply oblivious to the higher levels of reality; he is therefore not in a position to engage meaningfully with those in the Pythagorean tradition.

A second strategy employed by Syrianus is plain old knock-about sarcasm – which is, after all, only dealing out to Aristotle a taste of his own medicine, Books 13 and 14 being pervaded by mischievous and sophistical arguments. To take one example, let us look at his response to the passage 1079a14-19, where Aristotle is presenting a rather obscure, because very allusive, argument against the Platonists, to the effect that, in propounding the theory of Forms, they actually undermine their own theory of First Principles – presumably the One and the Great-and-Small, or Greater-and-Smaller:

> And in general the arguments for the Forms do away with things which are more important to the exponents of the Forms than the existence of the Ideas themselves; for the consequence is that it is not the Two (*or* Dyad) that is primary, but Number, and of this the relative (*to pros ti*), this in turn being prior to the absolute (*to kath' hauto*) – and all the other ways in which people, by following up the views held about the Forms, have gone against the first principles.

It sounds here as if Aristotle is trying to extract some illegitimate mileage out of the denomination of Plato's second principle as 'the Greater and Smaller', being regarded a sort of relative number, but one cannot be sure. At any rate, Syrianus is not going to let him get away with it. He first sets out the true Platonist doctrine (112,14ff.):

> Now these men (sc. the Platonists) claimed that, after the single First Principle of all things, which they were pleased to term the Good and the supra-essential One, there were two principles of everything, the Monad and the Dyad of infinite potency (*apeirodunamos*), and they apportioned these principles at each level of being in the mode proper to each. For this an element analogous to the Good in each realm of being and likewise entities assimilated to the primary Monad and Dyad.

This, of course, is not either old Pythagoreanism or early Platonism, but rather an exotic amalgam developed first, so far as we can discern, by Eudorus of Alexandria in the first century BC, on the basis of two alternative versions of early Pythagoreanism, and an interpretation of Plato's *Philebus*, and then taken up by a Neopythagorean sheltering behind the name of Archytas – which latter, rather than Eudorus, appears to be Syrianus' source. He then turns to deal with Aristotle:

> But our friend Aristotle declares that, in postulating the Essential Dyad and the Essential Monad among the Forms, first of all, since they are prone to award the highest honours to the formal causal principles (*eidêtikai aitiai*), in declaring these to be primary, they do away with the Monad and the Dyad among the first principles (for what monad and dyad could be superior to the primal Monad and Dyad?); and then, since the Essential Tetrad (*hê autotetras*) is double the Essential Dyad, and indeed the Essential Dyad is double the Essential Monad, and all these are numbers, not only is absolute number superior to the first principles, but even relative number; and in general he says that there are many such instances, in which they, in their desire to preserve their position about the Forms, all unwittingly find themselves in conflict with their own principles.

Aristotle is here trying to score points by systematically confusing Form-numbers (in which he does not believe) with mathematical or unitary numbers – the 'real' Tetrad, so to speak, is not double the 'real' Dyad, nor yet four times the Monad; it is simply 'Fourness', or what it is to be Four. Syrianus now turns on him (112,28ff.):

> Now that this is pretty sorry stuff (*phortikôs eirêtai*), and hardly comes to grips in any serious way with the position of those divine men, will be plain even before any argument to anyone of reasonable acuity. Nevertheless, it might well be demanded of us that we make an adequate response to this fallacious line of reasoning.

He then goes on to expound at some length the Platonic-Pythagorean doctrine of first principles, and their relation to the series of Form-numbers; but he has placed himself satisfactorily on a higher intellectual plane than Aristotle by such an introduction.

Another representative instance, from later in the work, occurs at 159,29ff., where Syrianus is provoked by Aristotle's dismissive conclusion to his analysis of Pythagorean-Platonic number theory in 13.9 (1086a18-21): 'We have now examined and analysed the questions concerning numbers to a sufficient extent; for although one who is already convinced might still be more convinced by a fuller treatment, he who is not convinced would be brought no nearer to conviction.' This calls forth the following response from an indignant Syrianus:

> Indeed our fine philosopher has rightly divined our situation, that, even if he were to fabricate such fooleries ten thousand times over against those who have been seized by the wonder of the ancient philosophy, he would achieve nothing: for he has produced all his arguments on the assumption of unitary numbers, whereas none of the divine numbers is of this sort, but, if any, only mathematical number. In fact, that he himself admits that he has made no points against their hypotheses, nor has engaged at all with Form-numbers, is borne witness to by what is said in Book 2 of his work *On Philosophy* (fr. 9 Rose) where we find the following: 'so that if the Forms are some other kind of number, and not the mathematical, we would have no knowledge of them; for who of at least the great majority of us understands any other sort of number?' So here too he has directed his refutations to the majority of people who do not recognise any other number than the unitary, but he has not begun to address the thought of those divine men.

There are many instances throughout the commentary of his treating Aristotle in this way,[41] but we may turn now to some examples of the third strategy that Syrianus repeatedly adopts, that of adducing Aristotle against himself. This is of course particularly effective in the ancient context, in which no serious philosopher, and in particular such divinely-inspired men as Pythagoras or Plato, or even, stretching a point, Aristotle himself, could be allowed any degree of inconsistency, or even of development in doctrine; so that any passage in any part of the philosopher's works may be adduced to reinforce (or confute) any other.

In the first instance which I have selected, Aristotle has been attacking, from 1076b39 to 1077a14, what may be termed 'the argument from objectivity', which claims that, for mathematics to be objectively true, there must exist objects correlative to the various mathematical sciences, which are other than physical objects. In this particular passage (1077a5-9), Aristotle is seeking to generate absurd consequences by focusing on the sciences of optics and harmonics, which should also have their proper objects:

> And similarly the objects of optics and harmonics will be distinct, for there will be sound and sight apart from the sensible and particular objects. Hence clearly the other senses and their objects will exist separately; for why should one class of objects do so rather than another? And if this is so, there will be separate living beings too, inasmuch as there will be separate senses.

The point here seems to be that, for there to be ideal objects of sight and sound, there must be ideal sense-organs to sense them, and therefore ideal living beings to possess the sense-organs, and this Aristotle is triumphantly presenting as an absurdity. Syrianus, however, does not regard this as an absurdity, and he proposes further to argue that, on the basis of his own utterances elsewhere, Aristotle cannot do so either (88,35ff.):

> There is actually nothing strange in all these things being present in reason-principles (*logoi*), and in the images of reason-principles, that is to say, objects of the imagination (*phantasmata*), not only prior to sensible objects, but also prior to the reason-principles in nature (*phusikoi logoi*) which give form to sensible objects. But he, though these facts are granted, adduces as the greatest of absurdities that there will be another set of living beings, if there are separate senses; but despite the fact that his own teacher (sc. Plato) had long ago told him that the Essential Living Being (*autozôion*), in comprehending within itself all the intelligible living beings, is the cause of the living beings both in the psychic and in the sensible realms, he pretends that he has never heard anything about such matters.

This is, of course, a reference to *Timaeus* 30C, which Aristotle, as a pupil of Plato's, should have duly taken on board; but, as he seems to have failed to absorb this doctrine, Syrianus proposes, first of all, to remind him of it, but then (89,18ff.) goes on to point out to him that he himself does actually accept the existence of living beings other than physical ones:

> And that I may not rely on the witness of what others have said, he himself, in Book K,[42] has called the Primal Intellect a living being. It is plain, then, that he should not, presumably, disdain to call each one of his other levels an intellective being, even if not a primary one. In the *Ethics*, furthermore, he clearly wishes man in the proper sense to be his intellect. If, then, the intellect in us is man in the proper sense, and every man is a living being, the conclusion is perfectly clear.

His strategy here is interesting, even if not entirely effective against

Aristotle's – admittedly rather sophistical – point. The passage in Book 12 – for it is Lambda, not Kappa – reads:

> Moreover, life belongs to God. For the actuality (*energeia*) of thought is life, and God is that actuality; and the essential actuality of God is life most good and eternal. *We hold, then, that God is a living being, eternal, supremely good*; and therefore life and a continuous eternal existence belong to God; for that is what God is.

The reference to the *Ethics* is somewhat less clear, but probably to some such passage as 10.7, 1177a12ff.,[43] where Aristotle is identifying happiness in the highest sense as the happiness of the highest element in us, which is the intellect, and Syrianus might reasonably draw the conclusion from that that man in the truest sense is to be identified with his intellect. So then, Syrianus is able to claim that Aristotle himself at least recognises such a thing as an immaterial living being, in the one case the Unmoved Mover (and all the other inferior planetary movers), in the other, the intellect of man, so that it is inconsistent of him here to ridicule the idea of an immaterial cogniser of mathematical, and even harmonic, truths which could also be described as a 'living being' (*zôion*).

Another example from later in the commentary occurs at 164,4-8 (Kroll), where he is responding to Aristotle's assertion in 13.10, 1087a11ff. that knowledge of universals is potential, while knowledge of particulars is actual. Among other arguments in confutation of this, he adduces the following:

> His statement that knowledge of universals is potential, while that of particulars is actualised, is clearly that of someone who, because of his antipathy towards his predecessors, is prepared to contradict what is said in his own *Analytics*, to the effect that it is not possible to have knowledge of particulars, never mind that this knowledge should be better and more perfect than that of universals.

Syrianus does actually seem to have a good point here, as is acknowledged e.g. by Ross in his commentary ad loc. (2, p. 466). Not only is this his position in the *Analytics* (*An. Post.* 1.24, 86a5-10; 1.31 *passim*), but one can adduce such passages as *De An.* 417b22 and *Met.* 7, 1039b27 in support of the same position. Ross does make the point, admittedly, that Aristotle on occasion advances the view that 'knowledge is of the universal *in the particular*, as he admits (*An. Post.* 87b28; *De An.* 424a21-24) that sensation is of that in the particular which is universal'. But nonetheless, for polemical purposes, Syrianus may be adjudged to have scored a palpable hit.

Again, these are only two of many instances of Syrianus' employment of such a strategy in the commentary,[44] but they will serve to illustrate his procedure. We may fitly end this survey, perhaps, by quoting Syrianus'

comment on the final lemma of Book 14, where Aristotle is aiming a final
dismissive crack at the Platonists:

> **1093b24-9** These then are the consequences of this theory, and
> perhaps yet more could be adduced. But it seems to be an indication
> of the fact that mathematicals are not separable from sensibles, as
> certain people claim, nor that these are principles, that many diffi-
> culties are experienced in explaining their generation, and that they
> have no way of connecting the various parts of their theory.

To which Syrianus acidly responds:

> But I would take as an indication of the fact that these divine men
> have done philosophy in the finest, best and most irrefutable way
> that you, Aristotle, the most ingenious and productive of those on
> record, should experience such difficulties in controversy with them,
> having said nothing that might even be persuasive, not to say conclu-
> sive, or indeed anything relevant to them at all, but in most of what
> you say employing alien hypotheses, in no way appropriate to the
> doctrines of your elders, while in a number of instances, when
> proposing to make some point against their true doctrine, you fail to
> come to grips with them at all.

Overall, I think it can be seen even from this brief overview that the
Commentary on the Metaphysics is remarkable among Neoplatonic commentaries on Aristotle for its strongly adversative tone. This, however, is
largely conditioned by the polemical nature of the subject matter. It does
not necessarily mean that Syrianus had withdrawn from the position
established by Porphyry of the basic concordance between Plato and
Aristotle; it is just that he is not prepared to let Aristotle get away with
the sort of sniping that he indulges in in *Metaphysics* 13 and 14. We may
deduce from Simplicius, after all, that Syrianus' *Commentary on the
Categories* was not notably polemical, despite the long tradition of hostile
commentary by Platonists and Stoics on that work. This work, then, seems
to stand alone, and it is all the more interesting for that.

5. Manuscripts and editions

The manuscript tradition of the *Commentary on the Metaphysics* is merci-
fully simple. The chief witness to the text is the codex *Parisinus Coislianus*
161 (C), of the fourteenth century (fol. 410^r-447^v), which follows a rather
curious order and procedure (though this itself may be conditioned by the
nature of Syrianus' commentary). In the MS, the commentary on *Met.*
Book 3 is followed, not by that on Book 4, but rather that on Books 13 and
14, while the commentary on Book 4, which follows this, is interwoven
with the commentary of Alexander. Certainly, as can readily be observed,

the commentary on Book 4 is of a rather different nature to those on the other three books, and this may have provoked this interesting anomaly. Specifically, Syrianus himself, at the outset (p. 54,11 Kroll), declares that he will not be commenting on all aspects of the book, since much has already been excellently dealt with by Alexander. Indeed, in the other manuscripts, which are copies of C, the commentary on Book 4 is omitted altogether.

Of these copies, although they amount to eighteen in all, the only ones worthy of note (since they were used by Usener in his edition) are *Parisinus graecus* 1896 (A) of the fifteenth century, and *Hamburgensis phil. gr.* 2 (H), of the same period. Of rather more use, in fact, is a Latin translation made by Hieronymus Bagolinus (Bagnoli),[45] and published in Venice in 1558. Though Bagolinus made use of an inferior copy of C, nonetheless he contributes a number of useful conjectures, which have been duly noted.

The work was edited first in 1870 by Hermann Usener, along with the other commentaries on the *Metaphysics*.[46] This was followed in 1902 by the edition of Wilhelm Kroll, in the *Commentaria in Aristotelem Graeca* series,[47] on which this translation is based. Kroll fully acknowledges his dependence on the edition of Usener, whose many acute emendations to the text are listed in his edition, and mainly adopted in this translation.

Other than this, the commentary has been accorded little attention, and no editions or translations into any modern tongue exist. However, even as this translation is appearing, there is also the prospect of an edition, with French translation and notes, by Concetta Luna, in the Budé series, which will constitute an important complement to the present work. Dr. Luna's battles with Leonardo Tarán, on the question of the relative dependence of Syrianus and ps.-Alexander, have been detailed earlier (section 3).

The present translation is based on the text of Kroll, while benefiting from the many excellent conjectures of Usener which he reports, as well as from a number of his own. Two controversial features of Kroll's edition, however, must be noted here. Firstly, it is the custom of Kroll, no doubt for reasons of space, to abbreviate lemmata of any length, whereas an inspection of the Coislianus would seem to indicate that Syrianus generally copied the text of Aristotle out in full. We have followed Syrianus here – with just two exceptions, 1086b14-1087a25 and 1088a15-1088b11, in either case because of the extreme length of the lemma concerned. Secondly, Kroll, in some places, notably between 1084b16 and 1086b14 lemmata which are then broken up into sub-lemmata, where, once again, inspection of the manuscripts suggests that Syrianus made no such distinction. Here, after some deliberation, I have followed Kroll in his employment of sub-lemmata on occasions where Syrianus seems to be providing, first, a general commentary on a given passage, and then some more particular comments on individual sentences or phrases, as this is a format attested from other commentators, and in any case, the dividing up of these lemmata into individual sentences and even phrases, even if that is the way that Syrianus in fact proceeded, makes the whole much more difficult to read. I hope that the reader, with this is mind, will forgive me for erring with Kroll.

A final issue is worth noting. The text of Aristotelian passages as quoted in the lemmata also differs in some minor respects from that of Jaeger's OCT edition. I confine myself, however, to noting variations that impact on Syrianus' interpretation. A full list of variants will no doubt be provided in due course by Concetta Luna in her edition.

As regards the apportionment of responsibility in this volume, the introduction has been composed by JD alone, and DO'M does not necessarily share his views, in particular, on the question of the relationship between Syrianus and ps.-Alexander discussed in section 3, or on the propriety of following Kroll in his treatment of Syrianus' 'sub-lemmata', as described above.[48] As regards the translation, JD is primarily responsible for pp. 80-175, and DO'M for the balance, but each has checked over the version of the other. DO'M is also primarily responsible for the Greek-English Index, though with additions and modifications from JD. Finally, we wish to express our gratitude to Michael Griffin for a fine job of editing, as well as for a number of valuable additions to the notes.

Notes

1. For such information as we possess, we are dependent upon Marinus' *Life of Proclus*, Damascius' *Philosophical History* (otherwise known as the *Life of Isidorus*), and the Byzantine encyclopaedia, the *Suda*. The best modern account of him is probably still that of Karl Praechter, s.v. *Syrianos,* in *RE* IVA, 1728-75.

2. What Damascius actually tells us is that Aedesia, who married Syrianus' pupil Hermeias, was a relative (*ên prosêkousa genei*) of Syrianus, and that she was 'the most beautiful and noble of the women of Alexandria'.

3. His other known pupil (apart from the shadowy Domninus), Hermeias (the author of a *Commentary on the Phaedrus*, which is generally agreed to be little more than a transcription of Syrianus' lectures on that dialogue) was also deeply influenced by him, but would seem to have associated with him for a longer period.

4. This work, a commentary on the *Peri Ideôn* and *Peri Staseôn* of Hermogenes, is edited by H. Rabe, 2 vols, Leipzig: Teubner, 1892-3. Rabe himself, it must be said, expresses some doubts as to the authorship, vol. II, iv-vii.

5. *in Cat.* 3,9-10 Kalbfleisch. There is some evidence also for comments by him on the *De Interpretatione, Prior Analytics, Physics, De Caelo* and *De Anima,* though these need not connote full-dress commentaries on these works. See Cardullo, 1986.

6. Now collected, with translation and commentary, by Sarah Klitenic Wear, *The Collected Fragments of Syrianus the Platonist on Plato's* Timaeus *and* Parmenides, unpublished PhD thesis, Trinity College, Dublin, 2005.

7. Proclus has a troublesome habit of referring to his Master in the imperfect (*elege*, 'he used to say'), as Wear has pointed out. Certainly, as mentioned already, Hermeias is relying in his commentary on oral communications of Syrianus in his seminar.

8. As discussed by Sheppard, 1980.

9. It is generally agreed that we have also the substance of a commentary by

him on the *Phaedrus*, in the surviving commentary of his student Hermeias on that dialogue. Hermeias indicates at various points in the text that he is essentially transcribing the contents of Syrianus' seminar.

10. For which see his remarks in the preface to Book 13.

11. Initially propounded, in Neoplatonic times, according to Hierocles (ap. Photius, *Bibl.* 214.2, 172a2-9), by Plotinus' teacher Ammonius Saccas, but copperfastened by the treatise of Porphyry on that very topic, now unfortunately lost.

12. On his various rhetorical strategies for dealing with Aristotle in these books, see section 4 of this Introduction.

13. We are grateful to Richard Sorabji for his valuable contribution to these remarks.

14. Again the classic article is by Ian Mueller in *Aristotle Transformed*, although he may not wish to be held responsible for the remarks added by Sorabji here.

15. It is a feature of later Platonism that philosophers can expound their doctrine at various levels of complexity in accordance with the nature of the audience, all of which are equally valid for their purposes, but which may not give a full insight into the whole range and depth of their thought. It is this, it has been argued persuasively by Ilsetraut Hadot in a series of works (most recently Hadot, 2004), that is the case with Proclus' contemporary, the Alexandrian Neoplatonist Hierocles, because of the nature of his surviving commentaries; and it is true to say that Iamblichus' *Pythagorean Sequence* and *Letters*, being in the realm of 'popular philosophy', give little hint of the deeper complexities of his thought.

16. It should be said, however, that this scheme of a supreme One presiding over a pair of Monad and Dyad can be traced back, on the one hand, to the Alexandrian Platonist Eudorus in the first century BC (ap. Simpl. *in Phys.* 181,10ff. Diels) – a source which, however, Syrianus gives no sign of acknowledging; and on the other, to a neo-Pythagorean writing *On First Principles,* attributed to 'Archytas' (ap. Stob. I 278-9 Wachsmuth), which he does (though, strangely, under the name of 'Archaenetus', 166,4 Kroll – this may, however, be merely a scribal error, as he gives evidence of knowing Archytas elsewhere in the commentary).

17. Or, conversely, on one theory, of expansion on the part of (ps.-)Alexander; see discussion below.

18. First in an article 'Syrianus and Pseudo-Alexander's Commentary on *Metaph.* E-N', in *Aristoteles Werk und Wirkung,* ed. J. Wiesner, vol. II, Berlin-New York, 1985, 215-32; and subsequently in a choleric review of Luna (next note), in *Gnomon* 77 (2004), 196-209.

19. *Trois études sur la tradition des commentaires anciens à la* Métaphysique *d'Aristote,* Leiden, 2001, 1-98 (with Appendices I-III).

20. In his review of M. Hayduck's edition of Michael of Ephesus, *In libros De partibus animalium, De animalium motione, De animalium incessu (CAG* 23: 2), *Göttingische Gelehrte Anzeigen* 168 (1906), 861-907; but this view goes back to Valentin Rose, in 1854 (*De Aristotelis librorum ordine et auctoritate commentatio,* Berlin), and has been adopted in more recent times by Paul Moraux (*Alexandre d'Aphrodise exégète de la noétique d'Aristote,* Liège-Paris, 1942, 14-19), and H.-D. Saffrey, *Le* Peri philosophias *d'Aristote et la théorie platonicienne des idées nombres,* Leiden, 1955, 18-19). One plausible basis for this view, apart from the linguistic arguments, which are impressive, is a scholion attached to the beginning of the commentary on Book 6 in the Paris MS (A), saying simply *michael tou ephesiou.* This attribution has been crossed out by the 'corrector' of the manuscript, but there it stands.

21. The period of Michael's activity as a commentator is fairly clearly delimited by what we know of Anna Comnena's life. Anna only formed her intellectual circle after she retired to a convent in 1118, and the commentaries were composed before she turned away from Aristotelian interests to write her memoirs in 1138.

22. Borrowed from Karl Praechter, and usefully assembled in her Appendix III.

23. This work is only available to us in the paraphrase of Psellus (222,90-3 O'Meara), but that preserves the tell-tale phrase.

24. Luna produces a third passage (Syr. 129, 5-25/ps.-Alex. 752,33-753,8), but the argument there, though ingenious, is more subjective; there once again seems no reason why both authors could not be adapting Alexander in their own ways.

25. *CAG* 22: 1,149,8-16.

26. There is the additional problem, raised by Tarán (op. cit., 230), of the knowledge of the commentary of Alexander on Book 12, in the Arabic tradition, by Averroes, who quotes him, and in a way which does not accord well with the surviving commentary of ps.-Alex. This material, however, plainly requires a good deal more examination than it has so far received.

27. Syrianus does, however, on a few occasions make references to Alexander which do not correspond to anything in ps.-Alexander, cf. 96,18; 100,4.10; 108,29; 111,34; 160,8; 166,27; 186,16 (in the case of the refs at 122,12.18, there is a corresponding passage in ps.-Alex.; and 195,12 is a general remark). In some cases, Kroll is able to point to relevant remarks at an earlier stage in the genuine commentary, but it is not necessary or probable to suppose that Syrianus is referring back to those.

28. Michael's action may perhaps usefully be viewed against the background of other Byzantine acts of plagiarism, such as Isaac Sebastocrator's appropriation of a number of the shorter treatises of Proclus, or Michael Psellus' of the later volumes of Iamblichus' *Pythagorean Sequence*, but in those cases the original works are borrowed without acknowledgement; here Michael seems to conceal himself behind the persona of Alexander (though we cannot be quite sure, after all, since his authorship was plainly known to some contemporaries or near-contemporaries).

29. The reader concerned may, of course, not be very much later; he could be a member of Michael's own circle, who edited his works.

30. A modified version of this section was delivered as a paper to the annual conference of the International Society for Neoplatonic Studies in New Orleans in June 2005.

31. This is alleged, indeed, by Hierocles (*ap.* Phot. *Bibl.* 214,2, 172a2-9), to be a characteristic of the teaching already of Ammonius Saccas, but we do not know much about that.

32. See on this the stimulating recent book of Lloyd Gerson, *Aristotle and Other Platonists*, Cornell University Press: Ithaca & London, 2005.

33. He composed a commentary also on Books 3 and 4, but they are not so controversial, and hew much closer to the previous commentary of the Aristotelian Alexander of Aphrodisias, so I leave them aside in the present context.

34. This, in fact, is something of an over-simplification (cf. Annas, p. 78). Only chs 4-5 of Book 13 are devoted to a criticism of the theory of forms as such. Chs 6-8 concern rather problems arising from the theory of Form-numbers, and chs 9-10 are rather disconnected and miscellaneous.

35. The topic of Syrianus' attitude to Aristotle, in general and in this commentary in particular, has been given a balanced appraisal by H.-D. Saffrey (1987), but he does not go into any detail as to Syrianus' rhetorical strategies.

36. Unless we count Hermeias' *Commentary on the Phaedrus*, which is largely a transcript of Syrianus' seminars on the dialogue. I am assuming, of course, that the *Commentary on Hermogenes* is in fact by him.

37. In fact, the true object of Aristotle's criticisms here remains obscure to modern commentators. Who, after all, in Plato's circle postulated that the mathematical entities *inhered in* sensible things? Julia Annas, in her commentary (pp. 137-8), refers to these people as 'partial Platonists', and suggests, reasonably, that the reference may actually be primarily to Eudoxus of Cnidos, who certainly was noted for holding that Forms inhered in particulars. But if that be so, Syrianus knows, or cares, nothing of it.

38. In her useful study, *Studies on the 5th and 6th Essays of Proclus' Commentary on the Republic*, Göttingen, 1980.

39. Preserving the MSS reading *hôs ousias,* secluded by Jaeger (with much justification); Syrianus, however, plainly read it, and strives to make sense of it.

40. We may note that the rhetorical technique of apostrophising one's opponent is practised quite frequently by Syrianus throughout these two books (nineteen examples in all); a full list is given by Luna, 2001, Appendice IX, p. 226.

41. One might instance 94,11-17; 108,9-11; 111,5-10 (Kroll).

42. This is actually a reference to Book L[12].7, 1072b29 – a strange error for Syrianus to make (but the K in the MSS may simply be a scribal error).

43. Kroll's suggestion ad loc. of 6.2, 1139b4 and 6.6, 1141a5 does not seem very useful. In both cases all that is being stated is that it is intellect that is the part of us that attains to the truth, but not that we are in the most proper sense our intellects.

44. e.g. 93,27ff.; 98,9-11; 111,23-7 (Kroll).

45. *Syriani antiquissimi philosophi interpretis in II, XIII et XIV libros Aristotelis Metaphysices commentarius, a Hier. Bagolini latinitate donatus,* Venetiis, 1558.

46. *Supplementum scholiorum: Syriani in* Metaphysica *commentaria,* Berlin: Academia Regia Borussica, 1870.

47. *Syriani in Metaphysica Commentaria,* ed. Guilielmus Kroll (*CAG* 6: 1), Berlin: Reimer Verlag, 1902.

48. It could be argued, of course, that Kroll is in this true to the intentions of Syrianus himself and the manuscript tradition deviant, but that is a rather far-fetched claim to make, so I would not press it.

Textual Emendations

86,17: Accepting Usener's suggestion, *dianoêtois*, for filling a small lacuna.

88,23: Adopting Usener's suggestion *prostithemenos* for *tithemenos*.

92,17: Accepting here Usener's tentative filling of a small lacuna.

94,25: Reading *prolêpsin* for *perilêpsin*, with Usener.

95,9: Reading *prôtôs* for *prôtôi*, with Kroll.

101,30: Reading *holôn* for *hoion* cl. Iambl. *DCMS*, 3,11.

102,20: Reading *poiêtikais* for *noêtikais*, with Usener.

107,31: Reading *mataioumenês* for *meteuomenês*, with Diels.

108,16: Reading *anereunêsai,* with Kroll.

109,14: Adopting Usener's filling of a lacuna.

110,11: Supplying *ta epistêta onta* with Bonitz.

111,14: Supplying a term opposite to *geitonos*, with Usener.

113,18: Reading *eidopepoiêmena* for *pepoiêmena*, with Usener.

116,10: Reading *hapasi* for *hapasês*, as suggested by Kroll.

117,5.6: Reading *têi epistêmêi* for *tês epistêmês*, as suggested by Kroll.

117,30: Reading *kai tou aidiou* for *kat' autôn*, with Usener.

118,37: Reading Usener's *tôn ontôs ontôn*.

121,33: Supplying *pasi* with Kroll.

122,3: Accepting Kroll's suggestion of *aulous* for *autous*.

123,15-17: Bracketed with Kroll, following Bagnoli.

123,31: Reading *prohuparkhein* for *pros sumpatheian*, with Usener.

126,32: Supplying *monadikôs*, with Usener.

128,19.20: Adopting here ps.-Alexander's version of the text.

131,27.28: Reading *hôs hupokeimenon ... noeitai* with Usener, and supplying *gar* after *noeitai*.

138,28: Reading *ousian* for *auto* with Usener.

141,30: We read *ton te eidêtikon arithmon <kai ton mathêmatikon ton> ekhonta ... .*

142,2: Reading *hê autê* before *theôria*, with Usener.

142,12: Reading *heterou* here for *hekaterou,* as suggested by Kroll.

142,20: We would be inclined to read *kata* before *taxin aluton*.

143,23: Reading *esti sustaseôs* for *episustaseôs* with Kroll.

143,31: Changing *hupethemetha, ênegkamen,* and *edoxamen* to third person singulars, with Usener.

144,5: Supplying *ê ex amphoin tôn* from ps.-Alexander.

145,13: Reading *autois* for *heautois*, with Usener.

147,12: Reading *teleutaion* for *teleutaiôn*, and excising *tôn*, with Usener.

147,33: Reading *kosmikôn* for *kosmôn*, with Usener.

149,6: I read *psukhêi* here, for the *tekhnêi* of the MSS.

149,13: Reading *tôi eph' hêmin kuriôs <arkhê estin hê boulêsis> tôn praxeôn.*

150,30-2: added from the parallel passage of ps.-Alex.

152,2: Inserting *monas* before *hekatera.*

159,14: Reading *taxeôn* for *lexeôn.*

159,32: Reading *eiper <ara>*, with Usener.

161,9: Reading *holikôterôn*, with Kroll.

162,20: Reading *mona,* with Kroll.

168,12: Reading *diataxeôs*, with Kroll, for the *dialexeôs* of the MSS.

169,32: Reading *energeiâi* for *energeia.*

172,10: Inserting *ek tou mê ontos* with Usener.

175,4: Reading *protei*, the conjecture of Usener.

182,3: Deleting *tis*, with Kroll.

186,23: Reading *<en> autêi,* as suggested by Kroll.

188,4: We suggest *isogônion* for the problematic *agônion.*

193,16: Perhaps read *psukhikous* for *theious*?

SYRIANUS
On Aristotle
Metaphysics 13-14

Translation

Syrianus, son of Philoxenus
Investigations of the Difficulties raised by Aristotle in Relation to Mathematics and Numbers in Books 13 and 14 of the *Metaphysics*

BOOK 13

Preface

I am not a natural controversialist, nor yet would I count myself as a disciple of Aristotle on merely a few or trivial topics; rather, I am one of 80,5
those who admire both his logical methodology overall and who would accept with enthusiasm his treatments of ethical and physical questions. And that I may not make a bore of myself by enumerating in detail all the excellent aspects of this man's philosophy, let me just ask why every intelligent person might not justly marvel at the apt re- marks, accompanied by demonstrations of the highest quality, to be 10
found in this most excellent treatise on the subject of both of the forms in matter and definitions, and of the divine and unmoved separable causal principles of the whole cosmos – although indeed they are beyond the reach of all synthetic treatment or too detailed exposition – and declare the author of such a philosophical enquiry a benefactor of the life of man. For all this he is owed the warmest thanks both from us and 15
from all those who can appreciate his acuity of mind.

However, since it is the fact that, for whatever reasons, both in other parts of his theological treatise[1] and especially in the last two books, 13 and 14, he has indulged in a good deal of criticism of the first principles of the Pythagoreans and the Platonists, while never presenting any 20
adequate justification for his position, and in many instances, if one may state the truth quite frankly, not even meeting them on their own ground, but rather basing his objections on hypotheses propounded by himself, it seemed reasonable, in fairness to the more unsophisticated students, lest, under the influence of the well-deserved reputation of the man, they be seduced into contempt for divine realities (*pragmata*) and the inspired philosophy of the ancients, to subject his remarks, to the 25
best of our ability, to a judicious and impartial examination, and to demonstrate that the doctrines of Pythagoras and Plato about the first principles remain free of disproof or refutation, while the arguments of Aristotle against them for the most part miss the mark and pursue lines of enquiry quite irrelevant to those divine men, while on the few occasions when they seek to make a direct attack on them, they are 81,1

unable to bring to bear any refutation, large or small. And necessarily so; for 'the truth is never refuted', in the words of that divine man,[2] and in assimilating their arguments about first principles to the realities,
5   the fathers of those arguments established them 'as firmly and unshakably as it is proper for arguments to be'.[3]

Chapter 1: Introduction

But that is enough by way of preface. Now that we have stated the purpose and the subject of this treatise, it is time to declare the contest (*agônes*) open.[4] For whether one wishes to call us contestants, in so far as we are providing a defence against a series of attacks on the fairest
10 and best of philosophical systems, or arbitrators between the purer and more intellectual approaches to the inspired doctrines of the school of Pythagoras and those difficulties raised against them from a logical point of view by that most ingenious of all recorded philosophers, Aristotle, we will not reject the title. Our only concern is to survive the challenge with due attention to justice and wisdom and devotion to truth.[5]
15   So let us begin from this point. Aristotle, having begun by stating (1076a12-15) that one must test and investigate the views of others about unmoving first principles, declares (1076a16-19) that there are two doctrines about first principles, that one that privileges mathematics and grants a separable status to them, and that which bestows supreme honour on the forms and assumes that all things have their
20 being in accordance with them and in relation to them. There arise, then, he says (1076a19-32), three topics for investigation: first, if mathematical objects exist, and if so, in what way they exist; secondly, if forms exist, and also the formal level of number (*eidêtikos arithmos*); and thirdly, if the first principles of beings are both numbers and forms. Taking these in order, then, he deals with the first question, refuting, so he imagines, those who assign real being to the objects of mathemat-
25 ics, and asserting his own view on this question, which grants mathematical objects whatever degree of existence they have by way of abstraction from sensible extensions and shapes. However, before dealing with his actual arguments against the more authentic doctrine on this question, it would be as well, perhaps, to present the true view of the ancient philosophy on these matters, that we may be in a position to discern whether it is against the real theory of these divine men that
30 this contentious[6] argument is directed, or rather whether in the text before us he is taking what is said [sc. by his opponents] in the light of his own particular assumptions, and then dishonestly setting out to overthrow them.

The divine Pythagoras, and all those who have genuinely received his doctrines into the purest recesses of their own thought,[7] declared that there are many levels (*taxeis*) of beings, the intelligible, the intellectual, the level of discursive intellection (*dianoêtikai*),[8] the physical or in

general vital, and further the bodily; for the procession (*proodos*) of
realities, and the declination inherent in this procession, being brought 35
to completion in accordance with a certain divine ordering, establishes
the power of Otherness (*heterotês*) in the classes of being, that is to say,
the ordered multiplicity, both continuous and discrete, of entities both
incorporeal and those which strike the senses. They declared that there
were, broadly, three levels of being, the intelligible, the dianoetic,[9] and 82,1
the sensible, and that there were manifested at each of them all the
forms, but in each case in a manner appropriate to the particular nature
of their existence (*huparxis*). And the intelligible forms are at the level
of the gods, and are efficient and paradigmatic and final causes of what
is below them; for if ever these three come together and are united with
one another, as Aristotle maintains they are,[10] this would not be ob- 5
served to be the case in the lowest works of nature, but rather in the
foremost and fairest and best causal principles of all things, which are
productive of all things by reason of their generative and demiurgic
power, while by reason of the fact that their products revert towards
themselves and are assimilated to themselves they are models
(*paradeigmata*) for all things; and since they create of themselves also 10
their own goodness, as the divine Plato says,[11] how would they not
manifest also the final cause?

The intelligible forms, then, being of this nature, and being productive of such great benefits to all things, fill the divine realms, but are
most generally to be viewed in connection with the demiurgic level of
reality, which is associated with Intellect proper (*peri tên demiourgikên
taxin tên noeran*).[12] The discursive forms (*ta dianoêta*) on the one hand
imitate what is above them and assimilate the psychic realm to the 15
intelligible, while on the other they embrace all things in a secondary
way, and those of them which are viewed by the divine and daemonic
souls are demiurgic, whereas those of them which are found among us
(humans) are only capable of cognition, since we no longer possess
demiurgic knowledge, by reason of our 'moulting' (*pterorrhuêsis*);[13] since
even our discursive nature,[14] as Plato testifies in the *Phaedrus,* when 20
brought to perfection and 'winged', traverses the heavens (*meteôropolei*)[15] and co-operates with the gods in administering the whole
cosmos.[16]

These discursive forms Plato clearly says in the *Timaeus*[17] that the
Demiurge implants in souls, structuring them by means of geometric
and arithmetic and harmonic proportions; while in the division of the
Line in the *Republic*[18] he declares that they are 'images' (*eikones*)[19] of
the intelligibles (and for this reason he has not disdained to call them
on occasion 'intelligible'),[20] but that they preside over sense-objects as 25
models (*paradeigmatikôs*); and in the *Phaedo*[21] he says that they are
causes for us of recollection – for what we learn are nothing else but
recollections of the median level of forms, which is the same as to say
the eternally-existent general reason-principles, not the 'later-born'

(*husterogenêis*)[22] concepts but rather those pre-existing essentially (*kat'*
ousian) in our souls, being inspired and guided by which those reason-
30   principles in nature are enabled to create individual things. In the
heavenly soul, for example, the fact that all the greatest circles in the
sphere bisect each other is pre-established effectively and creatively
(*drastêriôs kai dêmiourgikôs*), even as it is present in us only cognitively
(*gnôstikôs*), but in the heaven itself the zodiac and the equator and the
meridian, for example, and the horizons bisect each other, its soul both
35   embracing unitarily (*heniaiôs*) all these actions in its thought-processes
and bringing them about, while the body of the heaven takes in only
what it needs to of this dispartedly (*memerismenôs*).[23] For this reason
the proofs adduced by astronomers are composed of general and particular premisses, the general having its explanation in the fact that it
pre-exists in the soul which has brought the universe into existence,
83,1   while the particular is taken from the realm of sense-objects; for the
great Hephaistos inserted all things also into the sense-world, so far as
that was possible, as the divine Poem asserts:[24]

(With them then for nine years' space I forged much cunning
handiwork),
brooches, and spiral arm-bands, and rosettes and necklaces,
within their hollow cave.

5   and these are the third level of form, which the Pythagoreans considered to be the inseparable (*akhôrista*) causes of sensible objects, being
the ultimate images of the separable forms, and for this reason they did
not think it improper to call them by the same names as these latter. It
is by these that the soul which has fallen into the realm of generation
is roused and stirred up, and thus comes to reminiscence of the median
10   forms, and raises its own reason-principles to the intelligible and
primary paradigms. And thus do sight and hearing contribute to philosophy and the conversion of the soul.
        If these preliminary points are accepted, Plato and Pythagoras and
their followers are not at odds with each other about the theory of
Forms, as Aristotle asserts,[25] but the Pythagoreans, when primarily
15   discussing sensible objects, made use of the same terms, by analogy
transferring them to the median and then to the primal among beings;
for which reason they seemed – not to Aristotle, I would say, but to those
who give a more superficial account of their doctrines – to be talking
only about inseparable forms. Other thinkers, directing their attention
to the median reason-principles, have made demonstrations, starting
20   from them as images (*eikones*), about the intelligible Forms, and again,
using them as models (*paradeigmata*), about the forms that operate at
the level of the sense-world. These people are considered by the many[26]
to favour only mathematical being, since they have given mathematical
titles to the primary, median and lowest types of form; indeed, by some

of the more ill-conditioned critics, some of these are considered actually
to mix together and confuse the intelligible and discursive levels of
form, the teachers of such a doctrine themselves[27] having not committed 25
any such error, but a false view having been engendered in the minds
of some people by reason of the usage of terms in common (*dia tên tôn
onomatôn koinotêta*).[28] Plato, however, here also demonstrating his
generosity of spirit (*philanthrôpia*), made a terminological distinction
between the intelligible and discursive levels of reality, in order that not
even those asleep could misunderstand him. Hence it is that Aristotle
arraigns him[29] for postulating two types of separable substance – 30
whether justly or not will be clear already to those of intelligence, but
our examination of his argument, I believe, will demonstrate the matter
more clearly with the aid of a moderate degree of probing.

With this much, then, by way of preliminary cautioning, to wit, that
these men are not in disagreement in their hypotheses concerning the
Forms, even if they severally have made different kinds of deductions
about them, and that anyone who attacks any one of these authorities
is actually opposing all the friends of the Forms, let us now proceed to 35
follow the division and order of Aristotle's arraignment. We note, then,
that he puts forward three problems: (1) whether the objects of the
mathematical sciences (*mathêmata*) exist, and in what way they do; (2)
whether the Forms exist, and, if so, the number of the Forms; and (3)
whether these are first principles of beings. The first two problems we see[30]
him dealing with in Book 13, the third in Book 14. Of the former two, we 84,1
see that the first is that about the existence or non-existence of mathematical objects. Let us consider whether he lodges an adequate objection to the
separable nature of the existence of mathematical objects, seeing as it is
only a part of the universal reason-principles and the median forms
residing in the soul, but is customarily taken by those divine men as
representative of the intelligible nature as a whole. Aristotle, then, in his 5
attempt at refutation, approaches the question of their mode of existence
by employing the following division: (1076a33-6):[31]

'For', he says, 'if the objects of mathematics exist, they must
necessarily exist either in perceptible things, as some say, or
separate from perceptible things (there are some too who say this);
or, if neither one nor the other, either they do not exist at all, or
they exist in some other way.'

Now he is right in employing this division, except insofar as he has 10
postulated that there are some who have left mathematical objects as
inherent in perceptible things, and he has very well discerned and
expressed the conclusion to his hypothesis; for if they are neither
separate nor inseparable from perceptible things, then necessarily
either they do not exist at all, or they acquire whatever existence they
possess in some other way – that is, they are generated in us by

abstraction (*aphairesis*), which is in fact his own view. He attacks both the
15 position that they are inseparable from perceptible things and that they
have a separate existence, in order that either they may not exist in any
way at all, like the notorious 'thingummybob' (*skindapsos*),[32] or precisely
his own position will prevail, that they are derived from perceptible things
by abstraction. So he joins issue, then, first with those who do not separate
them from perceptible things, writing against them as follows.[33]

Chapter 2: The mode of existence of mathematical objects

20 **1076a38-b13** That the objects of mathematics cannot be in sensible things, and that moreover the theory that they are is
fantastical, has been observed already in our discussion of difficulties,[34] the reasons being that (1) it is impossible for two solids to
occupy the same space at the same time, and (2) that on this same
theory all other potentialities and characteristics would exist in
sensible things, and none of them would exist separately. This,
then, has already been stated; but in addition to this, it is clearly
impossible on this theory for any body to be divided. For it will
have to be divided along a plane, and the plane along a line, and
the line at a point; and therefore if the point is indivisible, so is the
line, and if the line is, so must the rest be also. So what difference
does it make whether perceptible bodies are objects of this kind,
or whether, while they are not, objects of this kind exist in them?
The consequence will be the same, for either they will be divided
when the perceptible objects are divided, or else not even the
perceptible objects can be divided.

Whether he constructs a strong or a weak argument in this passage is
nothing to the point; for neither any of the Pythagoreans nor Plato
himself nor any of the Platonists of his time postulated that geometrical
figures and magnitudes inhered in perceptible objects; if Severus,[35] or
some other of those who commented on Plato in later times, basing
themselves on the teaching of Aristotle himself, have made illegitimate
25 use of mathematical entities in their explanation of physical causes,
that has nothing to do with the ancients, whose doctrines he is here
attempting to refute; so that I will direct no response to him on this
question on behalf of those men.

Since,[36] however, he has referred us back to the difficulties raised in
B,[37] it must be said in response to what was said there that it is not
actually impossible according to all philosophers for two solid bodies to
be in the same place; and one would not be basing one's objection here
30 on an appeal to the Stoics, who do not actually dismiss the possibility of
even material masses interpenetrating one another,[38] but rather to
those who, postulating that extension pervades the whole cosmos,[39] and

has received into itself the whole nature of body, say that it neither cuts up other things nor is itself cut up and divided along with the air and the rest of bodies, but extends throughout the cosmos steadfast, firm, unmoved, and exempt from any alteration, providing a place and recep- 35 tacle and bound and circumscription and everything of that sort to the things that form the contents of the visible cosmos. These people do not say right out that such space and extension is a mathematical body, but 85,1 that it is akin to the mathematical in respect of its immateriality and immobility and intangibility, its freedom from resistance to the touch and its being exempt from all types of quality involving a capacity for being acted upon. Further, even as the mathematical body comes to be, when the reason-principle (*logos*)[40] is put forth, in discursive intellec- tion (*dianoia*) in virtue of the vital spirit (*pneuma*) and the imaging 5 faculty (*phantasia*) inherent in the spirit[41] (for at one and the same time the reason-principle of a sphere, for instance, comes to consciousness, and the imaging faculty beholds a mathematical sphere, endowed with immaterial bulk [*onkos*]), just so this spherical extension in the uni- verse possesses its substance in co-operation with the will and intellection of the cosmic Soul, Soul making it spherical through its vision of Intellect, while through its contemplation of all the Forms it 10 makes it capable of embracing all bodies, both each individually and the totality of them as one – as, after all, its intellections are both continu- ous and transitive – since the intelligible Forms in the Complete Living Being are both unified and distinct, although embraced by a single nature; and of these the (physical) cosmos, taking imprints (*mimêmata*), receives them in an extended mode and not devoid of magnitude (*amegethôs*).

But what provoked this whole line of argument was the point that, 15 neither according to these men[42] nor to those who postulate that imma- terial and simple bodies can interpenetrate each other indivisibly, is it impossible for two solid[43] bodies to come to be in the same place simultaneously, though they would maintain that for two material and resistant bodies to occupy the same place is a complete impossibility. But immaterial entities would seem to resemble instances of light 20 emitted by different lamps and extending throughout the whole of one and the same room, and interpenetrating each other without mixing and without dividing themselves; for these entities, even if one wants to call them incorporeal, nonetheless, spreading and extending them- selves, as they do, along with bodies in all three dimensions, are not prevented from occupying the same place as one another and the bodies concerned, for no other reason than that they are simple and immate- 25 rial and are not split up by being divided, but, while remaining connected to their source and dependent on this, are present when it is shining, and disappear along with it when it departs; which indeed is something that the immaterial bodies that are dependent on souls are not prevented from doing either.[44]

I make these points, in order that we may not be browbeaten by some
of the superficially impressive arguments of experts in physics, which
30 seek to extend the properties characteristic of material, passible, and
resistant bodies to the whole of extended nature. That this has no
relevance to the original subject of the treatise we have remarked
already.[45] For neither will anything be said (by me) in reply to him on
behalf of the Pythagoreans and Platonists, since he is not actually
attempting to set straight any doctrine of theirs, nor is Aristotle himself
35 in the present instance in dispute with those who are championing a
doctrine of extension (*diastêma*), but with those who wish, in the midst
of sensible bodies, to insert other bodies which are solid as regards being
three-dimensionally extended, but which are of mathematical nature.
We, as I say, are not aware of any respectable philosopher who maintains such a doctrine; for the five figures that are set out in the *Timaeus*
(58Cff.) as being employed for the construction of the elements of the
86,1 cosmos, while being presented in mathematical terms, yet hint at their
true character as active and creative forces in nature. And as for the
luminous vehicle (*augoeides okhêma*)[46] within us, even if it has been
described as three-dimensionally extended and yet not possessing solidity, it may be firmly maintained that this is not a geometrical body; for
5 how could someone classify something that is full of life and movement,
and indeed the most mobile of all elements within us according to the
definition of motion recognised by Aristotle himself, as being devoid of
motion by reason of being a geometrical entity? It is plain, in fact, that
the excellent[47] Aristotle is setting himself to refute a bogus theory, and
that our argument picks on one of his assertions as not being in all
10 respects absolutely and unqualifiedly true; since in what is said next,
to wit: 'that on this same theory all other potentialities and characteristics would exist in sensible things, and none of them would exist
separately' (1076b3-4), by 'other potentialities' he means to indicate the
limits of these, such as planes and lines, unless indeed he is taking in
also the proper objects of optics and harmonics and sciences akin to
15 these; but he adduces no necessity whatever for postulating that none
of them possess a separate nature; unless, after all, these things were
postulated to exist only in sensible objects, and not in <the objects of
discursive reason>[48] and outside sensible objects in certain reason-principles (*logoi*) which produce these. And he says that these objections
have been made previously in Book 3 against these positions.[49] His
20 objection here is something like the following: if, he says, the solid in
the sensible object were to be divided, inevitably it will be divided at a
plane surface; and the plane surface in turn will be divided at a line,
and the line at a point. Now if these were not subject to motion, as is
maintained by geometricians, no illogical result would follow; but in the
present case, since it is postulated that they inhere in sensible physical
bodies, when the line is subjected to motion by being divided, the point
25 will also necessarily be divided; and it makes no difference whether one

speaks of the actual physical points as being partless and indivisible, or one postulate such points[50] as being inherent in them. For it is obvious that what is in something is not divided without its substratum, when it is said to be in something 'as in a substratum'.

Such then is Aristotle's argument, directed against a false and implausible hypothesis, and refuting it boldly and convincingly. We, however, suspect that it may have been in one of the older philosophers 30 that he found this theory of a principle in nature that is indivisible and yet divided about bodies, and yet held to be both completely non-extended and thus partless, and that this gave him an excuse for fabricating this hypothesis, unless perhaps for the sake of making a comprehensive attack on all those who practise division[51] he chose to say something also against this theory.

But since he has made his point against those who place the objects 35 of geometry and the other mathematical sciences in sensible objects, let us see how he deals in turn with those who separate them from sensible objects.

1076b11-39 Nor again can objects of this kind exist in separation. 87,1 For if over and above sensible solids there are to be other solids which are separate from them and prior to the sensible solids, clearly besides sensible planes there must be other separate planes, and so too with points and lines; for the same argument applies. And if these exist, again besides the planes, lines and points of the mathematical solid, there must be others which are separate; for the incomposite is prior to the composite, and if prior to sensible bodies there are other non-sensible bodies, then by the same argument the planes which exist independently must be prior to those which are present in the immovable solids. Therefore there will be planes and lines distinct from those which co-exist with the separately-existent solids; for the latter co-exist with the mathematical solids, but the former are prior to the mathematical solids. Again, in these planes there will be lines, and by the same argument there must be other lines prior to these; and prior to the points which are in the prior lines there must be other points, although there will be no other points prior to these. Now the accumulation becomes absurd; for whereas we get only one class of solids besides sensible solids, we get three classes of planes beside sensible planes – those which exist separately from sensible planes, those which exist in the mathematical solids, and those which exist separately from these latter – four classes of lines, and five of points. With which of these, then, will the mathematical sciences deal? Not, surely, with the planes, lines and points in the immovable solid; for knowledge is always concerned with what is prior.

The same argument applies also to numbers: for there will be

other units over and above each class of points, and besides each
class of existing things, first the sensible and then the intelligible,
so that there will be {infinitely many}[52] kinds of mathematical
numbers.

In this passage, he tries to demolish a theory held by the philosophers
prior to him, but produces nothing in the way of scientific proof against
5 it, but only such points as would serve to confuse a non-expert who had
not penetrated the thought of those men. For if, he says, there are going
to be bodies over and above the sensible, there will also be two classes
of planes, those in those bodies and those subsisting on their own; and
three classes of line, those in the solid bodies, those in the planes, and
those on their own; and by the same reckoning four classes of points,
10 and five classes of units prior to the points, and in general always the
prior and more simple entities will be the more multifarious.

This sort of thing might serve for an attack on the doctrine which
might impress the general public, but it does not in fact succeed in
reducing it to absurdity; for the men concerned will accept that, at the
level of the essential reason-principles of the soul, these entities may
subsist in both distinct and unified modes, and there is nothing odd
about the fact that the point – or rather the reason-principle of the point
15 – might both be unmixed with what follows it and yet contribute to the
essence of the line and the plane and three-dimensional body; for these
men maintain firmly at more or less every level both the unity and the
dividedness of incorporeal forms. And further, the sameness of unity
and multiplicity might be conceded even at the level of sensible objects,
but particularly so at the level of the objects of discursive reason
20 (*dianoêta*), and even more so again this has been proved very clearly by
the older philosophers at the intellective level, and indeed this has been
given adequate treatment by ourselves in our commentary on Book 3,[53]
where we tried to spell out what sort of point is more honourable and
perfect than a line or a plane, and what sort is more imperfect and
inferior; for there is no problem about the one, as being more simple,
being more venerable and originative, while the other, as contributing
25 to establishing the definition and circumscription of something more
composite, being inferior – as, after all, in the case of the monad, one
sort comprehends within itself paradigmatically all number, both even
and odd, while the other is, if you will, just a small part of that quantity
which underlies numbers.

This much, then, is sufficient to present the truth on this topic. But
30 if one were to exceed the bounds of moderation in seeking to avoid the
criticism of the non-experts, and not grant that the principles of extended and non-extended entities exist in many ways in the soul, then
he could say in response to Aristotle that it is not necessary that there
be four classes of point, three of line, and two of plane. But even as the
letter A is to be found in a syllable and in a word and in a sentence,

though it remains one and the same in form and possesses the same 35
nature in all instances, even so do the point and the line preserve one
and the same form both on their own and as parts of more complex
entities; and even as the art of grammar, having recognised the force of
A on its own, knows also what it does in a syllable and in a sentence, in 88,1
this same way the mathematical sciences, in cognising their proper
objects on their own, recognise them also in combination with others.

Let this then be our reply to him in respect of what he considers his
inescapable premiss (*protasis*); for he raises the question, 'with which
of these will the mathematical sciences deal?' But how does he come to
the conclusion that there are many classes of mathematical numbers? 5
We may grant, indeed, that there are many classes of number, inasmuch as each order of beings is equipped with its proper numbers; but
as for classes of mathematical object, if one resolves to term only the
unitary (*monadikoi*) numbers mathematical and not their causal principle residing in the discursive intellect,[54] how would they be many?
Unless perhaps one wants to take the points as units (*monades*) and, 10
viewing them at four different levels, weave numbers out of all of them.
But this would amount to mere playing to the gallery,[55] rather than a
serious attempt at refutation (*elenkhos*).

1076b39-77a4 Again, how can we solve the problems which we
enumerated in our discussion of difficulties?[56] For the objects of
astronomy will similarly be distinct from sensible things, and so
will those of geometry; but how can a heaven and its parts (or
anything else which has motion) exist apart from the sensible
heaven?

Since all Forms in general are present both in divine and heavenly souls
and also in our own, in a manner proper to each,[57] even before the
corporeal level of the cosmos acquires them in an individualised mode 15
(*merikôs*), it is ridiculous to enquire, in respect of each item, where there
will be another heaven or another sun or anything else that goes to
make up the visible order. That these entities are to be found, not just
once, but I might almost say infinitely multiplied, is something asserted
from time immemorial by both theologians and philosophers, but he
chooses not to follow them in this, and advances it as a paradox that 20
there should be just one heaven over and above the sensible one. But if
one were to assert that the soul of the true philosopher pursues astronomy above the heaven and contemplates all reality on the intelligible
level, he will presumably object to this, since he does not accept[58] the
Forms, nor is willing to accept that the soul, operating as it does at the
level of discursive intellection, should possess the Forms in actuality,
but, if at all, potentially. But how, then, can the astronomers produce
proofs on the basis of appropriately primary causal principles, if they do 25
not proceed from general reason-principles, which our souls possess

cognitively, but the divine souls both cognitively and demiurgically? For either astronomers and all mathematicians, and indeed all physical philosophers, must give up hope of scientifically demonstrating any proposition, and abandon the idea that proofs derive from the causal
30   principle, not just of the conclusion, but of reality itself,[59] or, as long as both of these is maintained, it must be the case that the causal principles of all things that are produced both in the heavens and in the whole of nature pre-exist in some kind of universal reason-principles. And in general, those who maintain the existence of the sensible realm as real existence do not seem to realise that they are revealing the soul to be of less dignity than matter, as indeed is remarked by the worthy Amelius.[60]

35   **1077a5-9** And similarly the objects of optics and of harmonics will be distinct, for there will be sound and sight apart from the sensible and particular objects. Hence clearly the other senses and their objects will exist separately; for why should one class of objects do so rather than another? And if this is so, there will be separate living beings too, inasmuch as there will be separate senses.[61]

There is actually nothing strange in all these things being present in reason-principles, and in the images of reason-principles, that is to say, objects of imagination (*phantasmata*), not only prior to sensible objects,
89,1 but also prior to the reason-principles in nature which give form to the sensible objects. But he, though these facts are granted, adduces as the greatest of absurdities that there will be another set of living beings, if there are separate senses; but despite the fact his teacher had long ago told him that the Essential Living Being,[62] in comprehending within itself all the intelligible living beings, is the cause of the living beings
5   both in the psychic and in the sensible realms, he pretends that he has never heard anything about such matters.
It is possible, in any case, not to yield to his conclusions. For it does not follow, if sensible objects have causes prior to themselves, that sensation is necessarily connected with the causes of the sensible objects, nor, if sense-perception is present in distinct ways in the soul
10   and in the demiurgic intellect, that this by itself reveals the perceiving entity as a living being. For it is not presumably the case that every perceiving entity is a living being, but rather everything which is moved all at once by an external stimulus; nor is every cause of a sense-object grasped by perception, but rather that which is individual and inheres within its own product. It is possible also, agreeing to all this – since we learn that sense-perception occurs not only at the level of the rational
15   world soul, as Timaeus declares (37Aff.), but we also accept that there is a kind of demiurgic sense-perception celebrated by the theologians,[63] of which the heavenly bodies possess an image, themselves 'transmitting sense-perception to the worlds', as the Oracle has it – to accept the

conclusion that there are in fact other living beings. And that I may not rely on the witness of what others have said, he himself, in Book *Kappa*,[64] has called the primal Intellect a living being. It is plain, then, that he should not, presumably, disdain to call each one of the other levels an intellective being, even if not a primary one. In the *Ethics*,[65] furthermore, he clearly wishes man in the proper sense to be his intellect. If, then, the intellect in us is man in the proper sense, and every man is a living being, the conclusion is perfectly clear. 20

So then, once again, we accept the fact that there are other living beings besides sensible ones, but they exist in another mode and not in the same way as sensible ones; and if one wants to call their cognitions sense-perceptions and the objects of their cognitions sense-objects, in the sense that they are *causes* of sense-objects properly so-called, then we will not quibble about terms; only let it be made clear about which of them we are using each term on each occasion. 25

1077a9-14 Again, there are certain general theorems stated by mathematicians whose application is not restricted to these substances. Here, then, we shall have yet another kind of substance intermediate between and distinct from the Forms and the intermediates, which is neither number nor points nor spatial magnitude nor time. And if this is impossible, clearly it is also impossible that the former substances should exist separately from sensible objects.

'Stated' (*graphetai*)[66] here means 'demonstrated'. The argument (*epikheirêma*) as a whole is as follows: if some proposition is demonstrated by mathematicians or physicists by means of general principles and certain axioms (such as, for instance, 'if you take away equals from equals, equals remain', or 'if there are four elements in proportion, the product of the extremes is equal to the product of the median elements', and many other such axioms), it is necessary, he says, that, as there are separate magnitudes and numbers, so the things referred to by these axioms should be separate, being superior to mathematical magnitudes and numbers, while being inferior[67] to the Forms, being ranged between Magnitude Itself and mathematical magnitude. This he dismisses as an impossibility, in order to invalidate the premiss that the mathematicals are separate. But this is actually in a way true; for, among the reason-principles in the soul, some are more simple and general and comprehensive of the others, and for this reason closer to Intellect and clearer and more knowable than the more particular ones, while others are inferior in all these respects and are held together and structured and filled by their superiors. What is there strange, then, or rather how is it not necessary, if it is the case that our intuitions are true when they concord with the facts, and that axiom is true which declares that 'if one takes away equals from equals, equals remain', that there should be 30

35

90,1

5

10

some reason-principle (*logos*) to which this should primarily belong, which is a principle neither of magnitude nor of time, but which embraces all these and the rest of the things to which this axiom naturally pertains, but which is nonetheless not situated in any place nor in the sensible realm? For how should that which is general and

15 completely simple and thus indemonstrable be present in matter which is barely able to receive the individual reflection of the Forms? If, then, we are not prepared to accept this conclusion, how will that principle be preserved which declares that every demonstrative cause should primarily belong to some thing with which it is co-extensive and to which it pertains universally (*katholou*), in the way that you yourself understand the concept of the universal in the *Analytics*?[68]

20 For what reason, then, will the axioms be clearer and more cognisable than the more particular entities which are subjects of proof (*apodeikta*), if in fact we are to establish them, as being not previously existent, through induction from the lowest entities? And how will we come to agreement about them, if they are not essentially pre-existent in our conceptions? For what we derive from sense-objects, we do not necessarily have to be of one mind about, as for instance if I were to have

25 a sense-image (*phantasma*) of Socrates, and you of Alexander?[69] And how – to make use of a very valid principle of your own[70] – will actualised knowledge be identical with the object of knowledge, unless every object of cognition is co-ordinate to the relevant cognition, and especially that the most universal proposition (*logos*)[71] should be consubstantial with the conception of axioms, being the primal receptor of the intuiting (*epibolê*) and grasping of an axiom? For even as the Good itself both

30 brings into being intellection and unites it to the object of intellection, and as the child and offspring of the Good[72] produces both vision and the object of vision simultaneously and relates them to one another, even so that which occupies the plane of reality between these two, the much-revered Intellect,[73] produces scientific knowledge (*epistêmê*) and its object and brings them together and intertwines them with one another, in no case bringing into being one before the other, in order

35 that what is brought into being may not be maimed and imperfect and vacuous.

But we must not, by dwelling too long on these questions, get drawn into an enquiry extraneous to the main point. How – to return to that – will the intellect (a point explicitly granted by you) endow the soul with the first principles of scientific proof, if we do not have these already in our conceptions? For it is not of things that derive their generation from below them that the intellect is our provider. Either, then, proof is

91,1 circular, as we derive and substantiate the axioms on the basis of more particular truths, while the axioms in turn serve to provide scientific proof of such objects; or else, since proofs derive from principles higher than them, the simplest intuitions of axioms derive from Intellect, and from these in turn, when compounded together, the whole variety of the

Forms comes to be within us. And again, this whole variety is struc- 5
tured by Intellect and derives from Intellect (for what of those things
which we possess essentially is not from that source?), but in such a way
that more particular entities derive their existence from the more
simple levels of Form and reason-principle. It is only on this assumption
that we will find ourselves enjoying due consistency, when we admit
that proofs derive their validity from the primary causal principles.

1077a14-20 In general, consequences result which are contrary 10
both to the truth and to received opinion if one posits the objects of
mathematics thus as definite separately-existent entities. For if they
exist in this way, they would necessarily be prior to sensible magnitudes, whereas in fact they must be subsequent to them; for
incomplete magnitude is prior in point of generation, but subsequent
in point of substantiality, even as the inanimate is to the animate.

Those men are out of tune neither with themselves nor with reality; for
they consider as 'incomplete' (*ateles*) neither the Form of magnitude in
the mind (*dianoia*) nor that magnitude which arises in conjunction with
this Form in the imagination, nor yet as 'inanimate'.[74] For how could it
be, seeing as it is situated in the soul? And as for ourselves,[75] how are
we going to maintain positions concordant with ourselves, when we 15
both declare that there are causal principles of things through the
agency of which, subsisting in themselves, proofs arise, and yet we do
not grant them true existence (unless we are to postulate that the
non-existent can be the cause of existence), and when we repeatedly
maintain that universal entities are prior in the order of nature, on the
ground that they eliminate [what is below them] but are not themselves
eliminated,[76] while on the other hand we insist that these very entities
derive their existence by abstraction (*aphairesis*) from sensible objects?
For if you were to declare that the universal is of two sorts, the one
cause of the sensible, the other supervening upon it,[77] you would say 20
things dear both to your Father[78] and to all the progeny of Pythagoras;
and accept also that magnitude is of two sorts, the one residing in the
reasoning of discursive intellect (*dianoia*), along with which the form of
it in the imagination (*phantaston*) comes to be, the other arising by
abstraction from the sensible realm, and do not say that geometry
concerns itself with that which arises from abstraction; for it contains 25
nothing accurate, along with the fact that we have never seen any
polygons of such size and quality as geometry concerns itself with by
way of plane figures, nor such a variety of many-sided figures (*polu-
pleura*) as are examined by stereometry, or divisions of angles or sides
or surfaces (*embada*), and such things as have reason-principles replete
with theorems, but matter which does not admit of such; and say that
it[79] concerns itself with objects of the imagination, insofar as these arise 30
as a by-product of (*parhuphistatai*)[80] the essential reason-principles in

the discursive intellect, from precisely which it derives its demonstrative causality, or say rather that geometry aims to contemplate the actual partless reason-principles of the soul, but, being too feeble to employ intellections free of images (*aphantastoi*), it extends its powers[81] to imaged and extended shapes and magnitudes, and thus contemplates
35   in them those former entities. Just as, when even the imagination does not suffice for it, it resorts to the reckoning-board (*abakion*)[82] and there
92,1 makes a drawing of the theorem, and in that situation its primary object is certainly not to grasp the sensible and external diagram, but rather the internal, imagined one, of which the external one is a soulless imitation; so also when it directs itself to the object of imagination, it is not concerned with it in a primary way, but it is only because through
5   weakness of intellection it is unable to grasp the Form which transcends imagination that it studies this at the imaginative level. And the most powerful indication of this is that, whereas the proof is of the universal, every object of imagination is particular (*merikon*); therefore the primary concern was never with the object of imagination, but rather with the universal and absolutely immaterial. But if the universal is of one kind only, then how it can be both supervenient upon and cause of what
10   is more particular than it will be something difficult to prove – if one may term 'difficult' the utterly impossible!

1077a20-4 Again, in virtue of what can we possibly regard mathematical magnitudes as one? Things in this world of ours may be reasonably supposed to be one in virtue of soul or part of the soul, or some other influence; apart from this, they are a plurality and are disintegrated. But inasmuch as the former entities are divisible and quantitative, what is the cause of their unity and cohesion?

This seems to cut across the sequence of the argument; for it turns back again to his earlier point,[83] where he posed the question how mathematical objects can be both less perfect and prior to objects of sense. He
15   enquires here as to what the cause of unity is in mathematical magnitudes. In physical objects, after all, it is nature, or the enmattered form, or glue, or some form of binding; but what is it in mathematical entities?
     Our reply to him must be that the partless reason-principles of magnitudes are superior <to any sort of material bonding, while> the imaged magnitudes <which owe their existence to the Form>,[84] being dependent as they are on their own partless causal principle, will never be disintegrated, and, being still inherent in the soul, are held together
20   by it more than sensible objects are.

1077a24-31 Again, the ways in which the objects of mathematics are generated prove our point; for they are generated first in the dimension of length, then in that of breadth, and finally in that of depth, and this brings them to completion. Thus, if that which is later in point of generation is prior in substantiality, body will be prior to plane and line, and in this sense it will also be more truly complete and whole, because it can become animate; whereas how could a line or a plane become animate? The supposition would be beyond our powers of apprehension.

He goes back now to the beginning, where he sought to demonstrate that the sense-object is prior to the mathematical in substantiality (*ousia*).[85] But he does not here manage to demonstrate what he proposed to himself, since he makes the general assumption of generation in respect of things that are ungenerated (for mathematical objects are ungenerated), but if he proves anything at all, it is that, among sensible objects, a body 25 is both prior in essence to a plane and more perfect than it.

... because it can become animate ... beyond our powers of apprehension.

For you can see the line on the reckoning-board and the plane figure in the dust; and what, after all, could be more animate than entities inherent in the soul?

1077a31-6 Further, body is a kind of substance, since it already in some sense possesses completeness; but in what sense are lines substances? Neither as being a kind of form or shape, as perhaps soul is, nor as being matter, like the body; for it does not appear that anything can be composed either of lines or of planes or of points, whereas if they were a kind of material substance it would be apparent that things could be so composed.

This argument also is designed to show that lines and planes are 30 secondary to bodies; for if, he says, lines also are substances (*ousiai*), in what sense are they substances, as form or as matter? If on the other 93,1 hand they are non-substantial, they will be secondary to substances. Our reply to this must be that there is one type of substance that is non-extended, such as reason-principles and forms, and there is another, residing in the image-making faculty (*phantasia*), that is extended, serving as matter for either straight lines or curved ones. But even if one were to say that all substance at the imaged level resides as it were in the image-making faculty or the *pneuma*[86] as in a substratum, 5 one might be compelled to declare it to be secondary and less perfect than those particular entities, but not to sensible substance. For it is not the case that everything that is in a substratum is secondary to any sort of substance (for in that case the virtues and the items of scientific knowledge in the soul would be secondary to stones and all other material bodies), but it is secondary only to that in which it has its

10 being, and it is not secondary nor less perfect than some other inferior
    substance, unless one were, coming to close quarters,[87] in direct opposi-
    tion to the divine Plato, to declare that there was nothing odd in
    scientific knowledge or virtue being less perfect than body. But I
    presume that in fact soul and all to do with soul is superior to body[88]
    and all to do with body, and of these, soul is superior to those things that
    are in actuality sometimes present in it and sometimes not, while body
15 is of higher dignity than those things that are accidental to it. But
    surely it is inappropriate to set up a comparison between those things
    which are resident in the soul either permanently or occasionally and
    the body, and more inappropriate still, when making such a compari-
    son, to promote as prior to those things which have their place in the
    soul any material body, as being more perfect and more endowed with
    soul (*empsukhon*) than they; for this would be the most remarkable
    thing of all, if the body is to be more ensouled than those things whose
20 essence it is to be resident in the soul.

> **1077a36-b12** Let it be granted, then, that they are prior in defini-
> tion (*logos*); yet not everything that is prior in definition is prior in
> substance. Things are prior in substance which, when separated,
> have a superior power of existence; while things are prior in defini-
> tion from whose definitions the definitions of other things are
> compounded. And these do not always apply together. For if attrib-
> utes, such as 'moving' or 'white', do not exist apart from their
> substances, 'white' will be prior in definition to 'white man', but not
> in substance; for it cannot exist in separation, but always exists
> conjointly with the concrete whole – by which I mean 'white man'.
> Thus it is obvious that neither is the result of abstraction prior, nor
> the result of adding a determinant posterior; for it is as a result of
> adding a determinant to 'white' that we come to speak of 'white man'.

In this passage he grants that mathematical entities are prior in
definition to sense-objects, since someone propounding a definition of a
sensible body has need of the dimensions which bound a mathematical
entity, but that does not mean that they are prior in substance. And yet
25 according to the rules which he himself has laid down in Book 7[89] in
    relation to simple substances (I mean by 'simple' those taken without their
    accidents), that which is prior in definition is also demonstrated to be prior
    in substance; for the elements that are prior in definition in those entities
    are said to be prior in form, and what are prior in form are prior in
    substance. The conclusion from these two propositions is clear enough. So
30 the rule laid down by him in this passage demonstrates that mathematical
    entities are prior to sense-objects not only in definition (this, after all, he
    grants himself) but also in substance; for they are superior to them on
    the scale of being. Since, then, there is such a thing as a three-dimen-
    sional object with resistivity (*antitupia*), there must be also be prior to

this a three-dimensional object *tout court*,[90] and further, a two-dimensional object, and prior to that again an object with just one dimension; and the existence of these does not entail that of a sensible object. 35

But to pass on: what is the conclusion that he seeks to draw from these examples? What else than that that which is prior in definition is 94,1 not in all cases prior also in substance, and indeed that it is posterior. For 'white', whereas it is prior in definition to 'white man', is not according to him prior in substance. And yet one might make the point that, even though it is not prior to 'man', yet it should be senior to 'white man'. However, let it be admitted and laid down that there are some 5 things which, while being prior in definition, are coeval (*sundroma*) in substance with those things to which they are prior in definition. What do we conclude from this? Surely that geometrical entities, while being prior in definition, in respect of substance are neither prior nor posterior to sense-objects? And yet his whole argument is based on the assumption that mathematical matter[91] is derived from sense-objects by abstraction (*ex aphaireseôs*); this is why he produced such a conclu- 10 sion as: 'Thus it is obvious that neither is the result of abstraction prior, nor the result of adding a determinant posterior'. But nevertheless, making this premature move,[92] false as it is, and <employing it>[93] as a basis for his enquiry – we see what sort of conclusion he comes to. If he had wanted to give correct consideration to the dimensions with which geometry in fact concerns itself, he would have discovered that they are 15 in all respects vsuperior to material body – if, that is, we all agree that the immaterial is superior to the material, the general to the particular, and the eternal to the destructible.

1077b12-14 Thus[94] we have sufficiently shown (a) that (the objects of mathematics) are not more substantial than bodies; (b) that they are not prior in point of existence to sensible objects, but only in definition (*logos*); and (c) that they cannot in any way exist separately.

He takes this conclusion as something proved. We, however, have 20 demonstrated to the best of our ability that the reason-principles (*logoi*)[95] of these things are partless essences, and causal principles of the spatially-extended objects of imagination and sense-perception. We have also established with reasonable probability that the shapes and spatial extensions which arise in the imagination in association with partless reason-principles, inasmuch as they are in the soul as in a substratum, are themselves prior to the body and to bodily affections. But since what he has just said has created a presumption[96] towards 25 the conclusion, we must draw attention to the fact that the spatial dimensions in sense-objects have been shown to be prior to bodies in definition (*logôi*), but not posterior in substance (*ousiâi*), so that there is perhaps nothing odd about describing these as 'non-substantial'.

Chapter 3: The mode of existence of mathematical objects, continued[97]

1077b14-1078a13 Since we have seen that they cannot exist in sensible things, it is clear that either they do not exist at all, or they exist only in a certain way, and therefore not absolutely; for we use 'exist' in several senses.

Just as the general propositions in mathematics are not concerned with objects which exist separately apart from magnitudes and numbers, but are about these, only not as possessing magnitude or being divisible, clearly it is also possible for there to be statements and proofs about perceptible magnitudes, not qua sensible, but qua having certain characteristics. For just as there can be many propositions about things merely qua movable, without any reference to the essential nature of each one or to their attributes, and it does not necessarily follow from this either that there is something movable which exists in separation from sensible things, or that there is a distinct movable nature in sensible things; so too there will be propositions and branches of science about them, not as movable but as corporeal only; and again, as planes only and as lines only, and as divisible, and as indivisible but having position, and then as indivisible only.

Therefore since it is true to say in a general sense not only that things which are separable exist, but that things which are inseparable exist (e.g. that movable things exist), it is also true to say in a general sense that mathematical objects exist, and are such as they are said to be. And just as it is true to say generally of the other branches of science that they deal with a particular subject – not with that which is accidental to it (e.g. not with 'white', if the healthy is white, and the subject of the science in question is the healthy), but with that which is the subject of the particular science: with the healthy, if its subject of study is 'the healthy', and with man, if it studies it as man – so it is also true of geometry: if the things which it studies are accidentally sensible, although it does not study them qua sensible, it does not follow that the mathematical sciences study sensible objects – nor, on the other hand, that they study other things which exist independently apart from these.

Many attributes are essential properties of things as possessing a particular characteristic – for instance there are attributes peculiar to an animal as being male or as being female (yet there is no such thing as male or female separate from animals). So there are also attributes which are peculiar to things merely as lines or as planes. And the more that the subject of study is prior in definition and simpler, the greater is its exactness (for simplicity implies exactness). Hence we find greater exactness where

there is no magnitude, and the greatest exactness where there is
no motion; or, if motion is involved, where it is primary, because
this is the simplest kind; and the simplest kind of prmary motion
is uniform motion.

Having said in what way he does not think that the objects of mathe- 30
matics exist, now he undertakes to tell us what sort of existence one
might suppose them to have. His preferred view is that mathematical
magnitudes and figures neither exist on their own nor in sense-objects
while being distinct from sense-objects, but that they are derived con-
ceptually from sense-objects by abstraction. For he says, '*Just as the
general propositions in mathematics are not concerned with objects* 95,1
*which exist separately apart from magnitudes and numbers, but are
about these, only not as such*' (as when we say, 'If the first has the same
ratio to the second as the third has to the fourth, then, even when they
are interchanged, the characteristic of having the same ratio will be
preserved'), so he says, a mathematical discussion, when conducted in 5
relation to magnitudes, is concducted in relation to sense-objects, but
not *qua* sense-objects. We, however, even as we earlier objected to this
position, saying that this should take a broader view of both magnitudes
and numbers, so now have the same objection to make. For if the
universal is that in which properties primarily[98] inhere, it is necessary
that that should exist independent of entities that are more specific
than it; for it is not the case that something inheres primarily in
something non-existent. But if someone declares that the universal
inheres in the things that are more specific than it, then he is looking 10
to the immanent universal, which is a part of its substratum, and not
to the separable, which is predicated of every form. Except that one may
truly admire Aristotle's consistency,[99] in this passage also, for making
a connexion between universals and mathematical entities; for as it is
with universals, so also with mathematicals. Both of them, in truth, are 15
present in the substantial reason-principles of souls, but according to
him in perceptible objects, and in concepts which abstract the common qualities from sensible objects. And since he made mention of
motion, in saying that many statements are made about motion
without implying the existence of motion as a separate entity (for
when we say, 'Things that move at an equal speed cover the same
distance in an equal time', we are not referring to the underlying 20
objects, but are talking only of their motion, but nonetheless we do
not for this reason postulate the existence of such a thing as separate
motion), we must reply that, first of all, it is not the same case with
motion as with shapes; for he who does not wish that there be motion
outside of sensible objects does not conceive of some more exact form
of motion in the immobile realm, whereas the geometer does conceive
of other shapes more exact than perceptible ones; and secondly, he is
understanding 'universe' in an invalid sense; for there is motion

among incorporeal entities as well as shape and size, but they are not
the same as in the sensible realm.

　　In general, in response to his overall view it must be said that we also
30　do not observe all shapes or all numbers as being inherent in sensible
objects, that is to say, all those with which the mathematical sciences
concern themselves, nor is it possible that things derived from sense-objects should enjoy such precision. And if he were to explain that we
ourselves add to them what is lacking and thus make them more exact
and then contemplate them as such, he will have to tell us first of all
35　whence we are able to confer perfection on these; for we would not find
any other truer cause of this than that propounded by the ancients, that
the soul in its essence has prior possession of the reason-principles of
all things. But then if we add anything to what has been abstracted
from sensible objects, we will not end up with a more accurate or truer
result, but rather a more artificial one. At any rate, when receiving an
impression of the form of Socrates, if one retains it in one's imagination
40　as one has received it from the perceptible Socrates, one would acquire
96,1　a more accurate knowledge of him; while if you were to wish to alter it
so as to make it more comely, you would end up contemplating inwardly
anything rather than the form of Socrates. In the case of equal and
similar numbers and (geometrical) figures, however, we do not have the
same experience, but the more we adjust them in the direction of
5　greater accuracy and perfection, the more, by coming ever nearer to
their partless form, do they become clear and comprehensible to us. And
in general while we may admit that our mind is provoked to recollection
from sensible objects, it is really almost sacrilegious[100] to say that we
take in shape from that source; for the forms that are conveyed to us
through sense-perception can extend only as far as the imaginative
faculty, and indeed even in the imaginative faculty they tend to remain
10　individual and such as when they first entered. But when conceptual
thought subsequently transfers itself from these to the universal and to
those objects which are contemplated by exact reasoning, it is plain
that it is viewing its proper objects. For this reason this activity is
admirable and not concerned with business other than its own,[101] and
is such as to stimulate the eye of the soul, blinded as it is and buried
in a multitude of practical concerns.[102] But how could it achieve that
15　if it concerned itself with the products of abstraction? It would surely
have done rather the opposite: blinded what was previously sighted
in the mind, welded it to the body, and obscured the impulse that
would lead it towards true reality[103] – if, in the words of Alexander of
Aphrodisias,[104] it fabricates for itself certain objects of intellection,
which are not by their own nature intelligible, and then toys futilely
with them. For if they postulated that these entities were devoid of
20　substance, but similar to intellectual forms, this would be a matter
for great wonder, how things that had no substance bore any resemblance to them. The only line that it remains for them to take is to

say that, once the intellect has exercised itself on these objects, it will eventually be able to relate also to the intelligible forms, even as orators, by practising orations on various imaginary themes, gain experi- 25
ence for real contests, by reason of the similarity of the fabricated situations to real cases in the lawcourts.

But since they are not willing to accept the existence of either Ideas[105] or of mathematicals as images of the divine forms, nor even to grant them existence at all except by abstraction from sensible things, I do not see how on this hypothesis this process would any longer contribute to the ascent of our soul, or be analogous to bridges[106] conveying us from the realm of sense-objects to that of true intellection, and how it would 30
not be better to grasp sensible magnitude, as would be natural, by means of sense-perception, rather than, while surreptitiously depriv-
ing[107] it of its substratum, to apply to it a degree of scientific accuracy that neither exists nor could exist, and to consider it, not as it is, but in a mode in which it neither is nor could be.

It is just in view of his suspicion of this consequence that Aristotle, lest in saying that geometry does not concern itself with sensible objects 35
he be compelled to admit that it is inferior to sense-perception, declares that it does not concern itself with sense-objects except incidentally (*kata sumbebêkos*): even as a doctor does not concern himself with white things, even if all healthy things are white, but with healthy things, so also geometry concerns itself with magnitudes and shapes, even if no magnitude or shape has any existence outside of the sense-realm.   97,1

But first of all, medical science would not have covered matters concerning health without postulating the existence of its underlying subject-matter, if the soul did not possess the reason-principle (*logos*)[108] of each form, which it explicates discursively,[109] and thus generates the scientific knowledge of that very form. For otherwise whence would arise the general principles cognised by doctors and all other men of science, if not from the explication of the form as contemplated by them? 5
And then the example given is not at all similar. For medicine, inas-
much as it is a productive (*poiêtikê*) science and possesses a sense-perceptible end, necessarily concerns itself with the realm of sense-perception, but geometry, being theoretical[110] and independent,[111] if it does not concern itself with beings that are real, and real in a stronger sense than sense-objects, would not achieve anything worth- 10
while. And further, the science of medicine does not have anything to assert as to white things, insofar as relates to its own theoretical principles, but geometry makes demonstrations about the heavenly bodies – which it would not do, if it were not concerned with reason-principles (*logoi*) more perfect and more comprehensive than they; for why does a particular proposition about the heavenly realm come to be demonstrated by means of a universal one, if not because something universal contains the causal principle of the contents of the heavens, 15
which is also present in our own souls as an object of contemplation

(*theôrêtikôs*), while being in heavenly souls, additionally, as a creative principle (*dêmiourgikôs*). So much, then, for this line of argument.

But since, accepting that geometry deals with essential properties of magnitudes, he says that it is possible, even if the magnitudes are not
20 separable from sensible objects, for it to focus on essential properties of inseparable entities (for after all, he says, things pertain essentially to other inseparable entities: 'female' and 'male', for instance, are inseparable from living things, but yet have distinctive attributes, e.g. that the latter is generative, while the former is nutritive and receptive of seminal reason-principles), our reply will be that, first of all, the attrib
25 utes 'female' and 'male' are to be found at every level of reality and not just in sensible living beings – after all, they occur among the gods and in the classes of being superior to us, and even mortal nature would not possess them in the way proper to it if they did not proceed to it from above. And then, what is proved about celestial or divine realities by the accurate understanding of matters concerning male and female in this realm, in the way that one learns about celestial matters through geometrical proofs? But again, knowing how much geometrical proce
30 dures excel in accuracy, a quality which they would not have possessed, were they not concerned with a subject-matter which is serious and pure, he gives credit for their accuracy to the fact that their subject-matter is simpler. We would reply to that that if this simpler subject-matter were also prior in essence and more honourable than the more complex, it
35 would admit of exact study, even as the uniform motion of the heavenly bodies is more knowable than the more contorted and complex movements of mortal animals; but if this simpler subject-matter were to be more imperfect than the more complex, how would it admit of a more serious and truer account (*logoi*)? For it is not possible to construct such proofs about whiteness or fragrance; and yet all qualities and all
98,1 relations are simpler than the bodies which possess the qualities and are receptive of the relation. So one of two consequences follows: either mathematical proofs are not more accurate than accounts of natural phenomena,[112] or mathematical proofs are concerned with a more real subject-matter than are physical speculations; for it does not make sense that that which exists in a truer sense should be dimmer with
5 respect to knowability, or that the less real should be knowable with greater clarity. In fact, when this happens in respect of any intelligible object, it comes about by reason of our feebleness, not because of what is proper to the object; for the position of the divine Plato is on this question entirely correct,[113] that, just to the extent that each thing partakes of truth and reality, such is its position as regards clarity and knowability. And the very same point is clearly made by
10 our present philosopher in Book 2 of his *Metaphysics*;[114] so that we should not distance ourselves one whit from the doctrine common to him and to Plato.

1078a14-17 The same account applies to harmonics and optics; neither studies its objects as vision or as sound, but as lines and numbers (these latter being proper attributes of the former); and the same is true of mechanics.

Let it be agreed that the expert on optics does not concern himself with the actual form of vision, nor the expert on harmonics with that of sound, but the former with (visual) rays, and the latter with relative 15 (*pros ti*) numbers,[115] which are essential attributes of vision and sounds respectively; yet nevertheless this much in true, that the science of optics assimilates the rays sent out from our luciform spirit (*augoeides pneuma*)[116] onto visible objects to the lines that subsist in our imaging faculty (*phantasia*) and in the spirit itself. And for this reason Aristotle himself elsewhere[117] declares that the expert in optics treats physical lines as mathematical, and that he is right to do so, and to refer images 20 back to their immediate models (*paradeigmata*), since there is no way to attain knowledge of the imaged object other than by reference back to its more paradigmatic cause. And the expert in harmonics also refers back the numbers which have their subsistence in the substratum and in other things (than themselves) to separate ones, which are generative of them and serve as paradigms for them, as being able to partake 25 of accuracy from that source alone and from nowhere else. And similarly the specialist in mechanics, when structuring his material, relates all his creations back to immaterial structures (*skhêmata*), which subsist in the imaging faculty in the mode of extension (*diastatôs*), but in the intellect (*dianoia*) partlessly; for all these branches of science (*methodoi*), even if they have recourse to matter and turn their attention to 30 what is external to them, nevertheless, inasmuch as they are subordinate to the mathematical sciences, refer back to them and employ their theorems as paradigms.

1078a17-22 Thus if one posits objects independently of their attributes, and studies them as such, one will not for this reason assert a falsehood, any more than when one draws a line on the ground and calls it a foot long when it is not; because the error is not in the premises. Indeed, the best way of studying each object would be this: to take what is not separate and posit it as separate, which is just what is done by the arithmetician and the geometer.

In this case, however, we would maintain that this comes about not for the reason that he proposes, but because the scientist transfers his thought from the related structure to the unrelated,[118] and from the 35 particular and material to the universal and immaterial, in which also there becomes manifest the variety of reason-principles and the multiplicity of theorems.   99,1

Any more than … in the premisses.

This case is not like the former; for the quantity of the line that has been
drawn is not reckoned into the premiss, but recollection is experienced
of general principles (*ta katholou*), and the proof is constructed on the
5　basis of general principles; so that the primary discourse of the mathematician concerns them, and not magnitudes and figures inhering in
sensible objects.

Indeed, the best way of studying each object … and posit it as
separate.

This is by no means universally true. For that which has its essence in
a substratum and has no single separable causal principle would rather
be best viewed in its substratum; as for instance the shape of Socrates
10　would be more clearly viewed rather in the body of Socrates than if one
separated it off and viewed it by itself. And when in fact this is the case
(for it is the case with all common characteristics (*koinotêtes*) inherent
in bodies), the best perception of them as separable comes about for no
other reason than because we possess forms of each of them within
ourselves, in the unfolding of which we generate the sciences relative to
15　each one.

1078a22-31 And this is just what the arithmetician or the geometrician does. For man, qua man, is one indivisible thing; and the
arithmetician assumes man to be one indivisible thing, and then
considers whether there is any attribute of man qua indivisible.
The geometer, on the other hand, considers man neither qua man
nor qua indivisible, but qua solid. For clearly the attributes which
would have belonged to man, even if man were somehow not
indivisible, can belong to him even apart from these characteristics [sc. humanity and indivisibility]. So for this reason the
geometricians take a correct position, and deal with what really
exists; for what is real is so in one of two senses, either in actuality
or as matter.

Here he is concerned to counter an objection that has been brought
against his own position; for if, they say, you do not agree to the
existence of separable numbers or figures, then the mathematicians
will be concerning themselves with non-existent objects; for they will
20　not be dealing with entities inherent in sensible bodies (since such
things would be material), nor with separable entities, since there are
none such: so therefore with non-entities. His reply is that they are
dealing with things that do not exist in actuality, but potentially. Now
by way of informing us how these things are potentially and not
actually, he employs man as an example, and says that man is one and

indivisible in actuality, that is to say, in respect of his substratum; but 25
the arithmetician, in approaching him, concentrates on him as unitary
and indivisible, while the geometrician looks to him in his solidity and
extension in all three dimensions; for these qualities pertain to him as
well. So the geometrician does not lay emphasis on his indivisibility, but
on those attributes which apply to him along with his indivisibility, but
would apply to him even if he were not indivisible; so that he correctly
declares him to be extended in three dimensions and infinitely divisible, 30
and to possess all such attributes as the geometrician asserts and
demonstrates to be true of solids.

Our reply to this must be, first of all, to ask what it is that brings
figure and magnitude from potentiality to actuality. For the geometrician does not cognise the potential by keeping it potential, but by
making it actual; and if this is so, he does so by giving it shape and
making it more exact and perfect. How, then, could he do this if he did 35
not possess actualised entities within himself? For it is your principle,
Aristotle, that the potential is only brought to perfection and actuality
by the actual. And then again, geometry cannot take all its data from 100,1
sensible objects; for it deals with many shapes (*skhêmata*) and attributes of shapes which are not to be found in the sensible world. And
again, if these things exist in actuality in the sensible realm (for it is in
this sense that the Aphrodisian interprets the text here),[119] while being
studied in themselves only potentially, how can what is potential be 5
more exact than what is actual? It is to avoid this conclusion that the
younger Aristotle, the commentator on the philosopher Aristotle,[120]
declares that the Philosopher is actually saying the reverse of this, that
the one which is the object of the arithmetician's studies exists *potentially* in the sensible realm, and likewise the shape studied by the
geometrician, but they are studied in actuality by the sciences. And as
for myself, it would be my wish that the Philosopher had taken up this 10
position, rather than[121] the one attributed to him by the Aphrodisian, in
order both that his doctrine might come to be in other respects purer,
and that we might with greater confidence demand that he tell us what
it is that confers completion on the potential and renders it actualised.

1078a31-b6 And since the good is distinct from the beautiful
(because the good is always found in some action, while the
beautiful is found also in unchanging things), those who say that
the mathematical branches of knowledge do not speak about the
beautiful or the good are wrong. They do speak about and demonstrate a good deal about them; just because they do not name them
in demonstrating their effects and relations, it does not follow that
they are not speaking about them. The main forms of the beautiful
are order, symmetry and definiteness, which are what the mathematical sciences demonstrate to the highest degree. Since these (I

mean order and definiteness, for instance) evidently are causes of
a lot of things, clearly they are in a sense speaking about this sort
of cause too – namely the beautiful as cause. But we will speak
about this more explicitly elsewhere.

15 In this passage he directs his aim, very properly, at Aristippus and
anyone else who depreciates the mathematical sciences as not focusing
to any extent on the beautiful or the good. And he says that the
mathematical sciences have no concern with the useful or the advanta-
geous in the sphere of action (for that is what he refers to as the good
here), since mathematics was not to any degree a disposition concerned
20 with political issues. The beautiful, however, is something that mathematicians have very much to do with, since they are concerned with
what is symmetrical and definite and well-ordered; for even if they do
not mention the beautiful by name in their proofs, yet it is plain that
their whole business is concerned with symmetries and likenesses and
analogies and instances of order; and indeed in nature also many things
have as their end the beautiful and the ordered and the definite.[122]

25   So then, accepting this from Aristotle, we will first of all ask him to
tell us whence the mathematical sciences derive their concern with the
beautiful and the well-ordered and the definite. For sensible things,
even if they be heavenly ones, partake only to a partial extent of these
attributes, and not with such a degree of exactness, while the intelligible realm is superior to this degree of division and deployment (*anelixis*)
of reason-principles. The remaining possibility, then, I think, is that
30 what possesses them is a nature intermediate between the intelligible
forms and those in matter, experiencing a greater degree of fragmentation and division and multiplicity than the intelligible, while being more
unified and ordered and measured than the sensible, being adorned
itself with certain general reason-principles and immaterial forms,
while conferring on the sensible realm its immediate structuring.

        In view of all this, we will speak frankly to him, and declare that
those who despise the mathematical sciences derive their charge of
35 worthlessness (*euteleia*) against them from nothing less than the fact of
not granting them a distinct reality (*ousia*), but taking it that they are
mere playthings (*athurmata*) of the imagination which derives them
from the sensible realm. If he himself were prepared to deny the validity
of this assumption, he would be in effect condemning those who lack any
101,1 consciousness of the beauty of the mathematical sciences, and hold
opinions about them more consonant with his own views; for in respect
of entities devoid of reality and later-born (*husterogenê*) and mere
likenesses of sensible objects, what degree of beauty or order could there
be? For as to the dimness and worthlessness and total unknowability of
the objects of conjecture (*eikasta*), even if we learn from nowhere else,
5 certainly we learn with accuracy from the division of the Line in the
Republic (509D-510A); and if one were to relegate the mathematical

sciences to this status as being mere images of sensible objects, what
sort of probativeness (*apodeixis*) or order or definition or beauty could
one any longer assign to them, if one wished to maintain a coherent
position? The necessity of the argument is plain enough, even if we were
to do nothing to buttress it; but nonetheless it will become clearer if it
is spelled out rather than passed over in silence. For if the subject   10
matter of the mathematical sciences derives from the sensible realm,
then they will have no beauty nor good order nor adornment with
definitions; for what subsists in the sensible realm is the lowest level of
beauty and the dimmest degree of order and the most inferior sort of
definitions – if there is anything coming after the nature of sensible
things, it must necessarily be quite devoid of beauty and order and
definition and essence. But if there is something that is a receptacle
(*hupodokhê*) of beauty and definition and every sort of ratio and a   15
variety of theorems and marvellous order, it would be better and
superior to sensible things, and in all respects more venerable than
they, to the extent that which is always and in all respects in the same
state is superior to things that are disposed this way and that at
different times; for after all, if there is anything in the sensible realm
that is always in the same state, it has acquired this characteristic
directly from no other source than the intermediate reason-principles
of the soul.   20

1078b7-9 As for mathematical objects, then – that they really
exist, and as to in what sense they exist, and in what sense they
are prior and in what sense they are not – the foregoing account
may be taken as sufficient.[123]

He grants, then, their existence, in deference both to the proofs they
contain and the common and unwavering opinion about them, but [he
claims] that they exist by abstraction (*ex aphaireseôs*), which is the
same as saying that they exist in a dimmer and more image-like way
than sensible objects, being prior in account to sensibles, but not in   25
essence.

As to what he says himself,[124] I think the validity of it will have
become obvious to at least my more discerning readers; but if one were
to acquaint himself with the genuine doctrines of the Pythagoreans, he
will come to learn clearly also the essence and the potency and the
actualities of mathematical science as a whole, what is the body of
theory common to all of it, and into how many sub-classes it extends;   30
what are the first principles of all the various sciences,[125] and in what
way they differ from the other principles, such as are first principles of
other beings, and how such principles provide a common mode of
causation (*aitia*) in respect of all the mathematical sciences.

And again, [he will learn] what are the particular first principles of
each of the mathematical sciences, as for instance of numbers, of

figures, and of harmonies, and what distinctive characteristics they
have in themselves, and what differences they have in respect of each
35   other, and in respect of all the other principles of any other types of
being whatsoever; what are the common presuppositions of the mathematical sciences, with which the Pythagoreans concern themselves, and
how it is possible to make a general study of them; what is the best use
102,1   to be made of mathematical studies, and to what end one should refer
the best practice of them, and what is the proper object of knowledge
which serves as subject matter for each of the mathematical sciences.
And further, what is the criterion common to all the mathematical
sciences, and how it can be discovered from the division of the line which
5   Archytas transmits to us,[126] whether it is in the soul primarily that is
to be found the definite being of the mathematicals, or rather indeed
prior to the soul, since the soul is motion, and these entities are immobile;
that the essence of the soul makes the mathematical reason-principles
(*logoi*) in the proper sense the sum-total (*plêrôma*) of its contents, even as
was set out by Plato and, before him, by the Pythagorean Timaeus;[127] what
is the function of mathematical theorising and how it comes about, and
10   how it is in accord with the name 'mathematics',[128] inasmuch as it generates within us the whole recollection of the forms.

[We also learn] what are the powers of mathematical science and
what order they follow among themselves, and in accordance with what
distinctions they are divided, and in how many ways we acquire a grasp
of them; what elements and genera there are of mathematical science,
and how these elements and genera are the same in imitation of the
15   genera of being, and in what respect they are distinct from intelligible
and generated beings respectively; and about the likenesses and unlikenesses in mathematics, what they are and how far they extend, and how
they differ from likenesses and unlikenesses in the intelligible and
sensible realms. And further, how the knowledge of mathematics pene-
trates through the whole of philosophy; and what benefits it contributes
to the arts (*tekhnai*) both in general and in respect of particular classes
20   of them, that is to say, the theoretical, the productive[129] and the practical; also, what is the proper order to be observed in mathematical
education, and if it comprehends both a natural order and a pedagogical
order, and whether each of these accords with the other. Again, what
are the particular methods of Pythagorean instruction in mathematics,
and how they employed them and in relation to whom, and that they
always applied their own distinctive perspective to both problems and
25   to students. Also, what is the mode of division propounded by the
Pythagoreans of the whole of mathematical science into its chief genera
and species; what is the definitory discipline in mathematics and how does
it come about, and what useful contribution does it make to knowledge,
and what is the demonstrative discipline (*apodeiktikê*), and whether
mathematics provides this from itself or from some other source.
30   Then, who are the leading figures in the area of Pythagorean mathe-

matics? What came to be the distinctive procedure in that school with regard to mathematics? What should we demand from the truly educated mathematician, how should we judge his theoretical prowess, and on the basis of what principles conclude his correctness? How is it that on occasion we discourse in mathematical terms both about the primary intelligibles and about sensible objects, and why is this prone to happen? 35

When one has received all this, and in addition to this the proofs proper to each area of mathematics, from the leaders of mathematical science, and when one has learned by experience how by virtue of these 'an organ of the soul of each of us is purified and kindled anew, which had been destroyed and blinded by our ordinary pursuits, a faculty 103,1 whose preservation outweighs that of ten thousand eyes',[130] one should be ashamed to drag down into a subject-matter which is devoid of true being a kind of study (*theôria*) which both works for our preservation and is so elegant and adorned with scientific and intellectual arguments. And if anyone has been inspired with a longing for the explication and more extensive exposition of those topics which I have 5 listed, he will be able to satiate that desire by turning both to the collections of Pythagorean doctrine put out by Nicomachus[131] and the treatises of the divine Iamblichus on the same topics, the one expounding all his topics with an eye to descriptive accuracy and truth, the other enriching them with constructive reasonings (*kataskeuai*) and proofs and more intellectual theorisings; and it is obvious which is which.[132] 10

So much, then, will suffice for the present both about Aristotle's remarks on mathematics and our considered response to him. We must now go on to examine the difficulties he has raised about the Forms.

Chapter 4: The argument about the Forms[133]

1078b9-12 Now as regards Forms, we must first examine the theory of the Form in itself, not connecting it at all with the nature of numbers, but just as the people who first said that there were Forms understood it at the outset.

Since Plato, following the Pythagoreans, used to call the Forms also 15 Form-numbers (*arithmoi eidêtikoi*), 'let us first', he says, 'examine the Forms themselves, without referring to numbers, as to whether there are such numbers or not, but referring back to the conception of the those who first imposed this term on separable Forms'. And yet for someone who was going to conduct a fair examination of what they had in mind, there was no need to make such a distinction; for in fact 'Form' 20 and 'Form-number' are not applied to different things, but if indeed the statement is sound that 'all things are like unto number',[134] it is quite clear that number is here given a paradigmatic role, and in particular formal number. And if one were to look at the question from the point of view of the power of names, then it is clear to everyone that in the 25 case of the Form (*idea*), it is by virtue of assimilating to itself those things that participate in it, and endowing them with form (*eidos*) and order and beauty and unity, that it comes by this name, inasmuch as it always preserves the same form, while extending its power to the widest possible compass, and conferring the same form eternally on those that participate in it; and that number, in turn, has gained its

30   appellation by introducing harmony and friendship into all things; for the ancients use *arsai* for 'to fit' (*harmosai*) – as in 'and thereon he had fitted (*arse*) the doorposts'[135] – and *anarsion* for what is 'unfit' (*anarmoston*), and *arthmos* for friendship, as in 'but they established friendship (*arthmon*) among themselves'.[136] It is as derivative from all these

104,1 that number gets its name,[137] through measuring all things and fitting them together and rendering them friendly, which we declare to be the proper role of the formal cause.

But these considerations, it may be, are somewhat far-fetched. Let us just say this by way of introduction, that he has brought upon himself various opportunities for complaint by making this initial division of topics. And now let us turn our attention to what he says

5   next about the Forms.

1078b12-32 The theory of Forms occurred to those who enunciated it because they were convinced as to the true nature of reality by arguments emanating from the school of Heraclitus, that all sensible things are always in a state of flux; so that if there is to be any knowledge or thought about anything, there must be certain other entities, besides sensible ones, which persist; for there can be no knowledge of those things which are in flux.

Now Socrates devoted his attention to the moral virtues, and tried in connection with them to arrive at general definitions. He was the first to do this, for among the natural scientists Democritus touched on this only slightly, and defined 'the hot' and 'the cold' after a fashion, while the Pythagoreans had already done this in respect of a few things, whose definitions they expressed in the form of numbers, e.g. what 'opportunity' is, or 'justice', or 'marriage'. But it was natural for Socrates to enquire into the essence of things (*to ti esti*), because he was trying to reason logically, and the starting-point of all logical reasoning is the essence. For at that time there was not yet the dialectical power to enable people to consider opposites apart from the essence, and whether the same branch of knowledge deals with contraries. For there are two things that may fairly be ascribed to Socrates, inductive reasoning and general definition; both of these are associated with the starting point of knowledge.

But whereas Socrates did not regard universals, nor yet definitions, as existing in separation, they [sc. the Platonists] gave them a separate existence, and they called such entities 'Forms'.

In this passage, it is alleged that the divine men concerned derived their concept of Forms from the doctrine of the Heracliteans – falsely; for neither is it the case that Socrates, Plato, and their followers are entirely in agreement with Heraclitus concerning the status of sensible objects, as is shown by the *Theaetetus*[138] and what is said in the 10 *Cratylus*; nor did they come to the doctrine of definite causal principles for beings because of the fact that these objects were in flux, but on the contrary they concluded that the confused and unstable and unsure and faulty state of things in this realm acquires a measure of distinctness and identity and permanent status and good order from that level of being, to the extent that it was proper for it to be brought to order by that most causally efficacious principle of all things. That there can be 15 no scientific knowledge of things in flux is the view not only of Socrates and Plato and the Pythagoreans, but also of the author of these words [sc. Aristotle]; but also that there can be no knowledge of particulars; and these, whether they be in total flux, as is the doctrine of Heraclitus, or are constantly coming to be and passing away, but enjoy permanence as a whole by virtue of their formal cause, as Plato would have it, or 20 whether one calls them true beings, as Aristotle is wont to do, or indeed declares them to be the sole realities, as is the position of the Stoics, nonetheless that there is knowledge of individuals is rejected on all sides, unless one wants to call sense-perception knowledge.[139]

But to pass over much of what is said here, viz. that Democritus only indulged minimally in definition, while the Pythagoreans, in place of 25 definitions, imposed the names of numbers on things – for instance, the number seven on 'opportunity' (*kairos*), five on 'justice', and six on 'marriage' – and the attribution to Socrates of the instituting of know-ledge- acquisition based on logical proof, but not the whole extent of that divine dialectic, elevative as it is of souls; and the fact that what he calls dialectic – <that which> Plato calls <'eristic'>[140] – did not have in the 30 hands of Socrates and Plato such power as to defeat the tribe of sophists with their fallacious and perverse arguments – as I say, to pass over this, since he himself is not actually laying his main stress on these topics, let me turn to what I regard as his most mischievous insinuation, I mean that Socrates proceeded to universals by means of his definitions and postulated these as immanent in things (*akhôrista*), while Plato, whether through ignorance or disregard of Socrates' understanding 35 (*khrêsis*) of universals, granted them a separable status; for neither is it the case that Socrates considered that only the objects of definition were universals, but also prior to these the reason-principles in the soul, as Plato makes plain in the *Phaedrus* and the *Phaedo* and in many other 105,1 places, he being a just man and the most trustworthy of all men to report to us the views of Socrates. There is no way that the man who

received his philosophy from Socrates would either have deviated on any point from what had been laid down by his master, nor, if he had,
5 that he would have attributed to him doctrines in no way belonging to him, but rather going contrary to his whole project. As it is, in fact, in the *Republic*, in the Tenth Book, he presents him as championing separable Forms inhering in the Divine,[141] and in the *Phaedrus* (247D) as telling of the souls in their ascent viewing Justice Itself, Moderation Itself, and even Knowledge Itself, and in the *Phaedo* (100Bff.) as constructing an argument for the immortality of the soul by means of the
10 hypothesis of the separable Forms. And indeed the philosopher [sc. Plato] declares that it is not with Socrates that this theory took its start, but that it goes back to Pythagoras and the leaders of the Eleatic School. For Timaeus, Pythagorean as he is, does not postulate the bringing to order of the realm of becoming from any other source than the separable Forms, demonstrating both that they exist and that they are causes of
15 the things of this realm. And Parmenides declares[142] that, if there is no such thing as Forms, one will not have anywhere left towards which to direct his thought. And in the *Sophist* (246Aff.) he likens those who contend against the Friends of the Forms to Giants, presumably because they are opposing themselves to Olympian souls, who traverse the heavens.

But not to dwell too long on the historical aspect of the question, since
20 that is obvious enough, let us just say in reply to him, in a word, about Socrates and Plato and the Parmenideans and the Pythagoreans, that the Forms, in the hands of these divine men, were neither introduced in connection with the use of names (*onomata*) in ordinary language,[143] as was later thought to be the case by Chrysippus and Archedemus[144] and the majority of the Stoics (for there are many differences between the separable Forms and names in ordinary language), nor do they arise
25 as a by-product (*parhuphistatai*)[145] in the intellect[146] analogous to the notorious 'sayables' (*lekta*), as Longinus[147] chose to maintain. For nothing whatever arises as a by-product in the intellect, at least if a by-product is taken as something unsubstantial. For how could the same thing be both an object of intellection (*noêton*)[148] and arise as a by-product? Nor yet are the Forms according to their doctrine mere concepts (*ennoêmata*), as Cleanthes later maintained; nor yet, as was the view of Antoninus,[149] combining the positions of Longinus and
30 Cleanthes, do they arise as a by-product in the intellect in accordance with the conceptual forms.[150] Nor yet is Form to be equated with the 'definitional account' (*horistikos logos*), nor with the form in matter as object of definition, as Aristotle claims, both here and elsewhere, to be the view of Socrates; for these latter are in a state of combination and division and multiplicity and involvement with the realm of generation and matter, whereas the Forms proper are entirely simple and partless
35 and uniform and ungenerated and immaterial. How then is it surprising if we Platonists separate from one another entities so disparate from

each other? We do not, after all, approve on this point the Platonists Plutarch and Atticus and Democritus,[151] because they consider that the Forms are the universal reason-principles subsisting eternally in the substance of the soul; for even if they distinguish them from the commonalities (*koinotêtes*) present in sensible objects, nevertheless one should not confuse together the reason-principles in the soul and the 40 so-called 'enmattered intellect (*enulos nous*)'[152] with paradigmatic and 106,1 immaterial Forms and demiurgic intellections; but even as the divine Plato says that our [mode of existence] is characterised by 'collecting into one by reasoning' and that we have recollection of what we once saw when we made our journey with God,[153] while the divine mode is to be always in the same state on the same terms, so they too should make this same distinction, as long as they wish to remain Platonists. 5

Boethus the Peripatetic[154] is also led astray by these false leads from Aristotle into identifying the Forms with generic concepts (*genika*); and with him it is quite reasonable to class Cornutus,[155] since he himself is not far from this doctrine. For if on the one hand generic concepts are prior to particulars, even so they are not prior in such a way as to transcend being related to them, nor so as to be the causes of their 10 existence, which is the case with the Forms; while if they are secondary to them, as most authorities are wont to maintain, in what way will things that are later-born and devoid of substance and coming to be as mere concepts be able to assume the dignity of demiurgic and beneficent Forms?

How, then, do the Forms come to subsist, according to the actual contemplators of Truth? In an intelligible and tetradic[156] mode in the 15 Essential Living Being, and in an intellectual and decadic mode in the demiurgic Intellect; for the divine Number[157]

goes forth
from the recesses of the unsullied monad, until it reaches
to the divine tetrad, which in turn gave birth to the mother of all,
the venerable universal Receptacle, who has fixed a limit about all
                                                                things,
the unchanging, the indefatigable; they call her the holy Decad, 20
both the immortal gods and earth-born mortals.

This is an entirely accurate statement on a Pythagorean and Orphic level; but if one must speak in a more familiar manner, let self-sufficient and perfect Intellect be ranked as the causal principle of all things; and of this let the most divine and pure be preserved as free from all 25 activities for the purpose of creation and the beneficent providential care of things in the cosmos. So this entity, being by virtue of its intellections filled with Forms, excludes the causeless and the accidental (*to automaton*) from its creation, and, imparting to its creations a share of all things good and beautiful, turns the universe towards itself and makes it like to itself, and creates things of such

30   a kind and quantity as it conceives of; and being all-perfect, it conceives
     of everything.
          So nothing of those things that truly exist are bereft of the essence of
     Intellect, but it situates the Forms always within it, not as other than
     itself and its essence, but filling out the totality of its being and
     bestowing on all things their efficient cause as well as their paradig-
     matic and final causes; for they create inasmuch as they are Intellect,
107,1 and they are paradigms as being Forms, and they create though them-
     selves and their own goodness. It is against such propositions that he
     should contend who would conduct an honest argument against the
     lovers of the Forms, instead of concocting empty causes and hypotheses
     and instituting a shadow-combat against these.

     1078b32-4 For it followed for them almost by the same argument
     that there are Forms of everything to which we apply general
     terms ...

5   The Forms are both universal – if we are to term 'universal' the causes
     of the most specific reason-principles – and they extend everywhere
     indivisibly in their creative activities (*dêmiourgiai*). However, these
     men do not claim that there are in all cases Forms of everything that
     can be conceived of; for there are not Forms of evil or base things,[158]
     since these arise incidentally in nature rather by deprivation of and
     departure from Forms, for which reason they are said to be contrary to
10   nature. Nor are there Forms of negativities, for these are destructive of
     the definition and limit that is bestowed by the Forms upon all things,
     and at the same time the characteristic (*pathos*) of unlimitedness is
     more akin to Matter than to Form. Nor yet are there Forms of those
     things that are different at different times; for these acquire their
     altered and changeable aspect from a changing cause, and not from the
     changeless and steady illumination of the Forms. Nor do they admit
15   Forms of parts which are not also wholes, such as a hand or a head or
     fingers or nose; for the causal principles of things, being complete in
     themselves, produce whole Forms, not being divided about the parts of
     these in line with the reason-principles of nature. Nor yet did they allot
     to Intellect distinct causes of the primary attributes (*sumbebêkota*) of
20   bodies, as for instance sweetness and whiteness; for they considered
     that the physical reason-principles were sufficient for the creation of
     the attributes of bodies. Nor yet (did they postulate Forms) of composite
     entities, as of 'wise man'; for the Forms, being simple, prescribe a simple
     essence for each thing, while that which shares in different Forms
     provokes our mind to combine this with that, or conversely to distin-
     guish this from that. It is, then, what admits of assertion or denial that
25   is involved in combination and distinction; the Forms, and the kind of
     intellection that is co-ordinate with them, transcend all these processes
     by reason of their extreme degree of simplicity. So then, (there are not

Forms either) of those entities which take their origin from a union of unlike species, nor should one postulate Forms of these, as for example jinnets and mules and hybrid products of different trees; for all these things are later-born and supervenient and not works of nature alone, nor in general of a nature that is proceeding according to its own 30 reason-principles, but as it were of one that is being wronged and frustrated[159] and forced to go beyond its bounds (*polupragmonein*).

So it is clear from this that every art that imitates nature and provides some contribution exclusively to mortal life falls short of the causal efficacy of Forms. Nor, again, do we associate such acts as are dependent upon choices made at the level of soul,[160] nor such as are the product of a conjunction of multiple causes, which we are accustomed 35 to describe as dependent on chance (*kata tukhên*), with the causality of Forms; for entities that are produced from that source are always existent and in the same state and transcend the nature of their recipients.

It remains, then, that the Forms relate to universal and perfect essences and to those things which contribute to the natural state 108,1 (*diathesis*) of such essences, such as man and anything that may be perfective of man – wisdom, for instance, or virtue; for as the Forms are causes which are generative and perfective of all things, they both bring them into being and perfect them and turn them towards themselves. It is clear, then, that they contain within themselves the causal princi- 5 ples of the essence and the perfection of these entities.

We have here, then, in the briefest compass, the responses to the questions of what things there are Forms in the theory of these men, and of what there are not, and that there are not Forms of absolutely everything, as our adversary alleges.

> **1078b34-1079a2** ... rather as if someone who wanted to count things thought that he would not be able to do so while there were only a few, but made more before counting them. For the Forms are, if anything, more numerous than perceptible particulars (though it was in seeking causes for the latter that they went on from them to Forms) ...

The first part of this passage is a mere jibe and not a serious attempt at refutation (*elenkhos*), while the latter part alleges that they allow 10 that there are Forms also of accidental attributes (*sumbebêkota*); the point being that if each of us possesses many attributes, the Forms will be more numerous than particular entities. But the claim is false; for neither are there Forms of individual entities according to the more accurate of the Platonists,[161] nor yet of accidental attributes of bodies. To the jibe we may reply that it will not be possible even to count horses, if we do not employ in our counting the monadic number which is 15 distinct from the number inherent in the things to be counted (*arith-*

mêta).[162] And in general, if we are not going to <confine ourselves to investigating>[163] material causes, but rather pursue those that are of primary efficacy (*prôtourgoi*) and such as transcend their effects, we must transfer our attention to other natures, which, filling all things as they do, eternally and unmovingly and by reason of their very being, with order and structure, embrace within themselves the cause of what
20 comes to be, being less in number than encosmic things, inasmuch as they are closer neighbours of the One and proceed immediately from the monad, but by reason of their ineffable power contain the unlimitedness of the whole of time and those things which come to be within it, by reason of a superiority to them which is separable and unconnected.[164]

> **1079a2-3** ... because in each case there is, over and above[165] each thing, something else with the same name, distinct from substances ...

25 It has been stated of what things there are Forms, to wit, that they are of universal substances and those [qualities] that are perfective of them; it is false, therefore, to state that 'over and above each entity, there is something else with the same name (*homônumon*)' – except that to this extent he has correctly stated, and we should bear it in mind, that the Forms are indeed homonymous with sensible particulars, and not synonymous with them, as Alexander represents him as assuming.[166]

30   **1079a3-4** ... and in the case of the rest of things[167] a one-over-many, both for things in our realm and for eternal things.

While there are many problems connected with the Forms, there are four which are most worthy of attention; first, whether they exist; what they are; what sort of things they are;[168] and why they are (I take all these to be actually one single problem; for they all centre on the question of their actual existence); secondly, of what things there are
109,1 Forms; thirdly, what things participate in Forms, whether they are generated things only or also eternal things; and if the latter, whether all eternal things or only some; and if some, whether only those eternal things that are corporeal, as for instance the heavenly bodies, or also some of the incorporeal entities; and fourthly, how the participants in the Forms participate in them. This argument (*epikheirêma*) seems to
5 relate to the third problem, namely as to whether these men postulate a Form common to both sensible and eternal things, as for instance the Form of Likeness or Equality or Sameness, which is participated in both by the heavens and by things in this realm. And this involves no strange conclusion; for even if that which is participated in is the same, yet the mode of participation may exhibit difference; for each entity partici-
10 pates in its ruling causal principles in a mode proper to its order of being. But that we may not be thrown into confusion by these argu-

ments of his, let us take on board the views of the best of the Platonists as regards what things participate. It is the view, then, of Numenius and Cronius and Amelius that both all intelligible and all sensible entities participate in the Forms, while Porphyry considers that only sensible do so, <and Iamblichus considers that neither intelligibles exclusively or sensibles exclusively do so>,[169] but that the first and best among the intelligibles are the proper objects of participation, while   15 those things that are generated from these are what participate in the Forms, that is to say the realm of Soul and the sensible realm. And there is nothing strange in the idea of Soul's participating in one way in the Form of Man and of the Equal and of Likeness, while Nature partici- pates in another way, the aetherial realm in yet another, and the realm of generation in yet another; and that there should be structural connections (*suntaxeis*) and lines of sympathy and conformities in their   20 participation in a single Form, while the secondary entities are always dependent upon their priors, and that thus the Form, while not going forth from itself, is present without division (*ameristôs*) to all those things that are capable of participating in it, while the participating entities are constantly being brought to order by those prior to them and being led back towards the Form itself, body through nature, and this through soul, and soul in turn through its own proper intellect, which is ultimately inseparable (*anekphoitêtos*) from that realm and is united   25 to the divine Forms in a mode superior to the otherness characteristic of participants.

1079a4-7 Again, not one of the ways in which it is attempted to prove that the Forms exist demonstrates their point; from some of them no necessary conclusion follows, and from others it follows that there are Forms of things of which they hold that there are no Forms.

In some cases those men employed intellectual apprehensions (*epibolai noerai*), and it is probably for this reason that he says that they sometimes 'do not demonstrate their point' (*ou ... sullogizesthai*); but on occasion also they attempted to establish the existence of the Forms by   30 means of proofs (*apodeixeis*), without falling in with any untoward consequences. That the argument of our opponent is untrue is shown by the fact that there are many modes of argument employed by them in order to demonstrate the existence of Forms, and they pertain only to the ones that they want. One of these goes as follows: that which brings about the existence of the universe is God; everything that is, God creates by virtue of his very existence; everything that makes by virtue of its very existence makes a likeness (*homoiôma*) of itself; that which   35 brings about the existence of the universe makes the world an image of itself; if this is the case, it possesses within itself in a paradigmatic mode the causal principles of the universe, and these are the Forms.[170]

There are, of course, many other arguments to be found in them: that
which ranks what is perfect before what is imperfect; that which ranks
the monad prior to multiplicity; the partless prior to that which has
110,1   parts; that which is always in the same state prior to what is subject to
change – in which they demonstrate that reality does not take its origin
from what is worse, but rather ends in this, and takes its beginning
from what is most perfect and best and finest. For it cannot after all be
the case that our thoughts can grasp the properly equal and the
5   properly like and all such things, while the demiurgic Intellect does not
possess within itself Equality Itself and Justice Itself and Beauty Itself
and Good, and likewise all such entities.

1079a7-9 For according to the arguments from the sciences there
will be Forms of all things of which there are sciences ...

This claim used to be made also by these men: if the sciences are
10   concerned with real objects, universal entities (*ta katholou*) exist; for
the sciences are concerned with universals. This, then, is a syllogism in
the third figure: the objects of knowledge are universal; <the objects of
knowledge are real objects;>[171] so therefore, there are some existent
universals. For not all universals exist – not, for instance, the 'later-
born', nor those that inhere in individuals. But there is nothing strange
in the claim that all objects of knowledge are real, if one takes that to
refer to the objects of the proper (*kuriôs*) sciences,[172] not, for instance,
15   the objects of medicine, or carpentry; for these are not sciences in the
proper sense, but one might justly term such only those which concern
themselves with objects which are eternal and exist by themselves and
are always in the same state.

1079a9-10 ... and according to the 'One over Many' argument,
there will be Forms even of negations ...

That they ranked the One as prior to Multiplicity, is plain; but this
relates to 'one' insofar as it is substantial and generative of multiplicity,
not in that aspect which involves privation (*sterêsis*). For this latter is
20   a 'later-born' phenomenon, as for instance when the soul, in surveying
the common privation represented by 'what are not men', produces
within itself the concept of 'not-man'; for it is not the case that, even as
there is a formal and definitive causal principle in the universe that
makes horses horses, and another that makes dogs dogs, and another
swans swans, so there is some principle that makes all these 'not-men';
for if there were, we would have said that there was a Form also of
25   Not-Man. As it is, however, our soul, on discerning throughout these
other entities the privation of the human form, assigns the common
'not-man' element in them in accordance with the Form of Otherness
within it. So then, we do not assimilate privations to the class of partless

entities; for it is not the case that characteristics primarily (*proêgoumenôs*) pertaining to things and features attributed to them merely in thought depend upon the same causal principle.

1079a10-11 ... and according to the argument that we have some   30
conception of what has perished, there will be Forms of perishable
things, because we have a mental picture of these things.

We said that those things which the intellect has as its objects are truly
existent; for the thoughts of intellect in the true sense are not devoid of
being. But he, by dragging the intellect down to the level of the imaginative faculty (for it is this that he calls elsewhere the 'passive intellect'),[173] would in view of this say that there would be a substance of
things that have perished; for one may have an image also of something
that has perished. And one can observe from this also to what devices   111,1
the opponents of the Forms are obliged to resort, as they are diverted
from real beings to privations, and from intellect in its actualised state
to imagination and opinion; for one may have an image of or an opinion
concerning even that which is not, but it is not proper to have intellection or scientific knowledge of that which is not.   5
     As for the phrase 'we have a mental picture (*phantasma*) of these
things', if he is suggesting that that is an intellection, he must be joking
rather than serious; for that is to identify that as a motion of the divine
intellect which is precisely what our intellect seeks to purify itself from;
whereas if he proposes to identify it with a fictive (*plasmatôdes*) motion
of the imagination, when it is concerned with that which no longer
exists, then he has made a correct statement, but one that has nothing
to do with intellections that are always established in actuality.   10

1079a11-13 Further, of the most exact arguments, some establish
Forms of relations, of which they deny that there is an independent genus, and others state the 'Third Man' argument.

We do not claim that there are Forms of insubstantial relations, nor yet
of things involved in change, or of things which owe their existence to
some circumstance other than natural, as for instance 'above' and
'below', 'right' and 'left', 'nearby' <and 'far away'>,[174] and suchlike. But
such things as by reason of participation in some Form have come to be   15
relatives, as for instance 'like' or 'equal' or 'different', of these some are
endowed with relation to each other through participation in the genera
of Being, others through participation in at least one of the Forms. And
why should it occasion surprise if we declare that some things that are
relative entities (*pros ti*) in our realm should be perfected by virtue of
those [sc. Forms], when there also we are prepared to leave a place for
this relationship, though on the level of real being (*ousiôdê*) – and not
merely us, but also Aristotle himself? For when we postulate that one   20

thing is a cause or a principle or primary or more universal,[175] while
another is caused or derivative from a principle or secondary or more
particular (*periekhomenon*), what else are we doing than attempting to
indicate the order in accordance with which divine entities are mutually
related? Aristotle himself, after all, holds the view that, of the separable
Forms, on which he postulates that the spheres of the universe depend,
25 some are primary, others median, and others lowest, and some are more
comprehensive and others less so, if at least those also have that
ranking as between each other which the spheres of the aether exhibit
in relation to each other.

And how do they contrive to introduce the 'Third Man' argument? If
it is because all the Forms are manifested at every level of being, the
'men' will not only be three, but many, since all things are multi-layered
(*pollapla*); for they are manifested at the level of Intellect and individ-
30 ual intellects, in the single Soul and in souls, in universal Nature and
in particular natures; and then this Form would be present in heaven
and on earth and more or less in all the parts of the universe, in a mode
proper to the places receiving it. So there would be not three, but by my
reckoning an incalculable number. But if his point is that, because the
Essential Man is synonymous with men in this realm, as Alexander
35 states in his exegesis of this passage,[176] and all synonyms come to be
synonymous by virtue of their participation in some Form, a 'third man'
will manifest itself as being predicated of both the Form and things in
this realm, then the argument becomes ridiculous; for it is not the case
that things of this realm are synonymous with the relevant Form.
When, after all, would images become synonymous with their own
112,1 original (*paradeigma*)? Nor are we to imagine in general that the Form
(*idea*) participates in anything; for it is set forth for all as an object of
participation, inasmuch as it is the primary Form (*eidos*).[177] But if 'man'
is predicated of them homonymously, and there is nothing, in the case
of homonymous predications, that is adduced[178] by the utterance of the
word in addition to the subjects which are stated to be homonymous,
5 then how will there be any room for the Third Man, when the utterance
is, as it were, used up and split between the Essential Man and the
mortal man?

> **1079a14-15** And in general the arguments for the Forms do away
> with things which are more important to the exponents of the
> Forms than the existence of the Ideas ...

What he means is that the champions of this theory are more concerned
to preserve the first principles of beings than the doctrine of the Forms
10 (*ideai*), but in their enthusiasm for what they want less to exist they
succeed in destroying the first principles. And in truth, if that were the
case, they would indeed fall into this unwished-for situation. But let us
see if such is in fact their experience.

1079a15-19 For they imply that it is not the Dyad that is primary, but Number; and that the relative is prior to number, and therefore to the absolute – not to mention all the other conclusions in respect of which certain persons, by following up the views held about the Forms, have gone against the principles.

Now these men claimed that, after the single first principle of all things, which they were pleased to term the Good and the supra-essential One,   15
there were two principles of everything, the Monad and the Dyad of infinite potency (*apeirodunamos*), and they apportioned these principles at each level of being in the mode proper to each. For there is an element analogous to the Good in each realm of being and likewise entities assimilated to the primary Monad and Dyad. But our friend Aristotle declares that, in postulating the Essential Dyad and the Essential Monad among the Forms, first of all, since they are wont to   20
award the highest honours to the formal causal principles (*eidêtikai aitiai*), in declaring these to be primary, they do away with the Monad and the Dyad among the first principles (for what monad or dyad could be superior to the primal Monad and Dyad?); and then, since the Essential Tetrad is double the Essential Dyad, and indeeed the Essential Dyad is double the Essential Monad, and all these are numbers, not   25
only is absolute number superior to the first principles, but even relative number; and in general he says that there are many such instances, in which they, in their desire to preserve their position about the Forms, all unwittingly find themselves in conflict with their own principles.

Now that this is pretty sorry stuff, and hardly comes to grips in any serious way with the position of those divine men, will be plain even before any argument to anyone of reasonable acuity. Nevertheless, it   30
might well be demanded of us that we make an adequate refutation to this fallacious line of reasoning. We say, then, that the nature of principles is quite distinct from that of Forms, even if some connection of an homonymous nature should supervene in their regard, or rather, not in respect of them themselves (for how could anything supervene upon the most divine of beings?), but in respect of our treatment of them. For a start, the Dyad *qua* principle is the author for all things of   35
generative power and procession and multiplicity (*plêthos*) and multiplication (*pollaplasiasmos*), and rouses up all things and stirs them to   113,1
the generation of and forethought for and care of what is secondary to them, and further fills all the divine and intellective and psychic and natural and sensible realms (*diakosmoi*) with the numbers proper to them; and it does not grant that anything whatever is ungenerated of those things which are of a nature to come into existence. The Essential   5
Dyad, for example, confers its own form on all things, whether souls or natures or bodies; so that if the whole world is divided in two, or only the heavens, or the reason-principles of the soul, or, prior to the reason-

principles, the circles (for these are the first participants to be affected by the division into two), or some particular living thing that has two
10 eyes or hands or feet, or some other physical attribute, possesses throughout all of itself, along with its own Form, also the Dyad, we will say that this feature is present to them from no other ultimate cause than the Essential Dyad, which is on the one hand first among all the biform entities among the Forms and their cause, but is not for this reason the cause of the archetypal Dyad, by which both it and the whole
15 of Intellect is generated. And we say the same about the Monad; for there is a distinction between the archetypal Monad which, together with the Dyad, is the cause of existence to all things, bestowing upon everything self-identity and stability and coherence and eternal life, and the Essential Monad which holds first place of honour among the Forms, by participation in which all things which have been given form[179] enjoy unity and are held together by the principle of coherence (*hexis*) proper to them.

When, therefore, these men grant special prominence among the Forms to the Monad and the Dyad, they do not promote these with the
20 idea of eliminating their own first principles (for how could they, seeing as they declare that they themselves arise from the first principles, along with the whole of Intellect and the intelligible realm?), but for the reason that they govern the contents of the encosmic realm, and from one of them there emanates wholeness and unity to the cosmos as a whole and to (individual) souls and bodies, while from the other primary
25 division and duality – and it is plain which is which. The ploy of bringing number as unit (*monadikos*) into this, and on that basis maintaining that the Essential Dyad is twice the Essential Monad, is really very superficial; for it is not by reason of a given quantity of units that each of the numbers in that realm has acquired the title which it holds, but in virtue of a certain character of supremely divine and simple essence. Each thing participates in them according to its nature; for instance,
30 even as Essential Man, which is itself devoid of colour, structure, shape or parts, is participated in by the man of this realm, in the mode of structure, colour, shape and part, so the Essential Triad, which exhibits no quantity, is participated in by sensible entities possessing quantity. So seeking a multiplicity of units in formal numbers is like expecting to find a liver and a spleen and each of the other internal organs present
35 in the Essential Man. Therefore these men do not do away with their own first principles by postulating formal numbers, nor do they introduce relative numbers into the intelligible realm.

114,1 **1079a19-33** Again, according to the assumption by which they assert the existence of Forms, there will be Forms not only of substances but of many other things (since there is a single concept not only in the case of substances but in the case of non-substantial things as well; and there can be sciences not only of substances but also of other things; and there are a myriad of other similar consequences); but it follows necessarily from the views generally held about them that if the Forms are participated in, there can only be Forms of substances, since they are not participated in accidentally; things can only participate in a Form insofar as it is not predicated of a subject. I mean, for example, that if a thing participates in the Essential Double, it participates in something eternal, but only accidentally; because it is an accident of 'Double' to be eternal. Thus the Forms will be substance. But the same terms denote substance in this world as in the other; otherwise what meaning will there be in saying that something exists besides the particulars, that is to say, the 'one over many'?

In this passage he has raised a more weighty problem. It has been specified both by earlier authorities and by myself earlier of what things there are Forms and of what there are not; and specifically, that there are Forms of universal essences, such as Man, or Horse, and of anything that confers perfection on essences, such as Virtue or Knowledge, and 5 of anything that is an attribute of souls or bodies or natures, such as Likeness, Equality, Largeness, and anything of that sort. On the other hand, accidents solely of bodies have distinct causes in the reason-principles of nature according to Iamblichus, whereas the divine Plotinus advances the view that a Form of Whiteness should be postulated in Intellect.[180] So it is not the case that if there is one given concept over many particulars, there is therefore a Form corresponding to this (for 10 in this case there would have been Forms also of things contrary to nature), but if there is a Form of a given thing, there will also be universal reason-principles of that thing, though the converse is not the case. Nor yet are there Forms of all those things of which there are sciences which are not so in the strict sense.

However, that things of this realm participate in things that are real essences (*ousiai*), this is well said. It is not the case, however, that if something participates in an essence, that thing is itself an essence; at any rate, we call Knowledge Itself and Justice Itself essences, but the 15 states corresponding to these present in us are not essences. And this further should be said, that in the case of the Forms, there is nothing inhering (as an accident) in a subject, but all aspects contribute to the completion of the essence; for in the case of the Double Itself, eternity is not an accidental attribute even according to Aristotle himself; at any rate, he clearly states in Book 1 of the present work[181] that nothing is perishable or imperishable accidentally. Rather one should state the 20 matter as follows, that every immaterial and divine Form, at the level of its non-multiple and uniform and supremely simple essence, is endowed with many powers, and is not participated in according to all of its powers by entities of this realm. So the Double Itself possesses in

virtue of its essence partlessness and intelligence and demiurgic power
and eternity, and none of these as attributes in a subject; but it is
25 participated in by the separable Soul in respect of a larger proportion of
these powers, and by our individual souls in respect of less, while bodies
or bodily faculties must be content with just one or two. Those things,
however, which partake in essences do not necessarily all themselves
have to be essences (we have adverted to this fact on many previous
occasions), but even as some things participate in partless things
dispartedly and in intellective things unintelligently, so things may
partake in essences without being essences (*anousiôs*). For the expres-
30 sion 'one over many' was not intended to imply that the 'one' is included
in the same category as those, but rather that that henad is distinguished by ineffable degrees of superiority from the multiplicity that
proceeds from it and is an image of it and is dependent upon it.

1079a33-b3 If, then, Forms and the things which participate in
them have the same form, they will have something in common
(for why should duality mean one and the same thing in the case
of the perishable twos and the twos which are many but eternal,
and not in the case of absolute Two and a particular two?). But if
the form is not the same, they will be merely homonymous; just as
though one were to call both Callias and a piece of wood 'man',
without remarking any property common to them.

35 But neither are the Forms synonymous with things of this realm (for it
would be absurd to raise this question, lest, apart from everything else,
115,1 one fall foul of what they call the 'Third Man' argument), nor are they
homonymous in any chance sense, but only in the way that a model is
related to an image of itself, and specifically when the model generates
the images in virtue of its essence, and causes them to revert to it.

1079b3-11 And if we postulate that in all other respects the
common definitions apply to the Forms, e.g. that 'plane figure' and
the other parts of the definition apply to the Circle Itself, only that
we must also state of what the Form is a Form, we must consider
whether this is not completely vacuous. For to what element of the
definition must the addition be made? To 'centre' or 'plane' or all
of them? For all the elements in the essence of a Form are Forms,
e.g. 'animal' and 'two-footed'. Further, it is obvious that 'being a
thing Itself', just like plane, must be a definite characteristic
which belongs as a genus to all the Forms.

5 What is being said here is more or less the following: if one were to say
that the Forms are neither absolutely synonymous nor absolutely homonymous with things of this realm, but that the same account might
fit both the Form and the thing that is its image, if one were just to add,

in the case of the Form, let us say, 'intelligible', and in the case of things of this realm, 'sensible', he will think that he is making some sense, but in truth he is making no sense at all. For to what element in the 10 definition would he apply 'intelligible' or 'sensible'? As for instance if one has in one's mind an image of a circle, whereas that which is the object of intellection is the Circle Itself, someone might say that each of these is a plane figure comprehended by a single line, in the direction of which from one point in the interior of the figure all straight lines proceed equal to one another, but he would say that the Circle Itself is an 15 intelligible figure, but the figure in our realm is an object of imagination or sense-perception, one must consider, he says, whether this utterance is nonsensical. For to what, he says, are the characterisations 'intelligible' or 'sensible' to be related? To 'shape' or 'plane surface' or 'line' or 'point'? For all the elements that are subsumed into the definition are essences, as is in the case of 'man': for 'animal' and 'two-footed' are such.

One must respond to him with all due frankness and say that he 20 should not have attempted to give a definition of a Form in the first place (for Forms, being partless and simple and intellective, transcend both definitional accounts and everything that involves discursive and analytical study, as the divine Plato has specified in the *Letters* in respect of the essential Circle,[182] saying that it itself is something different to what is the subject of definition and knowledge; and indeed the marvellous Aristotle himself, in Book 8 of the present work,[183] 25 declared that there can be no definition of utterly and completely simple Forms), but we may concede so much to him as to say in response to his particular points that, even if the Forms were definable, it would not be necessary that we should employ the same definitions in respect of things of this realm and of their paradigms; for indeed the same account is not to be given of the image of Socrates and of Socrates himself, even 30 though the image has come into being in accordance with the form[184] of Socrates. But if one were to give the same definition for both of them, what would prevent us, in respect of each of the entities mentioned, from understanding 'intelligible' in the case of the one set, and 'sensible' in the case of things of this realm? For it would be reasonable that all things should subsist in an intelligible mode, if they subsist at all, in respect of their Form, but in a natural mode (*phusikôs*) in respect of those things that are likenesses of the Form. So then, neither is the Form definable in the true sense, nor, if it were, would it be subject to 35 the same definition as its products, nor, if one were to agree to all these propositions, would there be anything preventing one from assigning them [sc. definitions] in an intelligible mode to paradigms, and on the level of imagination or nature to images; for there would be nothing 116,1 paradoxical in the fact that intelligibility should pertain to all separable Forms, in the same way as the generic plane figure to things falling under the same genus, as for example particular plane figures.

Chapter 5: Forms and particulars

1079b12-15 Above all one might raise the question what on earth
the Forms contribute to sensible things, whether eternal or subject to generation and decay; for they are not the cause of any
motion or change in them.

5   He raises a question here about the usefulness of the Forms, querying
whether they contribute anything to sense-objects even if one does
postulate their existence. One must reply to that that all divine things
both exist and are such as they are, by virtue of their own first principles
and of themselves; which is not, however, to deny that, since their
essence is of a nature both to generate and to exercise providential care
for what they generate, even if they do not exist for the sake of what is
secondary to themselves, yet they bestow on everything[185] that follows
10 them existence and power and perfection. And indeed it is by virtue of
the Forms that such sensible objects as are eternal[186] both exist and
remain eternal, being such through being stimulated by love of those
entities to ceaseless life and motion, while as for the mortal and
material creations of Nature, when would they receive their entry into
the ranks of existent things, were it not that Nature and those creative
15 causal principles that employ Nature related their creation to certain
definite and completely unalterable (models)? For why otherwise would
it come about that change does not occur randomly, but changes and
processes of development manifestly take on definite forms, if it were
not the case that there is a pre-existent order inhering in the reason-
principles of Nature, and prior to that order a partless causal principle
20 co-subsisting with the Creator of All? Indeed, it is the view of Aristotle
himself that the First Cause of all, while being itself motionless, is, if
not the paradigmatic, then at least the final cause of all motion throughout the cosmos (*perikosmios*).

1079b15-23 Moreover they are no help towards the knowledge of
the rest of things (for they are not the substance of these things,
otherwise they would be in them) or to their existence, since they
are not present in the things which participate in them. If they
were, they might perhaps seem to be causes, in the sense in which
the admixture of white causes a thing to be white. But this theory,
which was stated first by Anaxagoras and later by Eudoxus in his
survey of difficulties [sc. about the Forms], and by others also, is
very readily refuted; for it is easy to adduce plenty of impossibilities against such a view.

That the Theory of Forms contributes greatly to the knowledge of things
is demonstrated by the divine Plato in many places, but especially in
25 the *Parmenides*,[187] where he says that there will be nowhere towards

which to turn the eye of the mind, if it cannot look towards the definite causal principle constituted by the Forms. And further, in the *Phaedo*,[188] the most authoritative of the proofs the immortality of the soul draw upon the principle and hypothesis of the Forms. But over and above that, this might also be grasped without difficulty prior to any argument; for if we always cognise images by reference to their models, 30 how is it possible, when this sensible cosmos is an image of the intelligible, not to recognise the latter also through the medium of the former? The assertion, then, that this does not constitute a reason for the Theory of Forms contributing to our knowledge of things of this realm, because they are neither essences nor accidents of sensible things, is something least of all fitting for someone skilled in demonstrative science (*apodeiktikos*); for if demonstrative proofs are based on premisses which are prior and more causative, then any given thing would not be known 35 through its own proper elements (for these are not properly causes, 117,1 except insofar as they are indebted for their coming-to-be to truer causes), nor, far more so, through the accidents inhering in it.

As for the pronouncements of Anaxagoras about the homoeomeries, and the problems raised by Eudoxus about some similar entities,[189] let them be as 'readily refuted' as you please; the Forms, at any rate, as being causes of being for things of this realm, both of their well-being 5 and of their permanence, necessarily confer perfection upon our knowledge[190] of them also.

1079b23-4 Again, other things are not in any generally accepted sense derived from the Forms.

That we do not say that things of this realm derive their subsistence from the Forms in the sense that they would from matter, or from privation, or in the manner of composite things, or from enmattered form, is obvious, since none of these is a causal principle in the true 10 sense, but the Forms constitute the most proper and comprehensive and separable causes of all things within the cosmos, both demiurgic and paradigmatic and final.

1079b24-7 To say that the Forms are paradigms, and that other things participate in them, is to use empty phrases and poetical metaphors; for what is it that fashions things 'looking towards the Forms'?

Yes, but only if we take the Forms in an impressionistic and literal-minded sense;[191] in that case the expressions seem to be metaphors 15 taken from painters or other craftsmen in this realm of existence, since if someone thinks of a demiurgic Intellect which is creator (*hupostatês*) and cause of all things, postulating that it generates everything by virtue of its very being, in accordance with its own peculiar nature

(*idiotês*), and accords it providential care, one would not seek further either the efficient cause of everything or (to understand) in what sense
20 we call the creative agent (*to poioun*) and its contents the paradigm of the ordered world. But how can he, when Plato states explicitly,[192] 'According, then, as Intellect perceives Forms existing in the Essential Living Creature, so many and suchlike as exist therein did he determine that this world should also possess', as if nothing of this sort had been said, now raise the question, 'what is it that creates looking towards the paradigm?'; for he should not just blandly ignore what Plato says, but if he had some objection to make to it, he should have made
25 reference to the doctrine in employing relevant arguments in refutation of it. He, however, is so far from having anything to say against the true theory of Plato as to be compelled willy-nilly to say the same things as him in another way. For the separable Forms, according to his theory, are final causes and objects of striving for all things, and causes of the
30 well-being and order and eternity[193] of the cosmos; but it is then obvious to anyone who looks at the text with proper understanding that they would also be creative causes of things in this realm; for it cannot be that one thing is cause of something's essence and form, and another thing of its being brought to completion. And if indeed the heavenly bodies are of infinite power by reason of their appetition (*ephesis*) towards the Forms, either it is from themselves that they possess this
118,1 appetition and infinite power, or both from those, or at any rate the second is bestowed upon them by those. But they could not be causes for themselves of infinite power; for in the case of every finite entity, the power is also finite. But if either both or only the second is from that
5 source, being as they are providers of natural power and eternity, and causes of existence, to those entities empowered by them, entities that might otherwise not have enjoyed existence, had they not received power from that source. It is for this reason that Plato says[194] that 'all the heaven and all generation will collapse and come to a stand' if there were not this incorporeal Form which inclined towards itself, and primarily exerts its activity towards itself, while secondarily it stirs up and sets in motion those things that are dependent on its beauty.
10 In this way, then, the separable Forms, even in his system, will be seen to possess also a creative causality, whether he cares to admit it or deny it. For as long as they are bestowers of both appetition and power immediately or rather of power through appetition, or of power alone, and they are also in addition to this causes of goodness and order
15 and eternity, how can they not also be the prior possessors of the primal cause of being?

Further, that, according to his own postulates, they will be paradigmatic causes of things of this realm, is plain from the following considerations.[195] The separable Forms, on his view, have eternally the same relation to one another as have the visible spheres in the aether. So then, either their likeness stems from chance, or there is some one cause prior to both of them of their single order, or the one class bestows a share of its own order upon the other.[196] But there can be no element 20 of randomness among the ruling causal principles, nor can there be anything higher, on his theory, than the separable Forms – for he denies the existence of a non-multiple and supra-essential One. The only remaining possibility, then, is that the one class of entities bestows on the other its own inherent order. And of these, it is plain that it is the separable Forms that act on sensible things; for it is not proper to suppose the reverse, even if he himself were entirely to assent that those are affected by the lowest class of beings. So then, the beings 25 There are paradigms and demiurgic causes of things of this realm, if, as is the case, they are both final causes and purveyors of power and eternity. How then does he have the face to attempt to refute his master, seeing that, on the basis of his own postulates, he is driven willy-nilly to adopt the same doctrine as he?

1079b27-31 Besides, anything may both be and come to be without being an image of something else; thus a man may become like Socrates whether Socrates exists or not, and even if Socrates were eternal, clearly the case would be the same.

But a purely chance likeness, even in the realm of perishable things, is 30 a very rare occurrence. To postulate, however, that eternal entities should be always unalterably the same, while generated things are created by Nature does not seem like an aimless enterprise, nor one that maintains sameness and likeness without due cause; since even in this realm something might be moved in a manner similar to both itself and another, but not for the same reason, whereas the circle of 35 the fixed stars also moves each of the heavenly bodies eternally and uniformly. So one should not adduce phenomena that occur only rarely at the level of the lowest of entities for the subversion of the order of true beings.[197]

1079b31-3 Also, there will be several paradigms (and therefore 119,1 Forms) of the same thing, e.g. Animal and Two-footed will be paradigms of man, and so too will the Form of Man.

One must not expect to be able to project individually (*diêirêmenôs*) all phenomena manifesting themselves in things of this realm back onto their primal and intelligible causes; rather, the man of this realm will be both a living thing and two-footed and rational and mortal and a 5 multitude of other things, but the Essential Man is none of these things, but contains within himself the partless causal principle of men at the psychic and natural and sensible levels, and he is equal to providing for the man of this realm, created on his model, all the attributes that contribute to his existence here. So it is not necessary, then, for the man

of this realm to partake in many Forms, insofar as he is man; but if,
10 because, inasmuch as he is sense-perceptible and partakes in the causal
principle of man in Nature and in Soul and in Intellect, in this way he
might be said to participate in a multiplicity of Forms, we may go along
with that; and there is nothing strange in the lowest level of beings
partaking in all the levels above them, even though they might be said
to participate properly only in the reason-principles in Nature, in the
view of the distinguished Amelius, to receive reflections (*emphaseis*)
15 from the Forms in Soul, and to exhibit rather just a likeness to the
actual intelligible causes.[198] If the argument is that, inasmuch as it has
this form, it is the product (*apotelesma*) of a number of Forms in virtue
of the distinction of reason-principles within it, one must not concede
the lumping of these two propositions together in this way, but one may
grant the division and fragmentation of reason-principles in their products, while still according the partless comprehension of wholes to the
20 separable causal principles.

1179b33-5 Further, the Forms will be paradigms not only of
sensible things but also of themselves, e.g. the genus will be a
paradigm for the species within the genus; hence the same thing
will be paradigm and image.

One must postulate that within Intellect there are more general causal
principles and others that are more particular, seeing as Aristotle
himself, in admitting that there is the same order pervading the visible
celestial spheres in the aether as is possessed by the intellectual causes
25 of the universe, is plainly agreeing that some of them are more comprehensive and others more particular. It does not, however, for this reason
follow for him, nor yet for us, that we can claim that the secondary ones
are images of their priors. Actually, as a general principle, the divine,
intellectual Forms might be said to be united with one another and to
interpenetrate one another purely and without mingling, but they
would never be said to participate in one another in the way that
30 secondary and lower natures participate in them. So all things in that
realm are primary and true and paradigms of what follow them, and
they admit into themselves no intrusion of the concept of 'image'.

1079b35-1080a2 Further, it would seem impossible for the essence and that of which it is the essence to exist in separation; then
how can the Forms, if they are the essences of things, exist in
separation from them?

The forms-in-matter, certainly, are inseparable from their substrata;
but it is not in this manner that the Forms were stated to be essences
(*ousiai*) of things, but because things in this realm possess their exist-

ence in accordance with them and through them and by their agency; 120,1
so necessarily they are separate from the realm of generation.

1080a2-4 In the *Phaedo*[199] it is put this way: Forms are causes
both of being and of coming into being. Yet, even assuming Forms
to exist, there is still no coming into being, unless there is something to initiate motion;

It is necessary that the sum-total of the creations of the divine Forms
should be actualised at any given time (and for this reason a whole 5
species can never disappear from the cosmos; for since the cause is of
infinite power by reason of its simplicity and partlessness, it follows
necessarily that its products will never fail); but the individual entity
would not participate in a Form, unless it possessed a matter that was
adapted to such participation. So the prior preparation of the material
causes circulating in motion assumes the role of necessary conditions 10
(*hôn ouk aneu*).

1080a4-9 and many other things are generated, like a house or a
ring, of which they say that there are no Forms. Thus it is clearly
possible that those things of which they say that there are Forms
may also exist and be generated through the same kinds of causes
as those of the things which we have just mentioned, and not
because of Forms.

These men did not reject the idea of demiurgic Forms of things that are
neither in nature nor created by nature; and this much at least he
reports correctly, that they did not consider that there were intellectual
and divine Forms of artificial objects; it was not only they who were of
the view that there reside in the souls of craftsmen artistic (*tekhnikoi*)
reason-principles which are more of the nature of models than their 15
products, but this is frequently propounded as a doctrine by Aristotle
himself. And this is a point that the friends of the Forms might fairly
make to him: how comes it that, whereas he grants that artificial objects
are brought about in accordance with models and in their case he does
not reject the concept of a paradigmatic cause, in the case of the works 20
of nature, which are after all the object of imitation for the arts, he
declares that they come about without a purpose, the creative activity
of nature being referred back to no definite causal principle? And yet in
various passages he himself declares that nature strives after form, but
he does not clarify his position. What sort of form, after all, one might
ask? Is it that which inheres in matter and is borne about in motion?
But this has never yet created anything, and is secondary to nature, and 25
involved with formlessness and shapelessness; and it is absurd, anyhow, for nature to be enamoured of that which is not yet existent and
which comes after it and is involved with privation, and therefore

devoid of beauty and attractiveness. But if he is referring to what is separable, so that it may direct its love towards that Form that is genuine and prior to itself and truly divine, it is absolutely necessary
30 that this be intellectual and immaterial and always in the same state and on the same conditions, in order that the love that imbues nature may be unquenchable and its creative activity unceasing.

Chapter 6: Return to the problem of numbers

1080a9-15 As regards the Forms, then, we can collect against them many objections similar to what we have just looked at, both in the manner we have just followed and by more formal and precise arguments.[200] But now that we have dealt with these problems, it would be well once again to turn to the investigation of the problems connected with numbers that follow from the theory that numbers are separate substances and primary causes of existing things.

That he has in fact nothing more than this to say by way of confutation of the theory of Forms is made plain both by the first book of the present
121,1 work, and by the two books which he composed *On the Forms*; for it is by hawking around everywhere pretty well these same footling dialectical arguments,[201] in some cases subdividing them and splitting them up, in others presenting them in summary form, that he attempts to confute the philosophers senior to him. But I imagine that it will not
5 escape the notice of the more alert reader that, even if such dialectical commonplaces as these were many times multiplied, they remain on a level proper to themselves, far removed from the science of divine things. However, since he declares that he proposes to turn his attention next to the theory of numbers, undertaking to refute those who accord them an intelligible essence, let us have a look now at the fellow's arguments concerning numbers.

10   **1080a15-b11** Now if number is a kind of nature, and its essence is nothing else but that very thing [sc. number], as some maintain, then it follows necessarily that either
  (i)   there must be some one part of number that is primary and some other part next in succession and so on, each part being different in kind – and this applies directly to units, any given unit being non-combinable with any other given unit; or
  (ii) they are all directly successive, and any units can be combined with any other units, as is held of mathematical number (for in mathematical number no unit is in any way different from another); or
  (iii) some units are combinable and others not, e.g. if after one

there is first two and then three and so on for the rest of the numbers, and the units in each number are combinable (those in the first two, for example, being combinable between themselves, and those in the first three among themselves, and so on with the other numbers), but those in the original Two are non-combinable with those in the original Three, and similarly with the other numbers in succession – this is why mathematical number is counted as follows: after one, two – another one added to the one before – and then three – another one added to those two – and the remaining numbers likewise; but this sort of number is counted as follows: after One a distinct Two not including the first One, and a Three not including the Two, and the other numbers similarly; or

(iv) one kind of number must be such as was first described, another like the sort spoken of by mathematicians, and a third is that mentioned last.

Again, these numbers must exist in separation from things, or not in separation, but in sensible things (not, however, in the way which we first considered,[202] but in the sense that sensible things are composed of numbers which are present in them) – either some of them and not others, or all of them.

These are of necessity the only ways in which the numbers can exist. Now of those who say that the One is the beginning and substance and element of all things, and that number is derived from it and something else, almost every one has described number in one of these ways (except that no one has maintained that all units are non-combinable); and this is natural enough, because there can be no other way apart from those which we have mentioned.

The first distinction made here is defectively stated, but yet has a certain validity. For it necessarily follows that, if Essential Number exists as a nature distinct from things that are subject to counting,[203] either each following number differs from its predecessor in species or it does not so differ. But this alternative 'or it does not so differ' would seem to be passed over. And further, the subsequent distinctions involving types of unit are all superfluous and pursue irrelevant lines of enquiry; for if those men had postulated that separable numbers had their being in a quantity of units,[204] it would have been proper to raise the question against them as to whether all the units are non-combinable, both those within the same number in relation to each other and those in different numbers in relation to those in another number, or whether they are all indistinguishable, as in the case of the units in mathematical number, or again, if some are indistinguishable, i.e. those in the same number in relation to each other, and others distinguishable and non-combinable, i.e. those in different numbers. But since according to them the numbers concerned are partless and devoid of quantity and identified with divine Forms, at least those of them that are separable from the cosmos, we consider that all such finicky logic-chopping is being dragged in inappositely.

25 The distinction made after this, on the other hand, we accept as substantial, in which he raises the question whether they postulated that the numbers were in separation or not in separation from bodies, but serving for the completion of sensible nature, or some in separation and others not. Since, then, the first and last distinctions he makes turn out to be substantial, we choose from the first one the alternative that

30 the different numbers are distinct in form, or rather that they are distinct Forms (for the pure and unsullied Forms are not separate from numbers); and from the second, that numbers are both separable and inseparable from sensible things. For this reason also it is logical that those who generate every class of number from the One and the Indefinite Dyad should seem to him to make use of <all>[205] these modes [sc. of existence]; for some concern themselves mainly with the

35 inseparable numbers only, on the basis of what is more immediately familiar to us making allusions to the higher causal principles, while others concentrate their attention on the separable numbers, in which they saw on a paradigmatic level those numbers also comprehended which proceed from nature, and yet others, in making distinctions between both, propounded as their own a clearer and more perfect doctrine.

122,1 And if we are to say anything also about the difference or lack of difference between units, one must not on any account assign quantitative units to the essential numbers; when we declare that the units are immaterial,[206] that will involve us in asserting that they all differ from one another by reason of otherness, and are indistinguishable in virtue

5 of sameness, and exhibit the combination of these characteristics through the operation of both of these genera of Being. It is plain, after all, that numbers in the same order (*taxis*) are controlled by sameness rather than otherness in their relation to one another, while those in various different orders exhibit great distinction by reason of the domination of otherness.

10 **1080b11-14** Some hold that both kinds of number exist, that which involves priority and posteriority being identical with the Forms, and mathematical number being distinct from Forms and sensible things, but both kinds being separable from sensible things.

It is plain that he is placing Plato in this category, as indeed is asserted by his commentator Alexander.[207] And we accept that Plato says this, and not only this; for he postulated also the existence of Form-number, the Forms having their order in it, and also mathematical number, this

latter being superior to physical number, but inferior to Form-number, 15
even as Soul is superior to Nature, but secondary to Intellect.

1080b14-16 Others hold that mathematical number alone exists, being primary among true realities and separate from sensible things.

Alexander declares that it is Xenocrates[208] who is alluded to here, since he makes mathematical number separate from sensible things. However, he does not regard it as the only sort of number (how could he, 20 after all, seeing as he was a Platonist and aspired to conform with Pythagorean principles, leave out of account numbers still more partless, that transcend the essence of Soul?); but in fact he is plainly, through the medium of mathematical terms, treating also of higher sorts of number.

1080b16-21 The Pythagoreans also believe in one kind of number, the mathematical; only they maintain that it is not separate, but that sensible objects are composed of it. For they construct the whole universe of numbers, but not of numbers consisting of abstract units; they suppose the units to be extended – but as for how the first extended unit was formed they appear to be at a loss.

That these men asserted that sensible objects were created by Nature 25 according to numbers[209] must be admitted; however, this was not according to mathematical numbers, but rather physical ones. In accordance with their method of symbolical exegesis, there was nothing inapposite about indicating truths concerning the particular characteristics of each sensible object through the employment of mathematical terms. But to attribute to them a knowledge only of physical numbers is not only ridiculous – it is downright impious. After all, how 30 is it not absurd to talk of people who, having received from Orpheus the theological first principles of intelligible and intellectual numbers, extended their significance very considerably, and demonstrated the extent of their dominance as far as the sensible world, while bearing constantly in mind the dictum, 'All things are like unto number',[210] as concerning themselves solely with bodies and the numbers associated 123,1 with bodies? And how could it be that Pythagoras himself, quite explicitly, in the *Sacred Discourse*, described number as 'the lord (*krantôr*) of shapes and forms', and 'cause of gods and daemons', and 'guide-rule and technical reason-principle for the God who is lord of all and most powerful craftsman' ('Number is established as intellect and guiding 5 principle of the constitution and generation of all things';[211] and how could Philolaus describe number as being the 'fundamental and self-generated principle of coherence of the eternal permanence of the things in the cosmos';[212] and how could Hippasus and all the acusmatics

wish to characterise number as 'the critical instrument of the creator God, and the paradigm according to which he fashioned the cosmos' –
10 were it not the case that they had in mind the separable, creative, and paradigmatic superiority of number over bodies?

1080b21-3 Another thinker holds that primary or Form-number is the only kind to exist, and some say, further, that mathematical number is the same as this.

It may be, in fact, that this thinker viewed all levels of number as being present in Form-number, those prior to it as it were proceeding into manifestation in it, while those subsequent to it are present in it as in
15 their paradigmatic cause.

And some say, further ...[213]

Some, he says, wished to eliminate mathematical number in its generally accepted sense, and, postulating one class of number, Form-number, called mathematical number the same as this. But one may say in reply that, since mathematical number is of two sorts, the one unitary
20 and the other substantial (*ousiôdês*), by means of which latter the Demiurge is said to structure the rational soul,[214] they did not think fit to call 'formal' that which is acknowledged by the general public to be non-substantial, but as for that which is substantially present in our souls, and which in turn by its innate power (*autophuôs*) generates unitary number, while not confusing it with Form-number, they nevertheless did not disdain to term it 'formal', in the same way as we are
25 accustomed to call the intermediate reason-principles in the soul 'forms'.

1080b23-33 The same applies in the case of lines, planes and solids. Some distinguish mathematical objects from those which 'come after the Forms'; and of those who treat the subject in a different manner, some speak of mathematical objects and in accordance with the principles of mathematics (namely those who do not make Forms numbers, and even deny that there are Forms), while others speak of mathematical objects, but not in a way appropriate to mathematics (for they claim that not every magnitude is divisible into magnitudes, and that not every two given units make a two). But all who hold that the One is an element and principle of existing things regard numbers as unitary, except the Pythagoreans: they regard number as having spatial magnitude, as has been previously stated.

We give the same account also in the case of geometrical terms: the figures occur in one way in Intellect, in another in Soul, but in each case without extension or shape, if it seems readily admissible for one pursuing his enquiries in accord with the peculiar character of the realities concerned, and not following the common meanings of words, 30 that shapeless shapes and partless magnitudes should subsist prior [sc. to their lower manifestations].[215] Now certainly some among those divine men,[216] in introducing for this reason indivisible lines and a non-quantitative dyad, have been indicted elsewhere as postulating impossibilities, and here as propounding unmathematical theories about mathematical entities. We also have received from the words of 124,1 the accuser the basis for mounting a defence of Xenocrates, who was not prepared to allow that the Essential Line could be divided, nor yet those lines manifested in the intermediate reason-principles of the soul; for which reason, seeing the numbers as reason-principles and Forms, he maintained their indivisibility – for indeed he viewed mathematical numbers rather in their formal aspect, and not in respect of the flux of 5 units underlying them.

As for his statement that everyone but the Pythagoreans regard numbers as consisting of units, whereas the Pythagoreans alone regard them as having extension and magnitude, he is wrong on both counts; for neither is it the case that everyone else declares all numbers to consist of units, but only mathematical number, nor did the Pythagoreans accord spatial magnitude to number, but, while they did indeed 10 generate magnitudes from the lowest level of numbers, they laid it down that numbers themselves were partless, both those that were generative of bodies and those that transcended the reason-principles in nature. And he himself chooses to take as positive evidence for numbers being regarded by everyone else as being composed of abstract units the fact that they derive them from the One, not allowing that the One in 15 their theory is not that which is generative of mathematical units, but rather that which is the causal principle of the Good and the absolutely best of beings.

1080b33-7 It is clear, then, from the foregoing account how many theories there can be about number, and also clear that all the ways have been mentioned. They are all impossible, but doubtless some are more so than others.

Some of these theories, he says, are comparatively plausible, others more impossible. Our reply must be that, if these men had postulated that all numbers were composed of abstract units, then your distinctions would have worked perfectly well; but as it is he distorts some of 20 the evidence, and puts the worst construction on other aspects, while in just a few instances one might discern some spark of a true understanding of their position.

Chapter 7: The problem of numbers, continued

1080b37-1081a5 First, then, we must enquire whether the units are combinable or non-combinable, and if non-combinable, in which of the two ways which we have distinguished. For it is possible either that any one unit is non-combinable to any other, or that the units in the Two Itself are non-combinable with respect to those in the Three Itself, and thus that the units in each primal number are non-combinable with one another in this way.

All this is futile bluster;[217] for none of the divine and intelligible num-
25 bers is unitary (*monadikos*).[218]

1081a5-9 Now if all units are combinable and undifferentiated, we get one type of number only, the mathematical, and the Forms cannot be numbers. For what sort of number will Man Itself be, or Animal Itself, or any other Form?

If every number is unitary, and all the units are undifferentiated, the conclusion stated here follows; for neither will there be any such thing as a Form-number (such a number cannot be unitary, after all; for it will be difficult to imagine how many units will constitute this Form or that), nor in general will there be any other type of number but the
30 mathematical. But if the whole hypothesis which states that every number is unitary is false, then nothing would be demonstrated from it. Indeed, it is possible to derive the opposite conclusion from what has been stated here; for if the conditional proposition adopted both by the Pythagoreans and by him is true, that, if every number is unitary, there is no such thing as a Form-number, since in fact there is such a thing as a Form-number, as those men have argued at length, it would not be
125,1 the case that every number is unitary. But the additional assumption (*proslêpsis*) which posits the antecedent in Aristotle's view and denies the consequent in their view needs further support (*sustasis*).[219] This one thing is agreed by both sides, that the Form-number is not unitary, and one must maintain this at all costs. For if it exists, as they
5 maintain, it is not unitary, and if it does not exist, as is the opinion of this fellow, it is at all events not unitary. So whoever either wishes to demonstrate that it is unitary or convicts it of being non-unitary is not sticking by the propositions mutually agreed.

1081a9-12 There is one Form of each thing, e.g. one of Man Itself, and another of Animal Itself; but the numbers which are similar and undifferentiated are infinitely many, so that this three is no more Man Itself than any other.

This argument is also adduced to prove the proposition that Forms are

not unitary numbers, since in fact units are undifferentiated. For if, he 10
says in effect, within the nine there is a first and middle and a last three,
then Man Itself, for example, would not be the first three in the nine
any more than it would be the middle or the last. But there must not be
a multiplicity of Forms of Man; so either none of the threes is it, or all
of them must be; but if it is impossible that all of them are, then none
of them is; so a Form would not be a unitary number, if indeed units are
undifferentiated. And we will say that there is nothing illogical about 15
these conclusions; for neither are they illogical, nor, even if they are
impossible, is this the result of anything other than the flawed nature
of the hypotheses.

1081a12-17 But if the Forms are not numbers, they cannot exist
at all; for from what principles can the Forms be derived? Number
is derived from the One and the Indefinite Dyad, and the principles and elements are said to be principles and elements of
number, and the Forms cannot be ranked as either prior or
posterior to numbers.

The proposition that, if the Forms are not numbers, they cannot exist
at all, seems to me to be well taken; but that they do not exist he has 20
not demonstrated, nor would it be capable of being demonstrated. That
the Forms are unitary numbers is something that he has assumed long
ago, but he is not prepared to argue for it. The three-stage argument,[220]
then, is more or less as follows: if the Forms are not unitary numbers,
i.e. numbers in which the units have no distinction from one another,
then they are not numbers at all; if the Forms are not numbers, then
they do not exist at all; <so if the Forms do exist, they are numbers.>[221]
He argues for the second inference as follows: all existent things derive, 25
according to them, from the One and the Indefinite Dyad; all things that
derive from the One and the Indefinite Dyad are numbers; therefore all
existent things are numbers. Both of the premises here are sound, and
the conclusion is true; but he does not take either 'One' or 'Dyad' or
'number' in the sense intended by these men. For they, with an eye to 30
both columns of the Table of Opposites[222] as they relate to each class of
being, used to declare that the better column was bestowed upon things
from the One, the inferior one from the Dyad. He, however, following
his usual strategy, understands the terms in a strictly mathematical –
or dare I say even vulgar? – sense. Again, those men termed the
products sometimes the Triad, indicating by the term 'triad' the arche- 126,1
typal nature of those numbers, and sometimes just Number; but he
twists this use of the term in the direction of unitary number. <...>[223]
since we neither reject the categorical syllogism, which shows most of
all that the Forms exist and that they are intellective and partless 5
numbers, if one is prepared to take the terms in the premises in the
proper sense, nor the three-stage argument, if someone refutes the

defective hypothesis by denying the consequent, since it is not possible
to establish the antecedent. If, then, the Forms exist, as those divine
men have demonstrated at length and we have made some modest
mention of also, the Forms would not be unitary numbers, if the units
10   are undifferentiated from one another – and I think even if it were
postulated that they are differentiated, unless one were to think up
some other meaning for 'unitary'.

It might somehow seem a good point to make that it is not possible
to rank the Forms either prior or posterior to numbers, if indeed Forms
are not numbers; for both are primary and proceed immediately from
15   the first principles; so that if they did not both exist, neither the one nor
the other would exist. Not but what it is not plain to anyone who has
attained an understanding of the theological doctrines of the Pythagoreans and the *Parmenides* of Plato[224] that there are numbers prior to the
Forms, to wit, the henadic and the really-existent, and these manifest
themselves in all the orders of divine entities; for the demiurgic Forms
are not absolutely the most primary of all things (for they are not, after
20   all, prior to the genera of Being),[225] but they are said to be prior to the
things in the cosmos, but not to hold the most primary position among
beings; and as immediate principles they do not have the primary
Monad and the first Dyad, from which there proceeds the triadic and
hidden level of Number, but those principles inhering in the very simple
thought of the Demiurge, 'from which leapt forth the Forms, bearing the
25   marks of body'.[226] And, while this is connected with another subject of
study (*theôria*), it is nonetheless less all now testimony to my position, if
the Forms would be shown to exist, but to that of Aristotle, if all number
were to be accepted as unitary, composed of undifferentiated units.

> **1081a17-25** But if the units are non-combinable in the sense that
> any one unit is non-combinable with any other, the number so
> composed can be neither mathematical number (since mathemati-
> cal numbers consists of units which do not differ, and the facts
> demonstrated of it fit in with this character) nor can it be Form-
> number. For on this view two will not be the first number
> generated from the One and the Indefinite Dyad, and then the
> other numbers in succession, as one says, 'two, three, four ...' –
> because the units in the primary Two are generated at the same
> time, whether, as the originator of the theory held, from unequals
> (coming into being when they were equalised), or otherwise ...

That if all the units are non-combinable with one another, both those in
30   the same number and those in different ones, and if furthermore every
number were unitary, then there will be neither mathematical nor
Form-number, is something that he takes as a logical consequence. For
mathematical number on the one hand is <unitary>,[227] but composed of
undifferentiated units (for it is thus that we can conceive of divisions

and additions and multiplications and all relationships proper to it); and Form-number cannot be composed of units which are non-combin- 127,1 able with each other – in truth, because it is simply not unitary, but according to him, because the two units of the Two, and the three monads of the Three, must be generated simultaneously from the first principles, and those things that are generated simultaneously from the first principles, he says, are indistinguishable. In this connection he refers also to actual statements of Plato, showing that according to him 5 each of the numbers is generated simultaneously by the first principles, being brought to equalisation from unequal sources. Now Plato did indeed in this statement allude to the fact that the divine entities are other than, and unequal to, each other by virtue of the Dyad and the procession from the Dyad, but the same as, and equal to, each other by virtue of the Monad and the reversion to the Monad[228] – unless one would prefer to describe it as the remaining prior to both procession and 10 return. But this fellow talks as if numbers, or the units in numbers, were originally unequal, but are now equalised. In fact, however, one must exclude unitary number from that realm of existence, and see the unequal and the equal, sameness and otherness, and that which re- mains and that which proceeds, as being altogether and unitedly pre- sent at that level.[229] And this follows from the hypotheses; but whence 15 comes the idea that all numbers are unitary? For he constantly assumes this, but in no way does he prove it.

1081a25-9 Then, even if one unit does come before the other, it will also come before the two made up of both. For whenever one thing is prior and another subsequent, a thing made up of both of them will be prior to the latter and subsequent to the former.

This[230] is also produced as a proof that the units in Form-numbers are not incombinable; for if the two units in the Two[231] are incombinable, 20 then the one of them will be prior and the other posterior; for certainly they cannot proceed simultaneously from the first principles if they are differentiated. But if this is the case, then the essential Two will be both prior to its posterior, and posterior to its prior. For there is a mingling of the two units; even as honey-wine is sweeter than wine, but more astringent than honey, so also the Two is posterior to the prior part of 25 itself, and prior to the posterior part. But I imagine that the more intelligent among my readers will realise that this is foolery and distraction rather than any attempt to present a serious exegesis of doctrine.

1081a29-35 Further, since the essential One is first, and then there is a one first among the others but second after it, and again a third, second after the second one and third after the first one, it follows that the units will come before the numbers after which they are named. For example, there will be a third unit in two before the three exists, and a fourth in three, and a fifth, before these numbers exist.

What is being said is more or less the following: if we postulate, after
30 the One that rules over and is generative of all things, the prior unit of the Two, there will be a twosome formed from the ruling One and this unit, even before the Two comes into being. And again, if we co-ordinate the two units of the Two with the first One, we will get a three, even before the Three comes into being; and so at each stage the quantity of units will anticipate the numbers proper to them. But that this is
128,1 foolery rather than serious argumentation, we have demonstrated many times before this; for to apply this sort of partibility and material division to entities that are partless and non-quantitative and entirely indivisible, and to practise upon them mixture and transposition of elements, and from firsts and seconds and all that follows on them to
5 create and generate one single thing by composition, is the action of a man who is not even aspiring to a true study of real being. And hence in what follows he actually gives an indication that he is making statements quite irrelevant to the doctrine of those men.

> **1081a35-b6** Nobody has in fact claimed that units are non-combinable in this way, but even this is reasonable, according to the principles held by those men, although in actual fact it is impossible. For assuming that there is a first unit and first one, it is reasonable for units to be prior and posterior; and similarly in the case of twos, if there is a first two. After the first, it is reasonable, indeed necessary, for there to be a second, and, if a second, a third, and similarly with the others in succession.

10 He himself accepts that nobody has maintained the doctrine of these non-combinable monads; for indeed according to their principles, he says, it is reasonable, but in actual fact it is impossible. But that they can be assumed according to their hypotheses, he tries to establish in the following way. If there exists, according to them, a first one and a first unit and a first two, then there is every necessity that there should
15 be a second one and second unit and a second two; for where there are firsts, there must also be seconds, and where there are these, there must also be thirds, and so on. But if this is the case, then necessarily the units are different from one another and non-combinable; for the third is different from the second, and the fourth different from the third.[232]

In fact, the type of game he is playing is quite clear; for if he were
20 calling 'units' each of the intelligible essences or the numbers proper to them, then there would be nothing odd, since there is an ordered

sequence in the divine realm, in the fact that some should be said to be first, and others stand in order after them. But since, having attributed mathematical units to the subject-matter, he then removes their particular quality again by postulating that they are non-combinable, and thus trifles[233] with divine things through these hypotheses, how would 25 one not suspect that he is not being serious here, but playing games?

1081b6-8 But to maintain at the same time both that after one there is a first and then a second unit, and that there is a first two, is impossible.

This remark he has cast into the midst of his argument, as much as to suggest that their doctrine concerning first principles is inconsequential;[234] for he does not consider it possible for both a one and a two to hold the first place after the One. For if the one is first, then by the same 30 token so is the two.[235]

But it has been stated above in what sense these men declared each of these principles[236] to be first, as each leading off and presiding over their own proper column of opposites (*sustoikhia*).

1081b8-10 But they postulate a first unit and a first one, but not a second and third, and a first two, but not a second and a third.

This is what he claimed followed for them of necessity, but not what was actually stated by them. And that it is indeed not stated may be 35 gathered from his own text; that it does not follow either may be 129,1 observed with a little attention. For in cases where the second follows on the first and the third on the second, and those following in turn on it, they are all co-ordinated with one another and of one nature, and their order, seeing as they are entities of like essence, accords due seniority to the first things. But nothing is of equal worth to the principles of all things; for it is one thing to be a principle and another 5 to derive from a principle; so that while they quite rightly postulated a first One and first monad and first dyad among the principles, as the one principle and the two (following it), they did not see fit to go on and assume seconds and thirds of the same sort. But if they were ever actually to say any such thing, they would obviously propound entities which proceeded analogously to these, which would serve as the immediate causes of median and ultimate types of being, which they would 10 certainly not describe as proceeding to infinity, but only to the extent that the descent of entities in procession (*proodos*) would be enabled to create the complete variety of beings, so as to be ultimate principles in nature of sensible things and generative of matter, thus constituting the lowest images of the first principles of all.

1081b10-21 It is also evident that it is not possible, if all units are non-combinable, for there to be an essential Two and Three, and so on with the other numbers; for whether the units are indistinguishable or each is different in kind from every other, numbers must be produced by addition, two, for example, by adding another one to one, three by adding another one to two, and four likewise. But if this is so, number cannot be generated as they generate it, from the Dyad and the One; for two becomes part of three, and three of four, and this happens in the same way to the following numbers.

15 There cannot, he says, be such a thing as a Form-number, that is to say, an essential Two or an essential Three, if it is assumed that units are non-combinable; for it follows upon this that there is no such thing as a Form-number. But this point he leaves in the air; instead he adduces the consideration that, whether units are combinable or non-combinable, there must be no such thing as an essential Three, by reason of the 20 fact that every number is counted and brought about by addition (so, for instance, the two becomes three by taking on a unit, and for this reason there are many twos, in the six, for example, or the eight, or the twelve, and two is the two-thirds part of three, and the half of four), but there is no such thing in the case of the Form-number (for it is generated, according to them, from the Monad and the Indefinite Dyad, and each 25 of them is one, and no one of them is part of another).[237]

Here he states correctly the properties of Form-number, but he does not act correctly in making the assumption that every number is measured and brought about by addition; for he should not have transposed the particular properties of unitary number to all classes of number. So there is no other conclusion to be arrived at in this context also but that it is quite imposible that the Essential Two be a unitary 30 number, which is something that more or less everybody would agree to prior to any argument.

1081b21-2 But according to them four was generated from the first two and the Indefinite Dyad...

This he states as if producing an objection to his own position. 'But those men', he says, 'from the essential Two (*autoduas*) – for this is what he means by the 'first two' – and the primal (*arkhikê*) Dyad,[238] which he terms the 'Indefinite Dyad' – produced the Four, not by combining them 35 nor increasing them by addition, but by the Indefinite Dyad's doubling the essential Two and thus bringing to birth the Four; so that they 130,1 would not be bringing about the number There by addition either. By producing, as it were, this self-contradiction, he admits one part of the truth, that they did not postulate the creation of number There by addition, and that one of the first principles is productive of duality (*duopoios*) and the generative cause of multiplicity and multiplication –

that one which turns all divine things back upon themselves and stirs
them up to the generation of secondary and tertiary levels of form.[239] He 5
counters this objection, then, in manner which he[240] regards as incisive,
but which in fact, as is plain to anyone, is illogical.[241]

1081b22-7 ...thus consisting of two twos apart from the essential
Two (otherwise the essential Two will be part of it, with the
addition of one other two). And two, also, will result from the
original One and another one – but if so, the other element cannot
be the Indefinite Dyad, because it generates one unit rather than
a definite two.

Even if, he says, they choose not to bring about number by addition,
nonetheless they will have to admit that there are two twos apart from
the essential Two in the four; but if they shrink from this conclusion, 10
they will consequently have to admit that the essential Two is a part of
the essential Four, and number will come about by addition, through
another two being added to the essential Two and thus bringing about
the essential Four. But if four is to derive from the essential Two and
another two, in accordance with the same analogy two will come to be
from the ruling One and another one. But if this is the case, it is not 15
possible that the other first principle should be the Indefinite Dyad; for
what is generated by the Indefinite Dyad should have been a two, but
as it is, what is generated is not a two but a unit, which along with the
One makes up the definite two. If then, he says, they do not accept that
in the essential Four there are two twos other than the essential Two,
they are liable to all these consequences, both that number is formed by
addition and that one of their first principles is eliminated. But that he 20
is managing to deduce these absurd conclusions by always presuppos-
ing that Form-number is unitary is something to which we have repeatedly drawn attention.[242]

1081b27-34 Again, how can there be other threes and twos besides
the essential Three and the essential Two, and in what way can
they be composed of prior and posterior units? All these theories
are absurd and fanciful, and it is in fact impossible for there to be
a first Two and then an essential Three. And yet there must be, if
we are to take the One and the Indefinite Dyad as elements. But
if the consequences are impossible, then it is impossible also that
these are the first principles.

These men postulated, as subsequent to intellective number, psychical
number and mathematical and physical number, but they did not speak 25
of them as unitary, nor did they talk of 'prior' and 'posterior' units as
going to make up their quantity. For all these classes of number, except
the mathematical, were according to them devoid of quantity; and they

viewed threes and fives and tens among them in terms of their powers
and their relationships to the divine numbers. For when they declared
30 that five, for example, represented justice in our realm, they did not
mean that it was formed out of five units, secondary to those in Intellect,
while superior to those in nature, but, from quite another perspective,
they associated the Form of Five with the Form of Justice, and that of
Seven with Occasion (*kairos*), and that of Six, both itself and its cube,[243]
131,1 with that of the Soul. So if someone is able in his mind to view these
matters according to their intentions, he will conclude that they are not
'absurd and fanciful', but rather that, of all beings of whatever type,
these have the greatest capacity for existence. And hence he himself
says that there must be prior and secondary threes and twos, if they are
produced from such first principles; and since this consequence is
5 impossible, he wishes also to demolish the first principles. But we are
quite prepared to accept that many orders of numbers emerge from
these principles, and the impossibility of the existence of different types
of numbers we neither see as a conclusion nor is it at all possible to
contemplate. For the truth cannot be refuted, nor can falsehood be
demonstrated.

> **1081b35-1082a15** If, then, any one unit differs in kind from any
> other, these and other similar consequences necessarily follow. If,
> on the other hand, while the units in different numbers are
> different, those which are in the same number are alone indistin-
> guishable from one another, even so the consequences are no less
> troublesome. For example, in the essential Ten there are ten units,
> and Ten is composed both of these and of two fives. Now since the
> essential Ten is not just any number, and is not composed of just
> any fives, any more than it is of just any units, the units in this
> Ten must be different. For if they are not different, the fives of
> which the Ten is composed will not be different; but since these are
> different, the units must be different too. Now if the units are
> different, will there or will there not be other fives in this Ten, and
> not only the two? If there are not, the thing is absurd; whereas if
> there are, what sort of ten will be composed of them? For there is
> not another ten in Ten besides the essential Ten.
>   Again, it must be true that four is not composed of just any
> twos. For according to them the Indefinite Dyad, taking on the
> definite two, made two twos; for it was capable of duplicating what
> it took on.

10 Having shown that, if all units are indistinguishable, there will be no
such thing as a Form-number, assuming that every number is unitary,
and that, if all are different, there will be neither mathematical number
nor Form-number, if in fact every number is unitary, now he turns to
the remaining arm of the division, and shows that, even if some of the

units are postulated to be indistinguishable, namely those of the same
number, and others distinct, namely those which make up different   15
numbers, not even so will Form-number exist, once it is again postulated that every number is unitary. For, although this hypothesis is
false and an object of ridicule to those who have studied the doctrines
of those men, he is not willing to give it up, since from it he can without
difficulty draw many absurd conclusions, just as if one considered the
Essential Man and the Essential Living Being to be composed, the   20
latter of soul and body, and the former of a particular kind of soul and
a particular kind of body, together with the quality of being capable of
laughter – and what could be found more deserving of ridicule than
that?

Most of this passage, then, where he is fabricating many fives and
many tens, may be set aside – our verdict on it will certainly be obvious
from what we have already said; but what is said at the end, that 'the   25
Indefinite Dyad, taking on the definite two, made two twos; for it was
capable of duplicating what it took on', while being derived from their
own customary statements, is at the same time polluted with sophistry
as a premiss.[244] For it is understood by the philosophers prior to him[245]
that the Indefinite Dyad, being as it is a motive principle, fills all the
Forms with generative power and multiplies them and provokes them   30
to the generation of secondary and tertiary immaterial forms; for it said
to be 'duplicative' (*duopoios*), inasmuch as, in the process of procession,
multiplicity increases by way of doubling, while power dissipates, and
at the same time because the principle of mathematical number,
through doubling all odd and even numbers, generates the even. For if
the Monad and the Dyad are the first principles of all numbers, yet we   35
know, nonetheless, that the Monad is of a masculine nature and hence
is productive of oddness, while the Dyad is feminine and hence the
patron and promoter of the even. It is possible, then, to view this by
analogy also in the case of the more senior types of number, setting   132,1
aside units and quantity, and looking at the types and powers of
separable numbers.

1082a15-26 Again, how is it possible that two can be a definite
entity existing over and above the two units, and three over and
above the three units? Either by participation of the one in the
other, as 'white man' exists besides 'white' and 'man', because it
partakes in these concepts; or when the one is a differentia of the
other, as 'man' exists besides 'animal' and 'two-footed'.

Again, some things are one by contact, others by mixture, and
others by position; but none of these alternatives can possibly
apply to the units of which two and three consist. Just as two men
do not constitute any one thing distinct from both of them, so it
must be with units too. The fact of their being indivisible will make

no difference; points are indivisible also, but still two of them do not make up anything over and above the two.

5   This objection is not relevant to divine numbers at all; for these are not unitary in such a way that we may ask in their case what each of them is over and above the units composing them. It is more properly directed against mathematical number. We shall reply to him then, in respect of mathematical number, that 'seeing as in each thing, according to you also, there is one element that is like matter and another like form, so also in the Five, the five units and in general the quantitative element

10   and the substratum come to numbers from the Dyad, whereas the form, as represented by the Five, is from the Monad; for every Form is itself a monad, and bestows definition on the underlying quantity, and so the Five is itself a sort of monad, because it proceeds from the ruling Monad, and it both gives shape to the quantity subject to it, which was hitherto formless, and binds it together to its own form. For we must understand

15   that there are in turn two principles of mathematical numbers existing in our souls, from which there is born the whole of mathematical number, the monad embracing within itself all the Forms of the numbers and assuming a role analogous to that of the Monad in the intelligible realm, while the dyad constitutes a sort of potency that is generative and formless and of infinite power, and for this reason serves as an image of the inexhaustible and intelligible Dyad, being itself

20   called indefinite. So then, as this runs over all things and extends itself indiscriminately, the monad is not found wanting, but constantly articulates and structures and forms the indefinite quantity that proceeds from it, adorning unceasingly with forms all its processions in order. And even as, in the encosmic realm, there is nothing formless or void

25   that insinuates itself between what is subject to form by reason of the providential care of the Demiurge, so also in the case of mathematical number there is no quantity left unstructured (for in that case the enforming power of the Monad would have been overcome by the indefinite Dyad), nor does anything else insinuate itself between the ordered sequence of numbers, by reason of the unfailing and orderly activity of the Monad.

30   So then, neither is it the case that Five is constituted from substance and accident, as with 'white man', nor yet from genus and differentia, as is 'man' from 'animal' and 'two-footed', nor by five units being in contact with each other, as in the case of a bundle of sticks, nor by being mixed together, like honey-wine,[246] nor by submitting to being placed in order (*thesis*), as in the case of stones going to make up a house. However, it is not so, as in the case of countable objects (*arithmêta*), that there is nothing over and above the individual objects; for let us grant

35   him for the moment that the conjunction of two men is nothing over and above each of them (although it is in fact Plato's view that all these combinations themselves receive the different numbers by virtue of

participation in some Form, as is written in the *Phaedo*;[247] but let this not be attributed to countable objects just for the moment); but it is not because numbers are composed of indivisible units that they have something other than those units (for the many points are indivisible, but nonetheless they are not considered to make up something else besides themselves as subjects), but because there is something in them analogous respectively to matter and to form.[248] For instance, when we add three to four and make seven, we express what we are doing in these terms, but our statement is actually not true; for the units when joined together with the other units make up the substratum of the number seven, but the actual seven is made up of this number of units and the Form of Seven (*heptas*). What is it, then, that applies the Form of Seven to the units? What is it, after all, that applies the Form of Bed to such and such a combination of pieces of wood? Surely it is plain that it is the soul of the carpenter that, in virtue of possessing the appropriate art, imposes form on bits of wood for the making of a bed; and it is the soul of the mathematician that, by possessing within itself the originative Monad, imposes form upon, and generates, all numbers. There is just this much difference, in that the art of carpentry is not ingrained in us naturally, and is in need of handicraft, since it is concerned with sense-perceptible material, while the science of arithmetic inheres in us by nature (which is why it is possessed by all) and has a subject-matter which is the object of discursive intellect (*dianoêtê*), whence it is able to shape it both easily and timelessly. And perhaps it is for this reason that the majority of people have been fooled into thinking that seven is nothing else besides the relevant number of units; for the imaginative faculty of non-experts, if it does not first see a state of disorder, and then the activity of the ordering agent extended over it, and then on top of that the object, whatever it may be, enformed and brought to perfection, does not believe that it is seeing two different natures, one formless, the other formal, and even beyond these that nature which bestows the form, but it speaks merely of a single, ungenerated subject, with no conception whatever of a cause of this.

133,1

5

10

15

20

It is for this reason, it seems to me, that the theologians and Plato have handed down to us accounts of the temporal generations of ungenerated entities,[249] and have declared the original state of things that are in fact eternally ordered to be disorderly and irregular and indefinite, that they may bring men to a conception of the formal and the efficient causes of things. It is no wonder, therefore, that, even though the seven units [sc. in seven] never exist independently of the Form of Seven, yet the seven should be described by the science that sets out these things to be something composite, containing one element analogous to Matter and substratum, another to Form and structure.

25

30   **1082a26-8** Moreover we must not fail to note the following also: that on this theory it follows that there are prior and posterior twos, and the same with the other numbers.

He has expressed himself elliptically here through a concern for conciseness, but the full version of his argument goes somewhat as follows: one must not fail to notice this consequence also, that, in accordance with this hypothesis, some twos are prior to others, and the same goes for the other numbers also, as for instance some threes appear as prior to
35   others. Let us now see how he proceeds to argue for this.

134,1   **1082a28-32** For suppose the twos in four come into being simultaneously; they are still prior to those in eight, and just as two generated them, so they generated the fours in the eight. So if the first two is a Form, these will themselves be kinds of Form.

This statement results from the following notion, according to which the latter of the two principles, being duplicative (*duopoios*), is said to double each of the numbers. But this has no relevance, not only to
5   formal and completely partless and non-quantitative number, but also to the mathematical and unitary type; for it is the quantities of the lesser numbers that are put together and subordinated to the form of the greater, as has been said, and not the numbers themselves. So then, even as when water is transformed into air, it is not the water that becomes air or the substratum of air, but rather that which was the
10   substratum of water becomes the substratum of air; and so, when three takes on two, it is not the forms of the numbers that mingle – except in the case of their immaterial reason-principles, in which there is no problem about things being united even when distinct – but it is the units that are linked up, and the matter put together. So three and four are each one thing, even in the case of mathematical number; for even if, in the case
15   of the nine, you think of a first and a middle and a last three, you are looking at one undifferentiated three taken three times; and in general, in any given nine you see nothing else than the Form of Nine imposed on a certain quantity, and even if you mentally divide up its substratum (for its form is indivisible), you straightway endow it with the forms proper to that
20   division;[250] for our soul is not capable of viewing the formless as unstructured, especially if it is itself instrumental in structuring it.

        1082a32-1082b1 The same argument applies to the units, since the units in the first two generate the four units in four, so that all the units become Forms, and a Form will be composed of Forms. Clearly, then, those things also of which these are Forms will be composite – as if, for example, one were to say that animals are composed of animals, if there are Forms of these.

Nor does any of this have any relevance to the doctrine of the ancients;
for neither is the number of the Forms (*ideai*) unitary, even if it is called
a unit (it is a number as being a pure form (*eidos*), assimilating to itself
those things that participate in it, but a unit as being the measure, and 25
indeed the prior measure,[251] of the forms both in the soul and in nature
and in sense-objects); nor, according to them, are Forms composed of
Forms, Horse, for instance, being composed of Man and Dog, so that the
horse of this realm should also be composed of various dissimilar
natures of this realm. All this, really, is more suitable to a comedian
than to a writer on serious subjects.

But not even at the level of mathematical number are the units
(*monades*) differentiated, but all the units underlying numbers are 30
undifferentiated, apart from that one [sc. the Monad] which, since it is
the first principle and fount and mother of all is so far from needing
anything to impose form on it that all the Forms actually proceed from
it into all numbers. However, the many units are not just homonymous
with the Monad, but also the definite two among the mathematical
numbers is homonymous with the Indefinite Dyad; for the Indefinite 35
Dyad is primary principle of all number, but particularly of the even, 135,1
while the definite two is in a different way a principle, not as being
generative, but rather as we say that the first bit of any thing is its
primary element, as in the case of Plato's *Republic*, the phrase 'I went
down yesterday to the Piraeus'.

1082b1-5 In general, to make units different in any way whatever
is absurd and far-fetched (and by 'far-fetched' I mean forced in
such a way as to fit one's assumptions). For we can see that one
unit differs from another neither in quantity nor in quality ...

This is well said in regard to the units which go to make up any number; 5
for neither will they differ in quantity, since all are minima, nor in
quality, for they are formless. And he also gives a good definition of
'far-fetched' (*plasmatôdes*).

1082b5-7 ... and a number must be either equal or unequal – this
applies to all numbers, but especially to unitary number.

This also is well said; for equality and inequality runs through all
number, whether natural or supernatural or mathematical. And one 10
should note this passage, in which he himself clearly admits that not all
numbers are unitary. For the phrase 'but especially to unitary number'
is a clear confirmation of the doctrine of the ancients; so nothing has
been demonstrated to us about non-unitary numbers, since he has
based all his arguments on the assumption of units.

15   **1082b7-11** Thus if a number is neither more nor less, it is equal;
and things which are equal and entirely undifferentiated we assume, in the sphere of number, to be identical. Otherwise, even the
twos in the original Ten will be undifferentiated, though they are
equal; for if anyone maintains that they are undifferentiated, what
reason will they be able to give?

This point is also very well taken concerning the multiplicity of units,
and shows that not only are they undifferentiated, but also numbers
that are equal to one another; so that, as we said, three would be just
one thing, even though it is taken many times in making up thirty; for
what are equal in the sphere of numbers are identical. So then the twos
20   in ten are also undifferentiated, not just because their units are undifferentiated (though this is also the case), but because their Form is one
– one, though, not as having given itself to undifferentiated subjects (for
it makes numerically only one single Ten),[252] but as having proceeded
from the original Monad and remaining itself purely one. For even if we
ourselves granted that the Ten was made up of five twos, even as it
25   contains ten units, it would have been necessary to agree that, while
there are many twos numerically, they are one in form; but since we do
not say that it is twos put together that make up the Ten (for the Forms
of numbers are simple and proceed from the Monad, so that that is the
case with the Ten), nor that the units underlying the Two, being
extended further, become the substratum of the Ten, which proceeds
30   from its own originating principle, and brings about a ten through being
combined with a substratum, we are not compelled to postulate numerically many Twos, that we may not be making them from numbers into
countables (*arithmêta*); since, after all, if there were many Twos, as he
136,1 himself asserts, and many Threes and many Tens, and in general each
of the unitary numbers would be infinitely many, it would necessarily
be the case also that mathematical number as a whole would not be one,
but that there would be infinitely many mathematical numbers; but in
fact there seems to be just one of any given mathematical number, for
it is a universal; so that this particular mathematical number, as for
5   instance Three and Four and each of the others, must be one, in order
that the total composed out of these may also remain one. For if
someone says that the totality of number exists only in infinite multiplicity, like individual things that are one only in form (*homoeidê*), we
will refer back once again to the single Form with which mathematics
concerns itself; and we will find one single Form of the totality of
10   mathematical number, embracing a single Two and a single Three and
not multiple versions of these, lest the totality once again become
multiple, and this proceed to infinity. Nor therefore will we divide the
Ten into five twos, but we will say rather that the subject-matter of the
two has been taken five times. Nor yet do we put together the Ten out
of five twos, lest we present its Form as being composite – something

that we do not see as happening even with sensible forms in the realm 15
of Nature. Nor in general do we say that Number is multiple as being
divided in accordance with its subject-matter, but rather that each
experiences manifold instantiations, if we are going to preserve it in its
pure state as Number, and not make it a countable.

1082b11-16 Again, if every unit plus another unit makes two, one
could make a two with a unit from the original Two plus one from
the original Three, which will thus be made up of differentiated
units; and would that then be prior or posterior to the Three? It
rather seems that it must be prior, because one of the units is
contemporaneous with Three, the other with Two.

This proposal about Form-numbers is as ridiculous now as it was then; 20
for it is not the case that two units serve as substratum to the Essential
Two, nor three units to the Essential Three, nor, if they did so serve,
would it be possible to separate one off from each and make some other
entity, since both sameness and difference inhere in either of them, and
it is not, forsooth, by removing difference from one or other of them, or
difference from one and sameness from the other, that you will construct some third thing as a mixture of them, and then enquire whether 25
it is posterior to both as being constituted from both, or posterior to the
former of them, and prior to the second, which he declares to be rather
the necessary conclusion.

All these questions, however, are taken from the realm of what is
material and generally divisible, and it is quite improper to apply them
to essences which are intellective and simple and absolutely indivisible.
If he wished to direct them against mathematical number, the attempt 30
would have stirred up much more of a problem, but even so on the basis
of the arguments advanced there would have been a solution here too;
for we should not be subtracting units either from the Two or from the
Three, in order to make up another two (for this is relevant to countables, as for instance to subtract from two horses or from three men; if,
then, we take one from each of those, we will make up a pair out of
dissimilar units), nor in general insofar as the Two is a two or the Three 35
a three, if each is what it is, will it be able to lose a unit. But all these
fantasies are dragged in to the realm of pure theorising by those who
declare numbers to be 'later-born' (*husterogeneis*)[253] and derived from
sensible objects, and each a multiplicity.   137,1

1082b16-19 We, after all, suppose that in general one and one
make two, whether they are equal or unequal – good and bad, for
instance, or man and horse; but supporters of this theory say that
not even any two units make two.

He treats these entities as if they were countables, and for this reason

5   uses as a measure in their regard unitary number. Those men, however,
     if they are claiming that the units underlying any given unitary number
     are different, would justly be subject to censure; but if what they are
     calling a 'unit' is in fact each one of the Forms, as being a prior measure
     of things in this realm, how is it not necessary, seeing as each of the
     Forms is different, that they should say that they are different units?
     And the Forms in Intellect would be different from one another by
10   reason of the otherness inherent in them, and much more so the Forms
     in Soul than those in Intellect, inasmuch as their distance from one
     another is greater, and again all are combinable (*sumblêtai*) in virtue of
     the unity emanating to them all from the Good and through the pre-
     dominance of sameness among the immaterial Forms. But this is
     matter for another enquiry. Of the units of which Aristotle is here
     setting himself up as the investigator, the Pythagoreans have neither
15   referred any to the Form-numbers, nor have they declared them to be
     different one from another.

> **1082b19-22** But if the number of the Essential Three is not
> greater than that of the Two, that would be surprising, and if it is
> greater, then clearly there is a number in it equal to the Two, so
> that this number will be undifferentiated from the Essential Two.

     First of all, you need not be surprised if, in positing the existence of the
     Essential Two and the Essential Three, they declare that the Three is
     not larger than the Two, and that the Two does not inhere in the Three;
     for neither do these numbers partake in quantity, nor does the Form of
20   Equality and Inequality[254] inhere in them as it does in unitary numbers.
     In the latter, after all, equal numbers are never unequal, nor unequal
     ones equal; whereas in the Form-numbers the same are both equal and
     unequal to each other, even as they are both same and different by
     reason of the presence in them of the genera of Being and the most
     comprehensive Forms, and they are involved in no contradiction by
25   reason of this; for they are not equal in the same sense as they are
     unequal, nor like in the same sense as they are unlike, nor the same in
     the same sense as they are different, but the like and equal and the
     same in virtue of Likeness and Equality and Sameness, and unlike and
     unequal and different in virtue of the Forms opposite to the former
     Forms. For there is no way that, when we have in the role of first
     principles a Monad and an Indefinite Dyad, those things that spring
30   from them should not receive the potencies of both. And furthermore
     one should bear in mind that this fellow is not postulating the number
     among the Forms as undifferentiated (how could he, after all, if the
     Forms partake of both equality and inequality?), but, if anything,
     number among the unitary numbers.

1082b22-4 But this is impossible, if there is a first and second   138,1
number; nor will the Forms be numbers.

He is quite right to say that it is not possible for two Twos to be
undifferentiated at the level of Form-number; but he is not prepared to
admit that it follows from his own hypothesis, which grants participation in unitary quantity to intellective forms.

1082b24-34 For on this particular point they are right who claim   5
that the units must be different if there are to be Forms, as has
been already stated. For a Form is unique, but if the units are
undifferentiated, the twos and threes will be undifferentiated also.
That is why they have to say that counting 'one, two, ...' does not
proceed by adding to what we have already; because if so number
will be not be generated from the Indefinite Dyad, nor is it possible
for it to be a Form, since then one Form will be present in another,
and all the Forms will be parts of a single Form. Thus from the
perspective of their hypothesis they are right, but absolutely they
are wrong, since their theories cause havoc.

Those people maintain, he says, an internal consistency who claim to
derive the total number of Forms from differentiated units, lest they be
constrained to postulate many Forms of the same thing, and to leave
twos in the four and the five and the six and in general in all numbers,
if the units are undifferentiated. And they maintain this correctly,   10
according to him, in relation to their own hypothesis, because one
should not create a three in that realm by adding a unit to two. For the
units in the two and in the three are not undifferentiated, but non-combinable; so that one must distinguish each of the numbers, and always
advance to the next one from a new starting-point. For if the numbers
are Forms, and Forms are not enveloped by other Forms in such a way   15
as to constitute a part of what envelops them, then neither would
numbers be parts of other numbers; but this will be the case with them,
if the units making them up were undifferentiated. But this conclusion,
he says, even if it preserves their hypothesis, nevertheless overturns
many of the theorems of arithmetic; and hence they speak correctly
from the perspective of their own hypothesis, but in absolute terms they
do not.[255]

However, that those men did not consider such units to be present at all   20
in Form-number, but that, by saying that the actual numbers were units
in another way, they admitted that they were differentiated both in
relation to themselves and to the nature of things, he is not willing to grant.

1082b34-7 For they will say that this point presents a difficulty:
when we count, and say 'one, two, three, ...', do we count by adding

on or by enumerating separate portions?[256] But we do it in both ways, which is why it is absurd to trace it back to such a great difference in essence.

They are wont, he says, to raise the difficulty as to whether one must 25 proceed from two to three, and then to four and five, and in general count by addition (*kata sunthesin*), or is it by division from the decad that they derive one, two, three, four; for neither of these alternatives finds favour with them. But we must declare, he says, that it is absurd, on the basis of such a superficial enquiry, to make each of the numbers an essence[257] and a Form. One must reply to them, then, that 'we do it 30 in both ways'; for when the greatest number is definite we divide, whereas when it is indefinite we add.[258]

But that this criticism cannot in any way be brought against Form-number, while against mathematical number it is in one way valid and in another not, we have frequently indicated; for it is both the 139,1 case that the difficulty raised by the ancients appears extremely intelligent, and yet the objection by Aristotle not entirely invalid; for the actualised Three, that which has received its Form, is one, and it could not, by taking to itself a further unit, become four (for how could the 5 Form of Three be transformed into that of Four?); but the potential three, as viewed in the three units, which is conceived of as without the Form of Three, if it were to take on a unit, would make up the substratum of four, which, insofar as it is formless, is not incapable of taking on another unit and making up the substratum of five, but, when dominated by the Form of Four, can only make up Four. So then, 10 divisions and multiplications are performed on the matter and quantity of numbers, not on their Forms; for these are not only in themselves unchanging, but also impose their one single shape on those things on which they supervene.

Chapter 8: Problems with the definition of number

1083a1-5 First of all, it would be well to define the differentia of a number, and of a unit, if it has one. Now units must differ either in quantity or in quality; and clearly neither of these alternatives can be true. But number, as number, one might say, differs in quantity. And indeed if units also differed in quantity, then a number could differ from another number even when equal in quantity of units.

It has been said often before that those men spoke of the Forms 15 themselves being units and numbers in one sense, while he advances objections which are proper to unitary number, and in relation to this he does a good job of making distinctions and decisions; for indeed if the units underlying mathematical number were differentiated, then Three and Five and each of the numbers will manifest itself in many different ways, and the three that seems to inhere in the seven will be different from that in the five or in the ten.

1083a6-11 Again, are the first units greater or smaller, and do the latter units increase in size, or the opposite? All these suggestions are absurd. Nor can units differ in quality; for no modification can ever be applicable to them, for they hold that even in numbers quality is a later attribute than quantity. 20

This also is very well said in respect of units in their usual sense. And indeed, if one imagines unitary numbers as coming into being, one will observe the Form that confers quality as coming later to shape the quantity underlying it.

1083a11-16 Further, the units cannot derive quality either from One or from the Two; because One has no quality, and the Two is productive of quantity,[259] because its nature causes things to be many. If, then, the units differ in some other way, they should most certainly state this at the outset, and explain, if possible, with regard to the differentia of the unit, why it must exist; or failing this, what differentia they mean. 25

That if any attribute is present in what follows on the first principles it must derive from those principles is a reasonable statement on his part; and as for his assertion that the arithmetical first principles[260] do not impose differentiation on units in their usually understood sense,[261] since they themselves contain no difference, this also is well said. But his refusal to allow that the One, which he takes to be the fundamental unit, even if he wishes it not to be itself qualified, is not the cause of quality, diverges both from the views of those men and from the truth, since after all the Indefinite Dyad must be rather the cause of quantification, not of both quantity and quality.[262] This assumption in turn follows from his view that the Three is nothing apart from the three units that comprise it; for in truth if this were the case, the Two that generates quantity would also have produced quality; but as it is, this latter generates the infinite succession of units, while the superior principle lays hold of them and shapes them by means of the Forms. 30

140,1

He does well also in demanding that they declare, not only that the units differ from each other, but what is the differentia of a unit. And they in turn have stated, not the differentia of the units making up a given number (for they do not grant that there is one), but rather the difference characterising these and their ruling causal principle. For when they say that the unit is the minimum element of quantity, or the primal and common part of quantity, they define it in its normal sense;[263] but when they say that the Unit [sc. the Monad] is the Form of Forms, they are identifying their ruling causal principle, that which 5

contains in itself on a preliminary level the Forms of all the numbers,
10 which the Stoics also do not scruple to term 'one-multiplicity (*hen plêthos*)';[264] since when they talk about the divine units (or monads), they define in one way the intelligible Monad, from which proceeds the primal Number, 'from the depths of the unsullied Monad',[265] but in another the intellective and demiurgic, which they also like to call Zeus, about which entities many of both ancient and modern authorities have
15 discoursed, but most clearly the divine Iamblichus, in the seventh book of his *Compendium of Pythagorean Doctrines*.[266] And if one is in a position to study with due comprehension the actual *Sacred Discourse (Hieros Logos)* of Pythagoras, one will find there all the orders of both units (*or* monads) and numbers comprehensively commemorated.

So we possess in their texts both the necessity of differentiating the units (*or* monads) from one another (for at each level of progression
20 (*proodos*) the monad which presides over the relevant order of being must needs exhibit a higher degree of multiplicity than those prior to it), and guidance as to what we should deem their differentiae to be; for the quantity and quality of the differentiae of the ruling monads must correspond to the number and variety of beings.

1083a17-20 Clearly, then, if the Forms are numbers, the units cannot all be combinable, nor can they all be incombinable in either sense.

25 If the Forms were unitary numbers, all the hypotheses concerning units are proved wrong in their regard; for if on the one hand their units were undifferentiated, many illogicalities would result (for there will be no difference between a Form-number and a mathematical number), and if they are different, the argument is preposterous, and this is true even if some units are assumed to be one way [sc. undifferentiated], and others the other. If, on the other hand, one were to say that number on the level of the Forms is not unitary, one will not be bothered by any of
30 his arguments; for none of them is directed towards this type of number.

1083a20-7 But then the way some other people speak about numbers is not correct either. These are people who believe that Forms do not exist, either as such or as being a kind of number, but that objects of mathematics exist, and the numbers are the first of existing things, and that their principle is the One itself. For it is absurd that if, as they say, there is a One which is the first of the ones, there should not be a Two which is the first of the twos, nor a Three of the threes; for the same argument applies to them all.

If indeed there were people who said this, they would be quite justly castigated by him.[267] But perhaps the fact is that, while they did not make use of the name of Forms, they hinted at the existence of divine

substances by employing the term 'mathematicals'; for how could they
have postulated the One and Number as prior to all other things, if they   35
were not in fact paying homage to the supra-essential One and the class
of Real Existents and the realm of the Forms? It is quite in consonance
with his own theory, then, that Aristotle should write as follows: '*For it*   141,1
is absurd ... to them all'. He correctly discerns the internal consistency
of the doctrine; for if there were henads occupying a fundamental
position within each order of beings, and all had proceeded from the
supra-essential and utterly separable One, then there must be such a
thing as a Form-number.   5

1083a27-b1 Now if this is truth with regard to number, and we
posit only mathematical number as existing, One is not a principle. For the One which is of this nature must differ from all the
other units; and if so, then there must be some Two which is first
of the twos, and similarly with the other numbers in succession.
But if One is a principle, then the truth about numbers must be
rather as Plato used to maintain; there must be a first Two and a
first Three, and those numbers must be non-combinable with one
another. But then again, if we assume this, many impossibilities
result, as has been already stated. And yet the truth must lie one
way or the other; so that if neither view is sound, number cannot
have a separate existence.

The whole argument here is as follows: if the mathematical is the only
type of number, then the One would not be the first principle of all
things. But if the One is the first principle, then Plato's view prevails,
and there is such a thing as Form-number, and one differs from the
other in essence. It would remain, however, our task to demonstrate   10
that the One is the first principle of all things, that which subsists
(*huparkhon*) neither as Intellect nor as Being nor as number, nor indeed
subsists at all, but transcending subsistence itself and Being itself, is
the cause of all good things and provides essence and unity to all; for if
this proposition is once established, it seems that Aristotle will be in
agreement with all the genuine doctrines of Pythagoras and Plato.   15

But then again ... as has been already stated.

There is in fact no impossibility here, if one makes correct postulates,
which are in accordance with those of the philosophers of old.

And yet ... a separate existence.

If number, he says, is separable, it follows necessarily that either
mathematical number is primary, or Form-number is. If neither of
these alternatives is accepted, then the premiss is invalidated. But the

conclusion is not entirely sound either (for there are other types of
20 number prior to the formal), nor has the minor premiss (*proslêpsis*) been
demonstrated – nor could it ever be.

> **1083b1-8** From these considerations it is also clear that the third
> alternative – that Form-number and mathematical number are
> the same – is the worst; for two errors have to be combined to make
> one theory. Mathematical number cannot be of this nature, but the
> propounder of this view has to spin it out by making assumptions
> peculiar to himself; and he has to admit also all the consequences
> of the theory that numbers are Forms.

Some people, he says, postulate two kinds of number and distinguish
them, like Plato (for he clearly states that mathematical number is
distinct from Form-number), while others recognise just one kind, the
mathematical, as do certain of the Pythagoreans, while yet others
25 recognise both kinds. He is perhaps alluding here to Speusippus and
Xenocrates, whom he describes as adopting the worst hypothesis, for
reasons that he clearly states.[268] But we ourselves have already stated our
views on this question, to the effect that, even if they used the same terms,
yet they understood the generic distinction between the different kinds of
30 number, since otherwise one who does not distinguish these but is confusing formal and mathematical number is making the creator (*hupostatês*)
of all the possessor within himself of mathematical number,[269] and is thus
attributing to the Father and Maker of all an arithmetical state of being
(*hexis*). But what could be more implausible than that?[270]

142,1 **1083b8-13** The Pythagorean view in one way contains fewer difficulties than the view described above, but in another way it
contains further difficulties peculiar to itself. By not regarding
number as separable, it disposes of many of the impossibilities; but
that bodies should be composed of numbers, and that these numbers should be mathematical, is impossible.

In truth, Plato and Pythagoras and those who have correctly received
their doctrines have the same[271] theory about numbers; but this fellow
makes divisions between them, and presents what each of them chiefly
5 concerned themselves with as being what they exclusively maintained.
For instance, he commends the Pythagoreans as asserting that numbers are inseparable from sensible objects; but he condemns them for
declaring that bodies are put together and created from them. But the
praise is based on a falsehood, and worse than the blame; or rather, both
are false, both the praise and the blame, but the former is based on an
10 hypothesis which is quite irrelevant to them, while the latter is based
on a true one; and it is obvious which is which. For who would not burst
out laughing on hearing that the Pythagoreans did not know that

numbers are separable? Pythagoras himself, after all, was accustomed
to give two different definitions of numbers, through one[272] of these
definitions demonstrating their completely separable and unsullied
nature, while through the other he taught us their creative and providential and preservative role; for when he says that number is 'the 15
extension and activation of seminal reason-principles inhering in the
monad',[273] he presents to us that number which proceeds self-generated
(*autogonôs*) and self-moved from its own first principle, and which is
established in itself and distinguished off into every sort of class; while
when he mentions 'that which subsists prior to all things in the divine
intellect, from which and out of which all things are constituted and
remain articulated in[274] an indissoluble structure,' he is celebrating that 20
number which is paradigmatic and demiurgic and father of gods and
daemons and of all mortal beings. Further, Hippasus and his school
define[275] number as 'the primary model for the creation of the cosmos',
and again, 'the critical instrument of discrimination (*organon kritikon*)
of the god who fashions the cosmos', while Philolaus maintains that
number is 'the self-generated and fundamental cause of cohesion
(*sunokhê*) for the eternal permanence of the contents of the cosmos', and 25
practically all the other Pythagoreans define their understanding of
number in obedience to these insights. And if then, just because they
say that bodies owe their substantiality to physical numbers,[276] either
one were to conceive that they were talking only about inseparable
numbers, or even according magnitude to numbers, it is plain that,
whether wittingly or unwittingly, he is disregarding their whole doctrine, and seeking to interpret the lowest level of their arithmetical 30
theory in the worst sense; for these men are not talking only about
physical numbers, nor are they mixing up the physical and mathematical levels of number, nor are they attributing three-dimensional magnitude (*megethos*) to the numbers that are the causal principles of
magnitude. But he takes this to be the case, and proceeds with the rest
of his argument on that basis.

1083b13-19 For it is not true to say that there are indivisible 143,1
magnitudes, and even granting fully that there were, units at least
have no magnitude. And how is it possible for a magnitude to be
composed of indivisible parts? Arithmetical number, at any rate, is
composed of abstract units. But those men [sc. the Pythagoreans] say
that things are number – at any rate they apply their theorems to
bodies as though the latter were made up of those bodies.

What those men say is unrefuted and remains true for all time; for, in
the words of the divine Socrates,[277] the truth is not refuted. The position
here being refuted relates in fact to anyone rather than the Pythagoreans; for neither do they claim that the number with which we measure 5
sensible objects is the cause of sensible objects, even if they discern in

it images of natural number (even as they used to maintain that the *bômiskos*[278] of 210 manifested the form of body, in the 1 the form of fire, in the 3 that of air, in the 7 that of earth, and in the 9 that of water; for these are taken to be in a certain analogical relation to one another, as
10 indications of natural powers); nor did they consider that the units in it either possessed indivisible magnitude or in any way inhered in sensible objects. But when they talk of indivisible magnitudes, they are directing us back to the reason-principles which are the causes of magnitudes and to the paradigmatic cause of large things, which that truly great man Plato used to term Largeness Itself (*automegethos*); whereas when they say that units have magnitude, they are celebrating
15 the universally extending power of the demiurgic monads; and again, when they say that magnitude owes its existence to indivisibles, they do not say this because atoms come together and as it were by coalescing create dimensions (for this Democritean doctrine goes against both geometrical and more or less all other areas of science), but because,
20 among indivisibles, such as are intellective, pure, demiurgic and life-giving Forms, these, while not departing from their own state, bring about at the lowest level all other things and in particular the mass (*onkos*) of bodies; while, as for those that inhere in nature and incline in their activities towards matter, they, although themelves being without mass and incorporeal, nonetheless, are the causes of bodily structure[279] through in some way or other coalescing with bodies, can be said for this reason to be inseparable from bodies. But the proposition
25 that a body should be created from bodies they rejected for many reasons; so that, if this is true, there is every necessity that bodies should derive their existence from indivisible entities, but not, however, that they are put together from indivisibles, nor yet dissolved into indivisibles, unless perhaps theoretically.

> **1083b19-23** So, if it is necessary for number to exist in one of the above-mentioned ways, if it exists independently, but none of these is possible, clearly number has no such character as is proposed for it by those who make it separable.

30 The argument here takes the form of a syllogism, but the inference is not valid; for if he once postulated that numbers are all unitary and extended the properties of the one sort to all, he would then seem to have a case against them.[280] Indeed, though, while those blessed men of old declared that even what possessed no order was brought to order by
144,1 means of numbers, the argument ranged against them brings confusion and disorder even to their divine insights about numbers.

> **1083b23-32** Again, does each unit come from the Great-and-Small, when they are equalised; or does one come from the Small

and another from the Great? If the latter, each thing is not composed of all the elements, nor are the units undifferentiated; for one contains the Great, and the other the Small, which is by nature contrary to the Great.

Besides, what about the units in the essential Three? For one of them is left over. But no doubt it is for this reason that in an odd number they make the essential One a median element. If on the other hand each of the units comes from both Great and Small, when they are equalised, how can the essential Two be a single entity composed of the Great and Small? And how will it differ from the unit?

The problem that he is raising is the following. They generate all other things, including mathematical units, from the One and the Indefinite 5 Dyad. Since, then, <they are generated either from the elements>[281] in the Indefinite Dyad, by which I mean the Great and the Small, or some from the Great and others from the Small, it will not be the case that each of the units is from all of the elements, nor will the units be equal, but, as well as being different, they will actually be opposed to one another, at least if some are going to be great and others small. And from which source does the three derive its third unit, from the Great 10 or from the Small? Indeed perhaps it is in response to this puzzle, he says, that they postulate the one in the three and in every odd number as a median element (*meson*), in order that the units may be equal deriving from the Great and the Small not only in the even, but also in the odd numbers. But if each unit derives from the Great and the Small, when they have been made equal to each other by blending, first of all, how will this Two arising from the Great and the Small become 15 one nature? For it is plain that, even if they are united subsequent to being equalised (*isastheisa*),[282] they were nevertheless before this unification two. And then, in what way will a single unit differ from a pair?[283] For if there is inherent in the unit a two which has been equalised, and the two, as such, is said to be a two, then how will they differ from one another?[284]

Now in the face of these objections of Aristotle's, we will lay it down that it is never the case that the Indefinite Dyad, whether one is 20 thinking of the primal one, or that at the level of Soul, or of Nature, or even that which is postulated as inhering in Matter, either operates or is operated upon in a divided manner, in accordance with the Great and the Small, but rather, in respect of each of those things generated by it, it introduces greatness and smallness in a manner proper to each level of beings; and the units, if we are focusing now on those in mathematical 25 number (since he is not prepared to recognise any other kinds), while being produced, certainly, from all the causal principles, including the One and the Indefinite Dyad, yet do not possess within themselves distinctly (*diêirêmenôs*) the Great and the Small, nor did they ever so

possess them, in such a way that we would have to pose the problem as to how each unit of the Essential Two differs [sc. from the other], but
30 they are, in relation both to all other numbers and to Two, formless and indefinite, but they are held together as such by the image of the One. But if on the other hand he were talking about immaterial monads (for one may call the intellectual Forms not only numbers, but also monads), we will far more strongly assert that each of them derives from all the causal principles, and they acquire from the One their unitary and monadic form, while from the Indefinite Dyad they derive their part-
35 lessness (*ameres*)[285] and their power of universal extension in respect of
145,1 their demiurgic and providential and preservative faculties; for it is in such terms that I feel that one should interpret 'smallness' and 'greatness' at the divine level.

> **1083b32-6** Again, the unit is prior to the two; because when it disappears the two disappears. Therefore the unit must be the Form of a Form, because prior to a Form, and must come into being before it. From what, then? The Indefinite Dyad, after all, is productive of duality.

That the unit is prior to the Essential Two (*autoduas*)[286] <is clear; for if the unit is eliminated, then the two is also eliminated. But that which eliminates is (ontologically) prior to that which is eliminated along with it; so that if the unit is prior to the Essential Two>, and the Essential
5 Two is a Form, then the unit which is senior to this is also a Form. From what, then, did it proceed? It did not come from the Indefinite Dyad; for that has the quality of doubling even simple things.

In this passage, in fact, he does not define what type of unit he is talking about, but it is obvious that he is propounding this difficulty about the unit in its normal sense, which has no place in Form-number, but is cast forth into the lowest level of mathematical number, and is
10 not absolutely senior to the unitary two, but, while perhaps being senior to it in point of generation, is certainly not so in essence; for of such a nature are the material causes. This unit has been produced – and the same goes for the whole substratum of the mathematical numbers – from all the causal principles, indeed, but most of all from the Dyad proper to them;[287] for this, where numbers are distinguished into form and matter, is rather the causal principle of their matter, and, where
15 they are divided into even and odd, is more fundamental over the even; and in virtue of this, and in addition to this many other marvellous things in respect of number, it is reasonably described as 'productive of duality' (*duopoios*). For all matter may be identified with the Dyad, and all even number and every non-square rectangle (*heteromêkês*), and anything else that belongs to this side of the Table of Opposites (*sustoikhia*).

1083b36-1084a2 Again, number must be infinite or finite (for they make number separable, so that one of these alternatives must be true).

The dichotomy is inescapable, and the reason for this is entirely com- 20
pelling; for while in the case of sensible things it is not possible to
declare either alternative definitively, but only that those things that
are bound to a single time are finite, while those that are in infinite time
are infinite, in the case of those things that are always in the same
relation and the same state,[288] in relation to which time has no function,
it is necessary to go for either the finite or the infinite. So one must say
that the divine entities are potentially infinite, but in fact are circum- 25
scribed by a finite number; what that number is, however, an individual
soul could not say, except that it is of such a size as the first principles
of these extend to in their wish to produce a different number for each
class of being. And if we should postulate in one case a triadic or tetradic
number, and in another a hebdomadic or decadic, it is not by counting
them in the way that one would count all other countable objects that
we declare the divine entities in that realm to be of such and such a 30
number, but since, while all are perfect and archetypal and ungenerated and comprehensive in advance (*prolêptika*) of all things, yet different characteristics manifest themselves in different ones, even if all are
in all – in those in which the primary degree of perfection is manifest,
their number we declare to be triadic; while in those which comprehend
archetypally all things in the cosmos, it is tetradic; in those which 146,1
ungeneratedly bestow providential care upon generated things, it is
hebdomadic; and in those which comprehend all things more discrimi-
natingly (*diakekrimenôs*) and indeed intellectually, it is decadic.

This, then, to encapsulate the greatest issues in the smallest possible
compass, is the sum-total of their doctrine on that subject. But Aristotle,
by mixing up the ordinary sort of units with the divine numbers of that 5
realm, takes pleasure in introducing total confusion into the subject.

1084a2-4 Now it is obvious that it cannot be infinite, because
infinite number is neither odd nor even, but numbers are always
generated either as odd or as even.

One might reasonably raise this problem rather in relation to mathematical number, but not to the divine or the formal; for in that realm
'odd' and 'even' have a different sense, not the one that he assumes here, 10
but rather in the way that the poets speak of the gods and goddesses:

'Hear me now, all you gods and all you goddesses!'[289]

For there the demiurgic Monad fills with divine and providential intellection each of the two tables of opposites (*sustoikhiai*). The problem

would have been in fact much more suitably raised in relation to
15 mathematical number; for either the number is finite, in which case its
procession will come to a stand, and thus each number will be either
even or odd; or there will be an infinite number that is even or odd. Now
in response to someone who raises such a problem about mathematical
number one may make the following valid point, that every number one
may take is limited, whether it be odd or even, but that number which has
20 not yet been picked out is unknown and formless and infinite, and, while
potentially of such or such a nature, in actuality neither even nor odd.[290]

Enough, then on this topic. Let us now see how Aristotle presents the
generation of number, in accordance with which every number necessarily comes to be either even or odd.

> **1084a4-7** By one process, when one is added to an even number,
> we get an odd number; by another, when one is multiplied by two,
> we get ascending powers of two; and by another, when powers of
> two are multiplied by odd numbers, we get the remaining even
> numbers.

25 According to him, then, One, by adding itself to (*empipton*) the Dyad,
makes three, while the Dyad, when it proceeds towards the One, makes
two, but when it has achieved that and then goes on in the same way,
it generates the even times even, while when it approaches the three
and the other odd numbers, it generates the even-odd numbers, and
adding itself to those in turn, the odd-even. Were this to be, as he states,
the view of the ancients, he correctly raises the problem; but if in fact he is
30 not correct in his investigation, it has no relevance to Form-number.

147,1 > **1084a7-10** Again, if every Form is a Form of something, and the
> numbers are Forms, then infinite number will also be a Form of
> something, either of a sense-object or of something else. This,
> however, is not possible, either according to the argument or on
> their own assumption, since they regard the Forms as they do.

This line of argument has somewhat more substance. In reply to this
the proponents of the infinity of paradigms declare that the sensible
world does not receive all the Forms simultaneously, and some of them
5 even say that not even in the infinite stretch of time does the world
receive images of all the formal causes – for such is the rash claim of
such people as Amelius, the follower of Plotinus.[291] Aristotle here,
however, seems rather to have hit on the position of the ancients; this
is why he adds 'it is not possible either according to the argument (*oude
kata ten thesin endekhetai*)', describing the doctrine of those men in just
these terms, presumably, as containing a certain degree of paradox.
10 And this, one may say, is an admirable feature of Aristotle's presentation, that he says that they declare that the Forms (*ideai*) are not

primarily of sensible things, but are of themselves,[292] while also being paradigms of the Forms (*eidê*) at the level of Soul and of Nature and, ultimately,[293] in the sensible realm, which is what he is hinting at by the phrase 'or of something else (*ê allou tinos*)'.

Let us grant, then, that he has demonstrated that the intelligible numbers are not infinite of their own nature, despite being unknowable and ungraspable from our perspective; for even if it were not for the 15 reasons that he states that one were to deny infinity to them, yet Philolaus has stated the situation with sufficient accuracy. 'For', he says, 'that which is knowable will not be a first principle, if all are infinite'.[294] If, then, the divine number knows itself, it is at all events because it is limited as far as it itself is concerned; and if it is just so great as the first principles wished it to be, then at all events it is 20 because its measure is pre-ordained to it by the will of the first principles;[295] so that it would not be infinite, except in the sense of being infinite in power (*apeirodunamos*), or in relation to us. Let us see, then, what oddities follow from its being finite.

1084a10-12 If, on the other hand, number is finite, how far does it go? In reply to this, we must not only assert the fact, but give the reason.

On the line of enquiry that you are pursuing, it is not possible to say; for divine entities are not countable by our nature. When, however, they 25 postulate triads and tetrads and hebdomads and decads, they have no lack of arguments pertinent to these speculations, as we have indicated just above.

1084a12-18 Now if number only goes up to Ten, as some hold, in the first place the Forms will soon run out. For example, if Three is the Essential Man, then what number will the Essential Horse be? For the Essential Numbers go up only as far as Ten, so it must be one of the numbers within this series (these being real objects and Forms), but they will still run out, since the Forms of animals will exceed them.

When those divine men declared that the Decad is the Form-number *par excellence*, as being the paradigm of the cosmos and 'a limit set 30 about all things',[296] and because even as the Decad contains within itself the whole of number no longer covertly, as does the Monad, or essentially, as does the Tetrad, but already with a greater degree of otherness and division, in this way also the intellectual creation embraces in advance within itself all the Forms of things in the cosmos.[297] And 148,1 whereas they have received this doctrine from Orpheus and Musaeus and those descended from them, Aristotle assumes that they postulate that the Forms are just ten in number, and proceeds to criticise their

views on that basis. And yet if they postulated that they were ten in number, but that each possessed powers limited in number, indeed, but of a quantity unknowable to us, not even so would the paradigmatic
5   causes be less than the species (*eidê*)[298] of living thing, nor in general than the species in this realm, if we specify that by *this* power of the triad, say, this is given its existence, and by *that* power that.

But enough of this. It is plain to us, once again, that the man is approaching the Decad celebrated by the ancients as if it were a unitary
10   number; and so his subsequent critique continues in the same vein.[299]

> **1084a18-21** At the same time it is clear that if in this way Three is the Essential Man, then so must the other threes also (for the threes in the same number are similar), so that there will be infinitely many men; and if each three is a Form, then each man will be the Essential Man; or if not, they will at any rate be men.

It has been said that not only is each of the Form-numbers one, but also each of the mathematical numbers, if that is taken to be the actualised number and that viewed in conjunction with its own form, while the
15   essential Three is not the paradigm of man or of anything else, but rather of all the threes following on itself; so that it is the single cause of many things, some nearer to itself, others situated at the lowest level of existence.

> **1084a21-5** And if the smaller number is part of the greater, when it is composed of units combinable in the same number, then if the Essential Four is the Form of something, e.g. Horse or White, then Man will be part of Horse, if Man is Two.

This too is ridiculous, and a cheap shot (*phortikôs*), which would only have any force if those men had postulated the number proper to the
20   Forms as unitary, and had said that each of the unitary numbers was instantiated on many levels, not only in itself but also in all the levels of being superior to it.

> **1084a25-7** It is absurd also that there should be a Form of Ten and not of Eleven, nor of the numbers following on that.

It is not absurd, if you bear in mind that Forms are of simple natures, and not of those things of like nature that are put together out of elements; and it is for this reason that they termed the totality of formal
25   number the Decad for the aforementioned reasons, while also postulating a Form of each of the unitary numbers up to ten; for these are distinctively simple, and exhibit formal differences between each other. Eleven, on the other hand, is a composite of two antecedent numbers.[300]

1084a27-9 Again, some things exist and come into being of which there are no Forms, so why are there not Forms of these too? So it would follow that Forms cannot be causes.

This is the way in which those who give over the universe to chance and   30
the spontaneous (*ek t'automatou*) might have argued; for since some
things arise spontaneously according to you also, what is there to stop
all things occurring according to chance? But I think you would say to
them that these things belong to the category of what may happen in a   149,1
minority of cases, whereas those things that come to fruition either for
the most part or always are the works of Nature and of Intellect, looking
towards some end. So assume that you heard such arguments first from
them [sc. the advocates of chance].

But what sort of things do you say come about without Forms? For of
those things which are primary in nature the Forms are substantial and   5
inherent in Intellect, while of the ultimate and insubstantial there is
nothing that is not brought about in accordance with natural reason-
principles, and as for manufactured objects (*tekhnêta*), you yourself
admit that they are created in accordance with the forms inherent in
the soul,[301] as is admitted in many places, but most clearly in Book 7 of
the present work.[302] Unless perhaps you mean either the products of
manufacture (*prakta*)[303] or those of chance and accident; for of these the
latter do not exist in the way customarily accepted by us (for none of   10
them arise without a cause); while the products of manufacture, even if
they do not have Forms pre-existing eternally in the same state, at least
they possess forms that pre-exist the manufacturing processes
(*praxeis*); for <our will>, awaking beforehand our whole mind-set in our
imaginative or opinionative faculties, <is the cause> in the strict sense
within us of our productive activities (?).[304]

1084a29-37 Again, it is absurd that number up to Ten should be
more really existent, and a Form, than Ten itself, although the
former is not generated as a unity, whereas the latter is. However,
they try to make out that the series up to Ten is a complete
number. At least they generate the derivatives, e.g. the void,
proportion, the odd, etc., from within the Ten. Some things, such
as motion, rest, good and evil, they attribute to the first principles;
the rest to the numbers. Hence they identify the odd with One;
because if oddness inhered essentially in Three, then how could
Five be odd?

What is left out of the argument is the conclusion, 'for it was the perfect   15
number'. Further, it is absurd if number does not extend to eleven, since
One, after all, is more truly existent than the Decad, and is its Form,
and so on. The Form of the Decad on their theory is not just any chance
one, but the originatory Monad, in defining which they term it the Form

of Forms,[305] because it contains within itself the Forms of all the numbers. But though it may indeed be the case that it is the Form of all the numerical Forms, nonetheless it may most of all be said to be that of the Decad; for the Decad is a representation of it, which is to say that, even as is the Monad in relation to all other numbers, so is it also in relation to the tens and hundreds and thousands after it – for which reason it is termed 'a second-level monad'.[306] So even as Intellect is the Form of all things, and especially of Soul, so the Monad, even though it is the Form of all numbers, is especially so of the Decad. It is to such a monad, then, that the epithet 'ungenerated' would most properly apply, not to that inhering in the number eleven. He knows himself, of course, the reason why they extended number up to Ten; for it was the ultimate perfection embracing the totality (*pan*)[307] within itself.

As for a paradigm of void, the more accurate of arguments do not allow for the possibility of it in numbers, since there is no void among existent things either, as Iamblichus has made clear in the fifth book of his *Compendium of Pythagorean Doctrines*.[308] The positions (*khôrai*)[309] of numbers and in particular their concordances (*harmoniai*), which are themselves in all cases filled by the numbers, they declared to be reminiscent of the 'place' of the universe, which may be regarded as empty when taken by itself,[310] but is in fact filled up by the demiurgic activity of Intellect and the circuit of the aether, which, by compressing and contracting all things towards each other, leaves no empty place in the universe, but presents the cosmos as concordant and interactive with itself throughout; even as, indeed, the Monad, in its generation of numbers, does not endure to leave any place empty, filling as it does all the arithmetical receptacles (*hupodokhai*) with an uninterrupted succession of numbers.

That every type of proportion (*analogia*) should be exhibited within the Decad is obvious enough; for arithmetical proportion occurs in the natural progression of numbers,[311] while geometrical is to be seen in 1, 2, 4, and 1, 3, 9, and the harmonic in 2, 3, 6 and 3, 4, 6. All things, then, he says, they attributed to the first principles, that is to say to the Monad and the Dyad, Rest and Good to the Monad, Motion and Evil to the Dyad. They could indeed give the title of first principles also to the two columns of opposites (*sustoikhiai*) in the numbers up to ten, and very aptly so, since even among real beings some depend on the first principles alone, the single One and the pair following upon it,[312] while others have taken on also a formal cause. Why this should be, though, is a rather long story.

As for the objection that he raises against them at the end, that is easily disposed of. 'If', he says, 'three comes about through the One, then why do not both five and all other odd numbers come about through three, even as every even number comes about through Two?' We shall reply that primary and incomposite number is likely to have been given form by the Monad alone, while secondary and composite number has another source of measurement over and above the Monad; hence the Monad acts as Form for all odd numbers, even as the Dyad does for all even ones. For in general it is not the Triad that should be analogous to the Dyad in respect of being a principle, but rather the Monad. Indeed, by these remarks he has made clear that according to him also there is   20 another cause by virtue of which they extend the paradigms of numbers as far as the Decad; for if they wish to view the causes of all things as being in them, and they see the causes of all in the numbers up to ten, then it would be superfluous to postulate paradigms of the numbers after that. And further, it would not be correct to say that eleven possesses, besides the Decad, the Monad that is the cause of the Decad, but rather the one that is as it were a part of ten and two and all the   25 other numbers.

> **1084a37-b2** Again, they hold that spatial magnitudes and the like
> have a certain limit, e.g. the first indivisible line, then the Two,
> then more of these up to Ten.

Again, he says,[313] they demonstrate from spatial magnitudes that one should extend number only as far as ten. For they said that the Monad creates the point, which he calls 'indivisible line',[314] the Dyad the line,   30 the Triad plane figure, <and the Tetrad solid body>,[315] and these suffice for <the universe; so that if these are the essence of the Decad (for if you add them together they make up the Decad), then the Decad suffices for> the universe. So let this causal principle be granted, even if it is rather lightweight[316] since taken merely in relation to mathematical number, and is many stages removed in rank from the more substantial types (of number), yet it is at least familiar in common parlance. For   35 there are four principles of creation as a whole, as has been demon-   151,1 strated elsewhere; and the Form of the Decad is derived in every case from the Tetraktys.

> **1084b2-13** Again, if number is separable, the question might be
> raised as to whether One is prior, or Three, or Two. Now if we
> regard number as composite, it is One that is prior; but if we
> regard the universal or form as prior, the number is, since each
> unit is a part of number as matter, while number is the form of the
> units. And there is a sense in which the right angle is prior to the
> acute angle, because it is determinate and because it is involved
> in the definition of the acute angle; and another sense in which the
> acute angle is prior, because it is a part of the other, i.e. the right
> angle is divided into acute angles. Thus, regarded as matter, the
> acute angle and element and the unit are prior, but with respect
> to form and substance in the sense of formula, the right angle, and
> the whole composed of matter and form, is prior. For the concrete

whole is nearer to the form or subject of the definition, although in point of generation it is posterior.

He has most aptly raised this problem, and then solved it on the basis
5 of their customary terminology; for the ruling Monad, bearing as it does an analogy to the divinity, which the members of this school[317] used to call the 'pinnacle' (*korupha*)[318] of all Forms and all geometrical figures, is in all respects primary among numbers; whereas that which fills the role of substratum with regard to numbers, which they defined as the minimum quantity,[319] is primary in point of generation, but not in substance. But he, although knowing these things and making such
10 dexterous use of these concepts himself,[320] is not prepared to countenance their transferral to numbers, but relying on the homonymous nature of the term *monas*,[321] tries to introduce confusion into a theory which actually treats excellently of all its elements. For listen to what he says next:

> **1084b13-16** In what sense, then, is the One a first principle? Because, they say, it is not divisible. But the universal and the particular and the element are also indivisible. Yes, but they are indivisible[322] in different senses, the one in definition, the other in time. In which sense then, is the One a principle?

So then, just as you make your distinctions, and say that the form or
15 the universal is indivisible in definition, while the element is so in time, since the time of a thing's generation begins from this, even so pray grant that they assume the same. What 'one', then, you ask – the ruling one, or that which is the least element in parts? But since there is, in their view, in general a distinction between One and monad, about which the older Pythagoreans had a good deal to say, as for instance Archytas, who says
20 that the One and the monad,[323] 'while akin, differ from one another',[324] and among the younger ones Moderatus and Nicomachus, why do we make this leap from the monad to the One, except for the purpose of making the intended meaning of those men more difficult to fathom?

> **1084b16-20** For, as we have just said, both the right angle seems to be prior to the acute angle, and the latter prior to the former; and each of them is one. Accordingly they make the One a principle in both ways. But this is impossible; for in the one sense it is the One as form or essence that is primary, and in the other the One as part or matter.

Thus, then, also the unit (*monas*) which fills the role of substratum to
25 numbers, taken as analogous to the acute angle, and being both prior and posterior to numbers, is in account later, but in point of generation older.

Accordingly, they make the One a principle in both ways.

But it is not the same thing, my fine fellow – the one, after all, is the ruling element in every sense, as being the cause of all things, while the other is the least of parts, as the acute angle is of the right angle.

But this is impossible.

The same thing, my fine fellow! And for that reason we will focus our attention on what follows, but we do not grant that it is directed against the doctrine of those men.[325] 30

For in the one sense ... as part or matter.

Number is prior as form and as essence, while the unit is as part and as matter; one might add that it serves as substratum to numbers.

1084b20-3 There is a sense in which each one of the two, number   152,1
and unit, are one; but in fact it is only potentially, and not in actuality – at least if the number is a unity and not like a heap, and if different numbers are made up of different units, as they say – that either of the two units exists.

He uses the phrases 'each one of the two' and 'either of the two <units>'[326] with reference to the units of the Two.[327] He says that, taken by themselves, each of these exists potentially and not in actuality, both in truth and according to the doctrine of the ancients; for if number is 5
not a heap of units, but each one, while being made up a definite number of underlying units, is constituted in accordance with the Form proper to itself, the unit in the Two would be nothing in actuality, before it was given order by the Form proper to it. One should take due note of this, then, that he is neither willing for number to be a system of units[328] nor indeed for units to be anything at all in actuality, until they are brought 10
to order by Forms; for even if it is for some other reason that he has picked on them, in a desire to show that they place the potential as prior to the whole and enformed not only in point of generation and time, but also in definition (*logos*) and essence (a position which we have actually countered earlier, when we said that the ruling monad, in their theory, is distinct from the unit that acts as matter), yet at any rate he preserves a sufficient degree of harmony with both the truth and with 15
the doctrine of the ancients.

1084b23-32 The cause of the error that befell them was the fact that they were pursuing their enquiry at one and the same time from the perspective of mathematics and from that of definitions of universals. Hence as a result of the former they conceived of the One, their first principle, as a point; for the unit is a point without position. So they too, just like certain others, put things together from a minimum element. As a result, the unit becomes the material element of numbers, and at the same time prior to the Two; but again also posterior to it, when the Two is regarded as a whole or unity or form. On the other hand, because they were looking for the universal, they treated the unity that is predicated of a given number as a part in the formal sense also. But these two characteristics cannot belong simultaneously to the same thing.

Your point that 'these two characteristics cannot belong simultaneously to the same thing' is well taken. However, it is simply not the case that those men claimed that the same unit (*monas*) was both comprehensive of all numbers and the least part of each,[329] but it has been said already that they held that the ruling monad was one thing, and the material

20 unit another. So then, they did not construct reality out of partless atoms, in the manner of Democritus and his followers, nor yet did they, inconsistently,[330] from a mathematical perspective, evince a low regard for the monad, while from a dialectical perspective they exhibit a high opinion of it, but, as been said already, they expressed these differing opinions about two different types of monad (or unit).

And do you take care, my fine fellow, lest you yourself become liable to the same accusation, by declaring that the animal and in general the

25 genus are now a part of the species and the individual (*atomon*), and now prior in nature and more comprehensive; for even if you make many different distinctions, and call the one 'generic' (*genikon*) and the other 'genus', as long as you do not grant substantial existence to the genus, there is no way that these things will not be mixed up with one another.

1084b32-1085a1 And if the One itself must be only without position (for it differs only in that it is a principle), and two is divisible whereas the unit is not, the unit will be more nearly akin to the One itself; and if this is so, it in turn will be more nearly akin to the unit than to two. Hence, each of the units in two will be prior to two. But this they deny; at least they make out that two is generated first.

30 Since, he says, the unit in two is more akin to the One itself – which is the same as saying the ruling Monad – than is two (for the latter is

153,1 divisible, while the former is indivisible), and that which is more akin to the first principle is prior, then the unit in two would be prior to two. 'But this they deny.' And rightly so, my fine fellow! For on this reckoning one could show that matter is prior to the whole cosmos, since it is simple and formless, and these properties are characteristic of the single first principle of all things. But I think that one should not make the antithetical homonymy of the lowest element in reality with the 5 first principles, viewed in the light of the much-vaunted principle of 'unlike likeness',[331] an excuse for standing the good order of things on its head.

1085a1-3 Further, if the Two itself and the Three itself are each one thing, both together make two. Whence, then, does this two derive?

Well, obviously, from the two Forms concerned; for it is generated in our minds by virtue of unitary number. But if, because each of the Forms is 10 co-ordinated with each of the others and with all simultaneously, one wished there to be a co-ordinating of the essential Two with the paradigm of Three at the level of true beings also, and were to enquire how the pair of them are two, we will say that they are possessed by the characteristic of the essential Two; for on every one which is co-ordinated to it the Two bestows its own peculiar character, as in turn does 15 the Three impart its own character to all the threes that wish to be united to one another. But nonetheless the primary beings do not participate in the formal measure of numbers in the same way as things in the cosmos, but, as we have said,[332] the divinities are united to one another and partake in one another by virtue of all being in all. This we must hold is the doctrine of the ancients.

He himself, indeed, might respond to a similar question as follows: if 20 the separable causal principle which moves the circle of the fixed stars is one, and that which moves the circle of Saturn is one, then both together are two. So then, from what derives this two? I think that you would say, 'From the two intellects; for we count them from without, approaching them not as numbers, but as things numbered.' So then also, if you in turn number two or three of the Forms, you are making them into things numbered, and you will say that they are composed of 25 Forms, treating each of the Forms as a unit.

Chapter 9: More difficulties with Form-numbers

1085a3-7 One might well raise this problem: since there is no contact in numbers, only succession, applying to units between which there is nothing – those in two, for example, or three – are these successive to the One Itself, or not? And is two first in succession, or one of the units in two?

The problem that he is raising here is the following. Is the first unit in the Two to be ranked next in succession to the primal One, or not? For if we do so rank it, then there will be a two prior to the Two; but if not, 30 then what would be the cause of this? And in general, are we to say that the Two Itself is next in succession to the One, or rather the unit in the Two, as being more akin to the One?[333]

We must say that in relation to Form-number problems about such units should not even be raised, as we have often indicated before this; but if the question is asked about mathematical number, we will say
35 that the units in each of the numbers, in themselves, are successive to nothing, seeing that they are not even actualised in themselves; but
154,1 when they are subjected to the Form of their proper number, then they are successive to each other, but they would not be said to be successive to the units in another number, but it is rather those numbers which are laid out in a natural series (*ekthesis*)[334] that would be said to lie in succession to one another.

1085a7-16 We find similar difficulties in the case of the genera posterior to number – line, plane and solid. Some derive these from the species of the Great and Small – lines, for example, from the Long and Short, planes from the Broad and Narrow, and solids from the Deep and Shallow (these being species of the Great and Small). The principle answering to the One is posited by different people in different forms. In these two we can see innumerable impossibilities, fictions and contradictions of all reasonable probability.

5 Wishing, he says, to generate magnitudes also from the two principles of One and Indefinite Dyad, they say that from the Dyad the line takes on the Long and Short, the plane the Broad and Narrow, and the solid the Deep and Shallow; for they called these 'species' of the Great and Small in the Indefinite Dyad. The principle corresponding to the One,
10 on the other hand, he says, they did not all introduce in the same way, but some said that the numbers themselves bestowed their forms on the various dimensions, as for instance the Dyad on the line, the Triad on the plane, and the Tetrad on the solid (for this is what he recounts in his treatise *On Philosophy* about Plato);[335] while others postulate that Form is conferred on the other magnitudes by participation in the One.[336]

All this, however, while not giving an entirely false account of the subject,[337] yet does not give a properly articulated account of the situ-
15 ation either; but nonetheless let us see what impossible consequences he declares to follow from this.

1085a16-19 For (a) we get the result that the geometrical forms are unconnected with each other, unless their principles also are so associated that the Broad and Narrow is also Long and Short; and if this is so, the plane will be a line and the solid a plane.

If on the one hand, he says, the first principles of magnitudes do not combine with one another, then their dimensions will be unconnected with one another (for entities which arise from different principles are not compelled to co-exist), so that there will be a plane without a line; but if on the other hand they do combine, then the line will be the same 20 as the plane and the plane as the solid.[338]

Now I am perfectly prepared to accept that, in writing this, he is sincere in[339] what he is saying; but nonetheless let him in turn take on board that it is their position that it is not necessary that they be exclusively either the same or distinct from each other, but there is an intermediate position, to wit, combining by reason of sameness, while being distinguished from one another through otherness.

And in general it is logical that the first principles, while being 25 together, should be distinguished by otherness, even as also the reason-principles in nature, while being all together in a mode of partlessness, are yet distinguished by otherness; and those things that proceed from the principles, being themselves simple, may also be viewed as distinct from the compounds deriving from them, while as they proceed further into complexity they nonetheless stand in need of their simpler forms. Hence a line may be considered independently of a plane, and this latter independently of a solid, but in the perfected magnitude all these must 30 be assumed.

1085a19-20 Moreover, how can angles and figures and suchlike be explained?

And further, he says, how can they construct these from their much-vaunted principles? For what is the excessive element, and what the deficient, in these? In the case of angles, at least, the answer is ready to hand: for it is plain that the right angle is to be associated rather with the Monad, while the acute and obtuse angles are to be ranked with the 155,1 Indefinite Dyad, from which derives the tendencies both to overreach and to be overreached. And of geometrical figures, those that are characterised by equality and sameness and likeness look rather to the Monad, while those characterised by inequality and otherness and unlikeness look to the Dyad.

By this, of course, I do not mean that each does not derive from both 5 of the two principles; for the sphere and the circle and the equilateral triangle and the square and the cube partake of the Dyad in virtue of their quantification and as it were their extension, and again *dokides* and *bômiskoi*[340] and scalene triangles and oblong rectangles (*het-eromêkê*) exhibit kinship to the Monad, inasmuch as they receive their form from that source. But, nonetheless, just as we were wont to say in the case of numbers, that each of them derives from both principles, yet 10 the odd is dominated rather by the character of the Monad, while the even is dominated by that of the Dyad; so also in the case of angles and figures we say that all derive from both of the two principles, but some are more akin to one or the other than others.

> **1085a20-3** And (b) the same result follows as in the case of number; for these concepts are attributes of magnitude, but magnitude is not generated from them, any more than a line is generated from the Straight and Crooked, or solids from the Smooth and Rough.

15 It must be granted that, just as the odd and the even are essential attributes (*pathê kath' hauta*) of numbers, so attributes of length are the round and the straight, of breadth the narrow and the broad, and of depth the short and the tall. But since these characteristics do not occur in them without a cause, it is plain that they come to them from the relevant principle, and so if it bestows upon them rectangularity and

20 stability, this proceeds to them rather from the Monad, as in the case of the right angle among the angles; but if it exhibits excess and deficiency, and is associated with the more and less, it derives this from the Dyad. So then, those men did not in fact maintain that the attributes in magnitudes were principles of those magnitudes, but rather those things from which these devolved onto magnitudes, of which one proper source is the Indefinite Dyad.

25   **1085a23-9** Common to all these theories is the same problem which presents itself in the case of the species of a genus, when we posit universals: is it the Essential Living Being that is present in the particular living being, or some other living being distinct from the Essential Living Being itself? This creates no difficulty if the universal is not separable; but if One and numbers are separate, as the people who hold this theory say, then it is not easy to solve − if one should apply the description 'not easy' to something impossible!

That, if universals are separable, then so are numbers, he grants, but he rejects the thesis of separability in the case of both the former and the latter, declaring that many impossibilities follow for those who separate them from sensible things. We, however, hold that there also exist universals that are inseparable from sensibles; for there inheres both in me and in you and in every individual that shares our form the

30 allotted reason-principle (*ton katatetagmenon logon*) of Man, and furthermore Living Being in the same way in lion and horse and man and dog, and Five in the fingers, and Two in the nostrils and eyes and hands, if you will, and feet. But since these phenomena do not occur without a cause, but are brought about through certain definite natural causes[341] (for they manifest themselves universally in all individuals not

35 maimed), there is every necessity that there exists also in nature as a

whole a Living Being separate from sensibles, in accordance with which this visible entity is crafted, and further in the nature of man a Five, in accordance with which the hand is always adorned with just so many 156,1 extremities, and a Two, in accordance which both the eyes and the nostrils are two; and if nature does not possess these things of itself, but they come to it from some other causal principle, even as they pass from it into matter, then even prior to nature there exist both universals and numbers, but not in the same mode as they exist in nature; for nature, 5 after all, did not possess them in the manner that it bestowed them upon matter, but partlessly and efficaciously (*drastikôs*), and the soul, again, possesses them in a mode more simple and immaterial, and what is superior to soul possesses them in a manner in accord with its superiority of essence and the communal life (*suzêsis*)[342] of the Forms. However, this at least should be retained as well said by him, that either both universals and numbers are separable, or both are insepa- rable; and from this proposition you could derive many others (for 10 whichever of these two propositions you establish, the other one would follow), and in particular this one, that if there are Forms, the Forms are numbers; for it is his position that, if there are universals, there are also Forms. And we accept this syllogism, not because the universals are Forms (for how could they be, when the one lot are in Soul, the other in Intellect?), but because, if there are unfolded Forms,[343] then there must also be what are more partless and more fundamental (*arkhê-* 15 *gikôtera*) than these. If, then, numbers are separable, there are univer- sals; and if there are universals, then there are Forms; if numbers are separable, then so also are Forms. So, even as one who accepts that Forms are separable does not leave off his ascent before he arrives at the simplest elements of reality, entities that no longer derive from other things and are secondary, but derive from themselves and are primary, so he who postulates separable number does not leave off his 20 ascent before, arriving at the Forms, he sees their unity with numbers; for unitary numbers possess the quantity of their Form as separate, but divine numbers possess the whole of their Form.

1085a29-35 For when one thinks of the one in Two, and in number generally, does one apprehend a Number Itself or something different? Some people, then, generate magnitudes from this kind of matter, while others generate them from the point (they regard the point not as the One but as analogous to the One) and another material principle similar to Multiplicity; yet in the case of this theory nonetheless we get the same difficulties.[344]

For when one thinks ... or something different?

Different, that is, from the fundamental monad, but not different from

25 some other, material unit; for the material units (*monades*) are indistinguishable from one another.

Some people, ... from this kind of matter, ...

From the opposing Dyad, he means, as for instance the Long and the Short, or the Narrow and the Broad, which we transfer from the fundamental Dyad to geometrical figures.

while others ... the same difficulties.

Others, he says,[345] declared that the first principles of numbers were not also the first principles of magnitudes, but they established the geomet-
30 rical principles as analogous to the arithmetical, postulating the point in place of the One, not as being identical with the One, <but ranked as analogous to the One, and something else not identical with the Dyad>,[346] but taken as analogous to this principle, which he describes as 'similar to Multiplicity'. Now that these people were actually saying the same as the previous group, albeit not employing the same formulations in their exposition, should be plain to all. Let us see, however,
35 what sort of 'absurdities' he declares to follow from their position.

157,1 **1085a35-b4 For if the matter is one, line, plane and solid will be the same; for the product of the same elements must be one and the same. If on the other hand there is more than one kind of matter – one of the line, another of the plane, and another of the solid – either the kinds imply one another, or not. Thus the same result will follow in this case also; for either the plane will not contain a line, or it will be a line.**

First of all, the latter of the principles does not serve as the matter of magnitudes, but rather as the generative principle of their matter, since it stands in an analogical relation to the Indefinite Dyad. And secondly, what necessity is there, in a situation where the matter is the same, that the same products should precisely result? They might come out
5 different, after all, by reason of their form-creating (*eidopoios*) cause, even as in the case of the elements of the cosmos; for fire and air, water and earth, employ the same matter, but they are by no means precisely identical with each other. Again, the syllable, the word and the sentence make use of the same materials (for the letters of the alphabet are the matter for all these), but nonetheless some of these are more simple,
10 and others are more complex; and of the more complex, none can come into being without the simpler, any more than the solid body can come into being without the plane and the line, while on the other hand the simpler entities can be considered also on their own, as for instance the line. But if the matters involved are in fact different, but those of the

simpler entities were to accord with the more complex ones, but not any longer those of the complex ones with those of the simpler ones, I do not see how the products of each will be either identical with or completely 15 disparate from one another. His distinguishing of alternatives, then, we accept, but what follows from his distinctions we will declare to have no compelling force.

1085b4-12 Further, no attempt is made to explain how number can be generated from the One and Multiplicity. Whatever they say, the same difficulties arise as for those who generate number from the One and the Indefinite Dyad. While one thinker generates number from multiplicity predicated in general, not from a particular multiplicity, another generates it from a particular multiplicity, namely the primal one (for the Dyad is a sort of primal multiplicity). So there is practically no difference between the two positions; the same difficulties will follow – does it involve mixture or juxtaposition or blending or generation, or whatever?

Both those who make Multiplicity the latter of two principles and those who make this the Dyad[347] have the same thing in mind, but employ 20 different terms to describe it; for they do not intend it to be either multiplicity in the sense of something generated, nor yet the Dyad as being a kind of multiplicity, but rather as generative of a quantity which is endowed with form from the Monad. As for the enquiry, in the context of a discussion of entities which are devoid of position or tangibility or materiality, as to whether we attribute the continuity of numbers to mixture or juxtaposition or blending or generation, we will say that such questions are such as could be only be raised by men who are focusing on physical bodies, and among such bodies, not even to the 25 more coherent of them; for it is plain that each (number) is one, and is assimilated to the unitary principle of numbers, by virtue of its own Form and through its own Form.

1085b12-23 We might very well ask the further question; if each unit is one, of what is it composed; for clearly each unit is not the One Itself? It must be generated from the One itself and Multiplicity, or at least a part of Multiplicity. Now we cannot hold that the unit is a multiplicity, because the unit is indivisible; but the view that it is derived from a part of multiplicity involves many further difficulties. For one thing, each part must be indivisible; otherwise it would be a multiplicity and the unit will be divisible, and unity and multiplicity will not be elements any longer, because each unit will not be generated from multiplicity and unity. Then, secondly, the exponent of this theory is merely introducing another number; because multiplicity is a number made up of indivisible parts.

30 He does well to enquire into the source of each of the material units, and
well also to dismiss the notion that the material is the same as the
fundamental, which he has termed 'the One Itself'; for this is just what
we have maintained ourselves all along. It is not the case, however, that
the conclusions which he draws necessarily follow; for we do not say
that it derives its existence from a *part* of the Dyad (for the whole
principle which is Multiplicity is indivisible), nor, if it derived its
35 existence from the Dyad, is it by virtue of that already a multiplicity;
for it is neither the case that the Dyad is itself a multiplicity, nor does
it generate something like itself.³⁴⁸ So one must reply to the first
158,1 question that this unit is given its existence from the causal principle
of numbers which generates its substratum, but it has something also
from the fundamental Monad, as he himself admits here ...³⁴⁹ and it
owes its existence to the first principles, and the Dyad is not divided
into parts, nor will there be a number in it prior to numbers, but it is
the cause of the matter of numbers. One could, after all, raise the same
5 problem also about the matter of generated things, and resolve the
problem by analogous answers. For if one were to enquire whether it
owed its existence to Multiplicity or to the One, we will say that it
proceeds from the same cause, generative of duality and possessed of
infinite power, but that it is receptive also of the imprint of the more
august principle, insofar as it is said to be to any extent one, possessing
10 a different oneness and a formlessness and non-essence distinct from
what resides in the fundamental One, and actually in a way antithetical
to that; indeed, that it receives the lowest imprints from that source, in
virtue of which it possesses a non-resembling resemblance to it.³⁵⁰

1085b23-7 Again, we must enquire from the exponent of this
theory whether the number is infinite or finite. There was, it
seems, a finite multiplicity from which, in combination with the
One, the finite units were generated; but different from that is
Multiplicity Itself, which is infinite multiplicity. Which sort of
multiplicity is it, then, that is, in combination with the One, the
element of number?

It is not about numbers now that he is enquiring whether they are finite
15 or not (for this question he had raised earlier),³⁵¹ but about the multiplicity inherent in the Dyad, from the disparting of which he postulated
that the units were generated. His intention is made clear from the
conclusion of his argument; for he says, 'Which sort of multiplicity is it,
then, that is, in combination with the One, the element of number?' Our
reply to that must be that there is absolutely no multiplicity in the Dyad
that can be distinguished into parts, even though it may on occasion be
20 termed 'multiplicity',³⁵² as possessing within itself and comprehending
the generative cause of multiplicity.

1085b27-34 We might ask a similar question with regard to the point, that is, the element out of which they create spatial magnitudes. This is surely not the one and only point – so what does each of the other points come from? Hardly from some extension and the Point Itself. Anyhow, the parts of the extension cannot be indivisible parts, as is the case with the parts of the multiplicity of which the units are composed; because although number is composed of indivisible parts, spatial magnitudes are not.

To enquire as to whence the many points and magnitudes derive their existence is a perfectly philosophical procedure, but to provide himself with such replies as these is the action of a man who is striving at all costs to reduce the positions of these men to bafflement (*aporia*). In fact, the many points are in an analogous position to the material units, so 25 that they have as a cause that which creates Matter,[353] but they also receive an imprint from the cause that creates Form; as for magnitudes, they take their extensions (*diastaseis*) from the former of the principles, that which creates Matter, but their reason-principles from the monadic cause. One should not, then, term 'extension' (*diastêma*) that principle which generates extension, nor conjure up (*epinoein*) parts of 30 this extension, from which points might derive; not only because there are no atomic parts of extension, but because the former of the two principles is not even extension, nor, in the case of the Dyad which generates multiplicity, do we call units those causes inherent in it of the units which proceed from it. All this, then, is maliciously fabricated by him in his desire to ridicule the first principles of the Pythagoreans.

1085b34-1086a11 All these and other similar considerations 159,1 make it clear that number and spatial magnitudes cannot exist separately. Further, the fact that the leading authorities disagree about numbers indicates that it is the misrepresentation of the facts themselves that produces this confusion in their views. For those who recognise only the objects of mathematics as existing besides sensible things saw the difficulties and artificialities surrounding the Forms, and so rejected Form-number and posited mathematical number; while others, wishing to maintain both Forms and numbers, but not seeing how, if one posits these as first principles, mathematical number can exist besides Form-number, identified Form-number with mathematical number – but only in theory, since in fact mathematical number is done away with (for the hypotheses which they make are peculiar to themselves, and unmathematical).[354]

That none of these arguments has proved to be worthy of credence in the refutation of those thinkers, I think has been adequately demonstrated by now. It is plain that such arguments as these, even if one heaps them up ten thousand-fold upon one another, will never be able to shake the truth from the minds of reasonably intelligent people.

5   Further ... in their views.

But perhaps it is the case rather that these are not in disagreement, but their successors in some cases did not understand what was being said, and in other cases pretended that they did not; for homonymous terms lend themselves to both possibilities.

For those who recognise ... posited mathematical number.

It has been said already that these men revered Form-number, seeing as they sought to assimilate themselves to the Pythagoreans, but since
10   they employed mathematical terms to characterise it, they gave an opening to those who wished to allege that they had abandoned what was primary and superior and had devoted themselves to what was secondary and inferior.

while others ... are peculiar to themselves, and unmathematical.

This allegation he aims at certain among the followers of Plato. But it has been said already that those men, even if they used the same terms
15   for different types of entity,[355] nonetheless maintained the distinction between them.

> **1086a11-18** But he who first postulated Forms, and that the Forms are numbers, and that there exist also objects of mathematics, quite rightly distinguished them. So the result is that all of them are correct to some extent, but overall they are not correct; and even they themselves admit as much by not agreeing but contradicting each other. The reason for this is that their assumptions and first principles are wrong; and it is difficult to propound a correct theory from faulty premises: to quote Epicharmus: 'no sooner is it said that it is seen to be wrong'.[356]

He praises Plato for distinguishing the objects of mathematics from the Forms, and states outright that all concerned are correct to some extent, but overall are in error; for he commends the first group for not
20   accepting Form-number, the middle group for declaring that there is only one kind of number (even if they mostly claim to speak of two types); and lastly those who distinguish Form-number from mathematical number; but he considers that all go astray from the truth, for the general reason that they postulated separable numbers. One must reply to this that his treatment of these men is defective, both in his praise of them, and far more so in his indictment of them.

The reason for this ... to quote Epicharmus ...

It is obvious that he was inclined to the comic mode even before he made   25
mention of Epicharmus!

'no sooner is it said that it is seen to be wrong'.

Quite the opposite, in fact: for their utterances are produced from a
depth of wisdom and on the basis of much testing, and it is only with
great effort, after much time, that the truth they contain is revealed to
a very few.

> **1086a18-21** But we have now examined and analysed the ques-
> tions concerning numbers to a sufficient extent; for although one
> who is already convinced might be still more convinced by a fuller
> treatment, he who is not convinced would be brought no nearer to
> conviction.

Indeed our fine philosopher has rightly divined our situation, that, even
if he were to fabricate such fooleries ten thousand times over against   30
those who have been seized by the wonder of the ancient philosophy, he
would achieve nothing: for he has produced all his arguments on the
assumption of unitary numbers, whereas none of the divine numbers
is of this sort, but, if any,[357] only mathematical number. In fact, that
he himself admits that he has made no points against their hypotheses, nor has engaged at all with Form-numbers, if indeed they were
to be taken as distinct from mathematical numbers, is borne witness   35
to by what is said in Book 2 of his work *On Philosophy*,[358] where we
find the following: 'so that if the Forms are some other kind of   160,1
number, and not the mathematical, we would have no knowledge of
them; for who of at least the great majority of us understands
another sort of number?' So here too he has directed his refutations
to the majority of people who do not recognise any other number than
the unitary, but he has not begun to address the thought of those   5
divine men.

   Some authorities, we may note, mark this as the end of Book 13, and
assign what follows, which belongs to the third subject of enquiry, to
Book 14; for he will go on now to enquire whether Forms and numbers
are first principles. However, the majority of texts, following the division of Alexander, make the cut between the books after what follows
on this.[359] It makes no difference for our purposes, in fact, whether the   10
books are divided here or below, just so long as we leave none of the
issues raised without examination.

1086a21-9 As for the first principles and causes and elements, the views expressed by those who discuss only sensible substance have either been described in the Physics or have no place in our present enquiry; but the views of those who assert that there are other substances besides sensible ones call for investigation next after those which we have just discussed. Since, then, some thinkers hold that the Forms and numbers are such substances, and that their elements are the elements and principles of reality, we must enquire what it is that they hold, and in what sense they hold it.

Concerning the first principles in Nature he has stated his views in the
15 *Physics*[360] and directed criticisms against the majority of his predecessors in *On Generation and Corruption*.[361] Concerning ethical or logical principles it is not relevant to the present enquiry to speak, but there has been discussion of these in the *Ethics* and in the *Analytics* (*Apodeiktika*) and in Book 4 of the present treatise.

But the views of those ... in what sense they hold it.

We have stated many times before this that in general the first principles are the One, and after it the Monad and the Indefinite Dyad, but that these manifest themselves appropriately within each order of
20 beings. But we must attend to what he says, and consider if he comes up with anything that tends to the overthrow of these hypotheses.

1086a29-35 The people who posit only numbers, and mathematical numbers at that, may be considered later; but as for those who speak of the Forms, we can observe at the same time their way of thinking and the difficulties which befall them. For they not only treat of the Forms as universal substances,[362] but also as separable and as particulars; but it has already been argued that this is not possible.

It is not surprising that they seem to you to say this, since you postulate that individuals are the only substances. They, on the other hand, rising
25 to an almost incomprehensible superiority over your sort of substances, postulate as substances the Forms, and declare that they actually embrace universals and in a unitary mode comprehend at a higher level the causes of both universals and individuals, being neither universals in the manner of the reason-principles at the level of soul, nor individuals and mathematically one in accordance with the appearances of the lowest level of images in Matter.

1086a35-b7 The reason why those who hold substances to be universal combined these two views was that they did not identify substances with sensible things. They considered that the particulars in the sensible world are in a state of flux, and that none of them persists, but that the universal exists besides them and is something distinct from them. This theory, as we have said in an earlier passage,[363] was initiated by Socrates as a result of his definitions, but he at least did not separate universal from particulars; and he was right in not separating them. This is evident from the facts; for without universals we cannot acquire knowledge, but the separation of them is the cause of the difficulties which we find with the Forms.

And we in turn have said before this both that it was not under the 30 influence of Heraclitus that they arrived at the theory of Forms,[364] nor is it valid to commend Socrates for not separating universals from sensibles; for he did not only consider that there were inseparable universals, but even that they were of just such a nature as the unlimited multiplicity of individuals.[365] However, he also regarded them as separable, as is indicated by the frequent use of the argument 161,1 from recollection by Socrates himself, 'that doctrine which you are accustomed frequently to expound',[366] and it would be much fairer to praise him for his contempt for the sensible realm and his inspired reversion to the divine realm of the Forms.

But I have said all this earlier. Since, however, he frankly admits 5 that it is not possible to acquire knowledge without universals, we must seek to learn from him what universals he has in mind. Does he mean inseparable ones? But these are mere parts of sensible objects, and fill the role of matter in relation to them, and are neither prior nor posterior to them; but we have often emphasised the fact that demonstrative proofs and scientific knowledge arise from causal principles which are both prior and more general.[367] And indeed we have derived from him 10 this piece of information, not only from other works, in which he is primarily concerned with such matters, but even from what he has said just a little before this, that that which is predicated universally is something different from what pertains to the individual as part of it, and could not ever become identical to it. If, then, all proofs are derived from universal predicates, they would not then derive from what in- 15 heres in particulars. Then again, if proofs are arrived at by means of inseparable universals, first of all, 'animal' will not be said of every man; for the animal in man will not, presumably, embrace also 'rational', 'capable of laughter', and 'mortal'.[368] And in general, if affirmative predication (*kataphasis*) is done away with, we know that all forms of syllogism also run the risk of being done away with, and proofs are 20 hardly likely to be left unscathed in the process. And then again, what are going to be the objects of proof, if those entities which are means of proof are inseparable universals? Those who make the means of proof separable, after all, at the same time demonstrate effects from causes, and are able to point to the objects of proof, that they both reside in separable substances and inhere in inseparable entities, while being more universal than these latter. But are we to make the means of proof

25 separable on the one hand, but 'later-born' and devoid of substance on the other, like the concept of man (*ho kat' epinoian anthrôpos*) which derives its existence in our imaginative or opinionative faculties on the basis of abstraction from sensibles? But in this case once again proofs will derive not from prior entities nor from causes, but from posterior ones and from effects, and furthermore it will result that we will come to know beings on the basis of non-beings, which is of all things the most

30 irrational. If, then, we are to be in harmony both with ourselves and with reality, we will rank natural reason-principles as prior to sense-objects, and as prior to these in turn our concepts which contemplate reality by virtue of the unfolding of the universal reason-principles, from which there derive both proof and every class of scientific knowledge, and prior to these in turn the formal essence of all things holding

35 sway in Intellect. And those criticisms which oppose these divine doctrines are some of them worthy of blind men, while others of them are not difficult of refutation.

162,1 **1086b7-14** Others, regarding it as necessary, if there are to be any substances besides those which are sensible and transitory, that they should be separable, and having no other substances, they set forth those substances which are said to be 'universally', with the result that universals and particulars come to be almost the same sort of thing. This in itself would be one difficulty for the view just described.

By 'set forth' he means, as it were, 'made individual'; for this is what 'setting forth' (*ekthesis*) implies. But as is obvious to the more discerning students, even though Plato and his school had a wealth of concepts available to them, nonetheless, owing to the fact that the procession of true reality produces images of the primal entities among the lowest

5 orders, they adopted the practice of applying these terms in their proper sense to divine beings, but in a secondary or even lower sense to sensibles.

... with the result that ... the view just described.

For it is not the case that the sensible realm has been endowed with all that is in Intellect, and furthermore some elements from this realm tend to become subsumed into the procession of realities,[369] such as extension and place and the ambivalence of free will (*prohairesis*) which

10 relates to our own essence. This, it seems to me, is the reason why he has inserted the 'almost' (*skhedon*).

It must be said, though, that not even in the case of those intelligible entities of which the sense-world possesses images is there a 'coming to be the same'; for an efficient and paradigmatic cause is one thing, while that which is produced by and in accordance with this is quite another; but if the lowest level of things may be assimilated to the median and the primal levels, what would be so strange about using the same names for all of them? For you yourself, after all, are prepared to use the term 15 'living being' (*zôion*) both for the primal God and for the sense-perceptible animal and for a painting of one,[370] and no one makes a 'difficulty' about that.

Chapter 10: A general problem about principles

1086b14-1087a25 Let us now discuss an issue which contains a problem both for those who believe in Forms and for those who do not, and which has already been mentioned at the start, in the Discussion of Problems.[371] If one does not suppose substances to be separate, in the way in which particular things are said to be separate, we shall do away with substance in the sense in which we wish to maintain it; but if one supposes substances to be separable, how is one to regard their elements and principles? If they are particular and not universal, there will be as many real things as there are elements, and the elements will not be knowable … If principles must be universal, so must what comes from them be universal, just as in the case of logical proofs; but if this is so, nothing will be separable or a real substance. But it is clear, at any rate, that knowledge is in one way universal and in another not.[372]

It is difficult to respond to what is said here by reason of the confusion of terminology; for he is using 'principles' (*arkhai*) and 'elements' (*stoikheia*) to refer to the same things, and one might perhaps further be in 20 doubt whether 'beings' (*onta*) refers to the intelligibles only[373] or to any and every sort of beings. For if the arguments here relate to real beings, we would not include among them elements in the proper sense, but we will say that they possess principles both final and efficient, but that elements properly so-called are not present among the perfectly simple Forms. If, on the other hand, he is including also sensible objects, then it must be granted that in the case of these there are both elements and 25 other sorts of principle; but nonetheless the same account is not to be given of all types of principle, but the elemental ones are inseparable, while the principles properly so-called are separable. But if, keeping before our minds the whole doctrinal position of the philosopher, we are to overlook the ambiguities of terminology, it seems to me that we must reject the abolition of separable substance, lest, once it has all been swept away, it carry along with it to oblivion also apparent substance 30 (and this very reasonably and consistently; for he has demonstrated elsewhere[374] that if there does not exist something of infinite power,

<then there will also be nothing>[375] that possesses limited power); and again, to accept the existence of separable substance seems to him to be a problem, since, if one were to postulate that its first principles were individual (*atomoi*), then he considers that there will be as many beings

163,1 as there are principles (for he sees them now as elements), and that will not allow any possibility of knowledge of them (for there is no knowledge of individuals, as is shown by proofs and definitions); but if they are universals, it is not reasonable that, when the substance is an individual, its principle should be something insubstantial; for it is his view that the universal is insubstantial.

5   We should say in response to this, to begin with, that the first principles of Forms are neither individuals nor yet universals in the manner of the forms in soul or those in nature or in sensible things or 'later-born' concepts of our imagination (*husterogenê phantasmata*), which are the only sorts of universal which one might justly describe as insubstantial; but they are prior to all these as causes of all things, and none of those things which are generated from them, seeing as not even

10 the Forms which proceed from them are either individuals or universals, but <they possess>[376] a form which transcends these and is intellective; for even as the individual is material (for it is only in Matter that reason-principles are divided up and, as it were, sliced into segments),[377] and the universal is proper to soul, so the partless is entirely intellective. Why then do we say that everything that is universal is insubstantial?

15 Of the problems he raises, then, some are perhaps sensibly put, but others have no force or truth-value in relation to the positions held (by these men); and in any case, his judgement is far too harsh; for he wishes to maintain that, even as the elements of speech produce an infinite number of sounds, while not being separable from the sounds, even so the first principles of beings, being inseparable from individuals, <are inherent in>[378] sensible substance. But first of all, those men

20 did not postulate the Monad and the Dyad as principles in this way; and then, just as in this realm it is discursive intellect (*dianoia*) and the speech-related imaginative faculty (*lektikê phantasia*) that variously structure the elements of speech and by means of such structuring produce all the different sounds, so on the universal level what is it that structures the elements of reality and preserves their eternal generation (*aeigenesia*)? For if it is something inferior to discursive intellect, then take care lest we make parts more august than wholes, and

25 accidents than substances, and the mortal than the divine, and than those things which are always uniformly actualised things which only come right occasionally[379] – unless we are going to say that entities at our level are governed by discursive intellect, while those in the universe are not even governed by reason.

But if it is some sort of intellect that effects this structuring, be it potential or actualised or even both together, it is plain that, if it creates

by its very essence, it contains the cause of its products within itself and 30
generates images of itself (for such is the nature of all things that create
by their very essence); but if it creates by choice (*prohairesis*) and
discursive intellection, once again (we must ask) by looking to what
aspects of the order and definition within it does it create these things?
For it does not do so impulsively and unreflectively, like those on our
level of existence who act at random. But in either event, it will possess
within itself the Forms of its creations; for not even in our case could we 35
generate from a limited set of twenty-four elements[380] an infinite number of words, were it not for the fact that we have within ourselves the
Form of each of them[381] and the reason-principles governing their 164,1
conjunction. For why is it that irrational animals have only a brief range
of sounds to express their feelings, whereas man never ceases putting
together individual utterances by employing thousands upon thousands of variations?

His statement that knowledge of universals is potential, while that 5
of particulars is actualised, is clearly that of someone who, because of
his contentiousness towards his predecessors, is prepared to contradict
what is said in his own *Analytics*,[382] to the effect that it is not possible
to have knowledge of particulars, never mind that this knowledge
should be better and more perfect than that of universals. And it would
seem, then, that the first mode of the first figure, that which derives a
conclusion from two universal premisses, which elsewhere he describes 10
as 'the most demonstrative',[383] would not form a perfect conclusion, nor
one that is scientific in actuality, but syllogisms formed from universal
and particular premisses will be more perfect, especially if the particular premiss be the minor one. Now one may grant that sense-perception
is primarily of the individual, and only incidentally of the common
element inherent in the particular; but to go on from that to claim that
grammar is primarily concerned with this particular A, and only inci- 15
dentally with the common A, is surely false. For it is the case rather that
the scientific arts and crafts (*tekhnai*)[384] concern what is universal; they
generate and evaluate the particular also by possessing the causes of
the common. The doctor, after all, knows how to cure a man, and not
just Callias;[385] but when man is actualised along with his matter, he
cures the individual by virtue of his previous mastery of the reason-
principles of health. Similarly, the grammarian knows the force of A, 20
both unaspirated and aspirated, both in its short and in its lengthened
form, both when uttered on its own and in combination with other
letters, in an initial position[386] among the vowels, both initially and
postpositively among the consonants; but when he wishes to express or
to judge the utterance of another, then he activates himself in relation
to the individual through his previous mastery of the reason-principles 25
of the universal.

All this, then, concerns the scientific arts and crafts, which are said[387]
to differ in this respect from the mere skills (*empeiriai*), in that they

know the cause of their respective efficacy, in this respect being perfectly in accord with the position of Aristotle himself also, when he
proclaims unequivocally in the *Rhetoric*[388] that 'no art or craft directs
its attention to the particular, as for instance medicine; for it is not
concerned with what is healthy for Socrates or Callias, but rather for
30 this sort of person, or these sorts of person; for it is this that is the
subject-matter of a scientific craft, whereas the particular, he says, is of
indefinite multiplicity and not a proper subject of scientific knowledge'.
And when we ascend to the level of the sciences, which relate to no
sensible object, but are concerned solely with the partless and immaterial Forms, how can one imagine in their case that they are not
primarily concerned with universals but with individuals?
35   Again, what is said at the end of the passage also is not to be accepted
without modification. For if, he says, the principles are universal, so
must what comes from them be universal, as in the case of logical
165,1 proofs. But in the case of logical proofs, one might say, the premisses
were principles of a material type, and did not establish the conclusion
while remaining in themselves, but contributing themselves to the
establishment of the proposition; but in the case of demiurgic principles,
it is not necessary for the products to be co-extensive with their causes.
5 For example, the sun, single entity as it is, creates all living things, and
yet nothing receives the totality of its power. One might make the point,
perhaps, that the immediate products of the universal principles[389] – I
mean by 'universal' not those in Intellect (for they are really prior to
universality and archetypes of principles [*autoarkhai*]), but those in
Soul – perhaps, then, these are primarily (*proêgoumenôs*) generative of
the reason-principles in nature, and only secondarily, through the
agency of the reason-principles in nature as they proceed into matter,
10 also of individuals; even as the universal premisses primarily conclude,
for example, that the angles of every triangle are equal to two right
angles, but secondarily that the angles of the scalene are so equal, and
finally, at many removes, that the same is true of the angles of this
particular scalene triangle. 'So then', as Archytas says,[390] 'once they
have obtained a good grasp of the universal, they are in a good position
to discern excellently also the nature of the particular.'
15   It is interesting to note, then, that despite being the most acute and
creative[391] of men, that marvellous fellow Aristotle was not able to
disdain the universals without being forced to utter sentiments at
variance both with himself and with the plain facts (*enargeia*); specifically, that the sciences are in actuality concerned with particulars and
not with universals, and that craftsmen have primarily knowledge of
20 the individual, and only incidentally of the common characteristic. To
employ once again that well-worn tag, 'Backwards the sacred rivers
take their course!'[392]
    This is as far as the Aphrodisian[393] would extend Book 13. What
follows he assigns to Book 14.

BOOK 14

Chapter 1: Further criticism of the Theory of Forms and Numbers

1087a29-b4 With regard to this kind of substance, then, let the foregoing account suffice. All thinkers make the first principles contraries; as in the realm of natural objects, so too in respect of the unchangeable substances. Now if nothing can be prior to the first principle of all things, that first principle cannot be a first principle if it is an attribute of something else. This would be as absurd as to say that 'white' is the first principle, not qua anything else but *qua* white, and yet that it is predicable of a subject, and is white because it is an attribute of something else; because the latter will be prior to it. Moreover, all things are generated from contraries as from a substrate, and therefore contraries must certainly have a substrate. Therefore all contraries are predicated of a subject, and none of them exists separately. But there is no contrary to substance; not only is this obvious, but it is borne out by reasoned consideration. Thus none of the contraries is strictly a first principle; the first principle is something different.

Here he launches an attack on those who make the first principles of 25 unchangeable things contraries, even as he himself has no compunction about employing contraries, along with a substratum, as first principles for sensible objects. He produces a syllogism in his usual manner: contraries inhere in a substratum; first principles are not in a substratum,[394] lest the insubstantial turn out to be prior to substances. And the conclusion is obvious: contraries, he says, are not principles. And if they are principles, it is at all events not *qua* contraries but *qua* something 30 else, as for instance intellect or body or whatever may be the substratum for them.

To this one may respond that those men do not in fact employ as their first principles contraries of such a sort as to be insubstantial in the sense of being inferior to substantiality, but if anything, in the sense of being superior; for the first principles of substantial reality must necessarily be supra-substantial. And in general, those men did not take their start from opposites as such, but they had knowledge of what was beyond the two tables of opposites, as Philolaus[395] bears witness to when 35 he says that God established Limit and Limitlessness, by 'limit' indicat- 166,1 ing the whole sequence of opposites more akin to the One, while by 'limitlessness' he indicates the sequence inferior to this, and prior again to these two principles they situated the unitary and completely separable cause, which Archaenetus[396] declares to be a 'cause above a cause', while Philolaus asserts that it is 'cause of all things',[397] and Brotinus as 5

'surpassing all intellect and substance in power and dignity'.[398] Taking his start from these, the divine Plato also, in the *Letters*, in the *Republic*, in the *Philebus*, and the *Parmenides*,[399] utters the same sentiments on the same topic. So then, his premises are not sound, since that one which states that 'contraries inhere in a substratum' is false (for if one
10 is to call entities above the level of nature 'contraries', they are at all events not insubstantial), and also that one which states that 'principles are substances' (for the principles in the proper sense and the principles of all things are actually supra-substantial); nor does the conclusion refute any doctrine maintained by those men; for they did not take their start from opposites as such, but ranked as prior to these the One which transcends both the principles and the columns of opposites.

15 **1087b4-9** They [sc. the Platonists] treat one of the contraries as matter, some opposing 'the unequal' to the One, (on the ground that the former is of the nature of Multiplicity) and others Multiplicity. For according to some, numbers are generated from the unequal dyad of the Great and Small, while according to another individual, from Multiplicity; but for both by One as their substance.

Neither is it the case that they identify the Dyad that is prior to all numbers as a material cause (for the divine class of numbers in general have no need at all of matter), nor does Plato, in representing the Indefinite Dyad as inequality, deviate from Pythagoras, who portrayed it as Multiplicity;[400] for each of them is seeking to relate its designation
20 to those characteristics which it bestows on numbers; and it has been said already that it is the cause of multiplicity and procession and productive power and differentiation, even as The One is cause to the divine Forms of self-identity and eternal permanence and of holding fast as they are: 'Eternity remaining in One', as he says,[401] indicating by that the cause of divine substance's remaining always uniform in the same state.

25 **1087b9-12** For he who speaks of 'the Unequal' and the One as elements, and describes the Unequal as a dyad composed of the Great and Small, speaks of the Unequal, that is the Great-and-Small, as one thing, not discerning the fact that they may be one in definition while not being one numerically.

For Plato, he maintains, should have said that these are two in definition, but one numerically;[402] for such would be a better explanation of the passage than that which Alexander assumed to be the meaning.[403] But, my fine fellow, we will say, Plato is not calling the second principle 'unequal' and 'dyad' and 'great-and-small' in the sense that you are
30 assuming here, but rather as being the cause of multiplicity and proces-

sions, and as generating all things both great and small. These terms, then, should be taken in a sense generally concordant with his doc- 167,1 trine.[404] And in general, if its substratum were something distinct from the reason-principles in it,[405] even as Socrates is different from 'the snub-nosed' and 'the potbellied', or if it were in one respect great and in another small, there would be some excuse for making it 'two in definition, but one in substratum'; but if in fact it transcends with an unutterable pre-eminence those things sprung from it, both great and 5 small, and is superior to any substratum, then what occasion is there for such terminological nitpicking?

1087b12-27 Again, they do not even give a good account of their first principles, or elements, as they call them. Some talk of the Great and the Small, along with the One – these amounting to three – as the elements of numbers, the first two filling the role of Matter, while the One serves as Form. Others talk of the 'Many and Few', because the Great and Small are in their nature more suited to be the principles and magnitude; while yet others use the more general term which covers these – 'the Exceeding and the Exceeded'. But none of these variations makes any appreciable difference with respect to some of the consequences of the theory; they only affect the formal difficulties, which they seek to escape because the proofs which they themselves put forward are formal. The only exception is the argument that makes the Exceeding and the Exceeded principles, and not the Great and Small: this implies that Number comes before Two from the elements, since in both cases you have the more universal coming first. But in fact they assert the one, but not the other. Others again oppose 'the different' and 'the other' to One, and yet others oppose Multiplicity to One.

All these men, according to him, call the more divine and 'paternal' principle of numbers 'One', while the 'maternal' principle some call 10 'Great and Small', like Plato, others 'Few and Many', in an attempt to correct him, others 'the Exceeding and Exceeded', having recourse to a more general term, others 'the Other', and others yet 'Multiplicity'. Now that all these are actually indicating the same entity is something that we have asserted repeatedly. But if he is asserting that this conse-quence follows for those who assume more general contraries in place of more specific ones, that they make Number, which is the genus of 15 Two, superior to Two, which is something that they do not want to do, then we will respond by asking 'Than *what* two?' and '*What* number?'. For if you mean the Indefinite Dyad, how on earth could Number be the genus of that, seeing as it is generated from it? But if you mean the Essential Two (*autoduas*), this itself is the first among the Form-numbers.

20   **1087b27-33** Now if, as they maintain, existing things are derived from contraries, and if there is either no contrary to the One, or if there is to be any contrary, it is Multiplicity (the unequal being contrary to the equal, the different to the same, and the other contrary to the self-identical), then those who oppose the One to Multiplicity have the best claim to credibility – but even their theory is inadequate, because the One will be a numerical mimimum;[406] for multiplicity is opposed to fewness, and many to few.

His purpose is plain, to pick out one thinker from all the others and discredit him, so that the others also may stand condemned into the bargain.[407] Our response to this must be that these men do not require an arbiter (for they are not at all in dispute with one another), nor do those who oppose Multiplicity to the One stand convicted by him of making the One a minimum (*oligon*); for if we recall what was said back

25   in Book 10 of the present work,[408] it was quite clearly stated there that it is not to every kind of multiplicity that the few constitutes a contrary, but to that kind which contains excess, nor is the One contrary to multiplicity and number, but rather in the way that relative things are opposed to one another. So even according to himself both these propositions, on the basis of which he derives the conclusion which is designed to refute these men, are false, both the one which declares that

30   the One is the contrary of multiplicity and that which lays down that everything that is contrary to multiplicity must be 'few', and we will not require any other authorities to counter these propositions of his, but have only to read over what he has written himself in Book 10. But why am I spending so much time on this topic? For neither does this fellow manage to refute the doctrine of the One held by those men, nor does he comprehend Multiplicity in the sense in which they expound it. What follows will provide further clarification of the irrelevant nature[409] of

35   the man's criticisms.

168,1   **1087b33-1088a14** That 'one' denotes a measure is obvious. And in every case there is something else which serves as substratum: in the musical scales, for instance, it is the quarter-tone; in spatial magnitude the finger or foot or something similar; in rhythms the foot or syllable; and similarly in weight a defined standard weight. So it is in all cases, a quality for qualities, a quantity for quantities (the measure being in each case indivisible – in kind for qualities, to perceptual test for quantities). This shows that 'one' is not in itself the substance of some one thing. And this is reasonable: 'one', after all, denotes a measure of some plurality, and a number denotes a measured plurality and a plurality of measures. (Hence too it stands to reason that one is not a number; for the measure is not measures, but rather the measure and one are first princi-

ples). But the measure must always be something which applies
to all alike, e.g. if things concerned are horses, the measure will be
a horse, if men, the measure will be a man; and if they are man,
horse and god, the measure will presumably be 'living being', and
the number of them living beings. If, on the other hand, the things
concerned are 'man', 'white' and 'walking', there will hardly be a
number proper to them, because they all belong to the same thing,
which is numerically one; however, their number will be a number
of 'genera', or some such term.

Whereas those divine men called God 'One' as being the causal principle
of unity for all things, and as being superior to all Being and all Life and
Intellect in its entirety, and 'measure of all things' as illuminating all 5
things with existence and purposiveness (*telos*), and as embracing and
defining all things by virtue of its ineffable superiority, which exceeds
in simplicity every kind of limit, this marvellous fellow,[410] choosing to
interpret this in the sense of the minimum element in a given quantity,
and that which through smallness is manifested as a common measure
among things of the same genus, asserts that nothing is either a
measure or a unit which is not inherent in some substratum. And it is
obvious how this argument, in very truth falling away from the single 10
first principle of beings or the monad which is attached to that, as from
some 'heavenly threshold',[411] has slid away from the whole incorporeal
order[412] of reality, and the whole encosmic plane, and has cast itself
headlong into the lowest level of bodily existence, through concerning
itself with the least of all solid bodies by reason of their smallness and
meanness, and for this reason declaring the measure of some things to
be same in species, as in the case of horses, of others the same in genus, 15
as with man, horse, and god, and in other cases – I don't know what to
say; for he himself expresses bafflement as to how one should reckon
the number arising from a conjunction of different categories, except to
suggest that it should be called a 'number of genera'.

It may be worthwhile, however, to set beside these speculations
either the position of Cleinias the Pythagorean,[413] who wishes to make
the One and the measure entirely separable not only over bodies or all 20
things in the cosmos, but also of the actual intelligibles, when, in paying
honour to it, he says that it is 'first principle of all things', and 'measure
of intelligibles', and 'ungenerated and eternal and single and dominant
(*kuriôdes*),[414] itself revealing itself'; or that of the divine Plato, where he
declares God to be the measure of all things, as containing within
himself the beginnings and ends and mid-points of things.[415] If one 25
bears this in mind, then, it is not difficult, I think, to see how far short
the 'one' and 'measure' produced by him here fall from the true Measure, though he can quite happily use those on occasion to perform
measurements, as being those things by means of which measurement
happens; for what measures ten horses is not 'horse', but rather our

consciousness (*dianoia*), or[416] if we make any use of 'horse' in this
30 context, it is not really horse that we are referring to, but the unitary
one and unitary number; but it is the true measures, as defining the
essence and the powers and the ends of the things measured, that
properly merit the term 'measures'. And this did not in fact escape the
notice of Aristotle himself; at any rate, he writes in the second book of
his *Statesman*,[417] in the very same terms as those of his predecessors in
35 philosophy, literally as follows: 'for of all things the most accurate
measure is the Good'. So it is plain that he is presenting his arguments
here rather in a pettifogging[418] and contentious mode, and it is thus fair
that we should address to him, in respect of each of them, the following
Homeric abjurgation: 'Indeed thou knowest how to devise a better word
than this!'[419]

169,1   **1088a15-1088b11** Those who regard the Unequal as a unity, and
the Dyad as an indeterminate compound of the great-and-small,
hold theories which are very far from being plausible or even
possible. For these terms represent affections and attributes,
rather than substrates, of numbers and magnitudes ...

For if there is a multiplicity of which one term, to wit 'few', is
always predicable, let us say 'two' (for if two is many, one will be
few), then there would be an absolute 'many' – for instance, 'ten'
would be many (if there is nothing more than ten), or 'ten thousand'. How then, in this light, can number be derived from Few
and Many? Either both ought to be predicated of it, or neither; but
according to this view only one or the other is predicated.[420]

The One and the Equal, if taken as the paternal principle, is neither
relative nor in general an attribute at all (*sumbebêkos*), but, if the truth
be told, a supra-essential entity which is cause for all things of unity
and equality, and which illuminates all things with stability and firm-
5 ness and steadfastness and immaculateness; even as in turn the Unequal, which this man distinguishes now into the 'great and the small',
now into the 'many and few', and sometimes into 'the exceeding and the
exceeded', when it is taken as the primary Dyad, symbolically indicates
the cause of increase for all things, but is established as superior not
10 only to attributes merely, but also to the substances that are generated
from it. It is utterly ridiculous, therefore, to attempt to refute the
doctrines of his predecessors by making appeal to senses of these terms
which are more familiar to the general public. We, on the other hand,
assert not just that they do not make an attribute superior to a substance, but that they assign, not only not a secondary, but not even a
15 much more remote rank among first principles and divine Forms to an
attribute; for in general, according to them, nothing in the realm of the
unchanging is of the nature of an attribute, but that realm is occupied
by such entities as Equality Itself and Knowledge Itself; Sameness,

then, Likeness, Otherness and all these things are substances, and
relate to themselves and not to something else. After all, we observe the
divine Plato writing of such entities in many places, but particularly in
the *Phaedrus*: 'It beholds Justice Itself, it beholds Moderation, it be-   20
holds Knowledge – not such knowledge as is subject to generation, nor
such as varies as it is associated with one or other of the things we call
realities, but that knowledge which exists in the realm of true being'
(247A). That is why he is accustomed to call each of the things in that
realm 'Such-and-such Itself', which in the view of some of the more exact
authorities is superior to 'relating to oneself and not to something else';
so that, even if there are in that realm causal agents and things caused,
these are not related as attributes, but as substances. And the same   25
goes for all so-called relations at that level; so that, of the things in the
higher realm (*ekei*), some are supra-essential and others are substances, whereas an attribute would occur, if anywhere, only in connexion with the soul in the realm of generation, and generation itself.

So much, then, may be said in reply to his argumentation as a whole.
However, to categorise either the Dyad at that level as 'few' or the
Decad as 'many' will in my view commend itself to nobody; for it is only   30
unitary number to which such characterisations might be attributed or
otherwise connected.

Chapter 2: No principles or elements of eternal things; problems about plurality

1088b14-28 But we must enquire in general whether eternal
things can be composed of elements. If so, they will contain matter,
since everything composed of elements is composite. Assuming,
then, that that which consists of anything, whether it has always
existed or came into being, must come into being out of that of
which it consists; and that everything comes to be that which it
comes to be out of that which it is potentially (for it could not have
come to be out of that which was not potentially such, nor could it
have consisted of it); and that the potential can either be actualised or not; then however everlasting number or anything else
which has matter may be, it would be possible for it not to exist,
just as that which is any number of years old is as capable of not
existing as that which is one day old. Therefore things which
contain matter cannot be eternal, as we have had occasion to say
elsewhere.[421] Now if what we have just been saying – that no
substance is eternal, unless it exists in actuality[422] – is true
universally, and the elements are the matter of substance, an
eternal substance can have no elements of which, as inherent in
it, it consists.

Now let us say at the outset – or rather, not us but the oldest and best

of the philosophers – before even he launches his argument against
Plato, that the divine Forms are not produced from material elements,
or generally from elements at all, if one is using the term 'elements' as
what are brought together for the construction of something else; for
170,1   that which is constructed from material elements is subject to generation and corruption, while that which is put together from immaterial
elements, even though it is ungenerated, yet it is composite; but the
divine Forms need to be simple and ungenerated, and not to be structured in the manner of the soul, nor *a fortiori* to be constructed in the
manner of this cosmos. So there is no need for us to refer back to the
5   first book of his work *On the Heavens*,[423] where it is demonstrated that
what is generated and in general that which is capable of not existing
is destructible and not eternal; but having readily granted him, even if
not all his particular points, at least that his conclusion is sound, we
declare that what the ancients meant by elements were the generative
causes of all things.

   While there are many statements in this passage which are deserving of examination, we should pay special attention to that assertion of
10   his that 'no substance is eternal unless it exists in actuality.' For if here
we were to read the dative, *energeiâi*, the consequence will be that for
him the aether is even now eternal, but this assertion does not agree
with his overall position;[424] for there is nothing preventing even something that is constructed out of elements and matter existing in
actuality. But if we read the nominative, *energeia*, he will be in danger
15   of asserting that the heavenly realm is not eternal, even if it is established for all time; for it is not always the case that the eternal is
straightway a separate Form.

   1088b28-35 There are some who, while making the element which
   acts conjointly with the One an Indefinite Dyad, object to 'the
   unequal', quite reasonably, on the score of the difficulties which it
   involves. But they are rid only of those difficulties which that
   theory involves because it makes the unequal and relative an
   element; all the difficulties which are independent of this view
   must apply to their theories also, whether it is Form-number or
   mathematical number that they construct out of these elements.

   It is not because of objecting to such a concept of 'unequal' as this, nor
   yet in fear of the marvellous logical manoeuvres of the dialecticians,
20   that they resolved to call the causal principle of multiplicity a 'dyad', but
   rather because they wished to make clear its affinity to the more august
   principle, and so when they termed that 'equal', they termed this
   'unequal', and when they called it 'One' or 'monad', they saw fit to call
   this 'dyad'; for what causes we have stated many times already, and also
   that there are one set of causes that constitute Form-number, and

another set that constitute mathematical number, far inferior to these, but nonetheless analogous to the former. 25

1088b35-1089a7 There are many causes for their resorting to these explanations, the chief being that they visualised the problem in an old-fashioned form. They supposed that all existing things would be one, absolute Being, unless one could come to grips with and refute Parmenides' words:

'This view shall ne'er prevail, that things which are not, are.'

They thought it necessary to prove that what is not, is; for only in this way – from that which is, and from something else – could existing things be composed, if they are many.

'Out upon it, truly, excellent though you be, you have spoken overweeningly!'[425] – supposing Plato were naïve in raising these problems, and particularly in presenting the hypotheses in the *Sophist* ....[426] And then, what common element does Not-Being possess, which the nature of Otherness, split as it is into fragments (*katakermatistheisa*), bestows upon it? The first principles, after all, are prior to the genera of Being, 30 both that of the Monad and that of the Indefinite Dyad.[427]

1089a7-15 However, in the first place, if 'being' has many senses (for sometimes it means substance, sometimes quality, sometimes quantity, and so on with the other categories), what sort of unity will all the things that are constitute, if there is no not-being? Will it be the substances that are one, or the affections (and similarly with the other categories), or all the categories together? Or will they all – 'this' and 'such' and 'so much' and everything else signifying one kind of thing – be one? But it is absurd, or rather impossible, that the introduction of one thing should account for the fact that 'what is' sometimes means 'this', sometimes 'such', sometimes 'so much', and sometimes 'somewhere'.

Plato's arguments are actually concerned primarily with beings of another kind; but if you want to drag these ten categories into the discussion, on the assumption that you can demonstrate multiplicity among beings without the postulate of not-being, then let me tell you in 171,1 turn that without otherness there would be no ten categories, nor even two, nor indeed anything else apart from what is numerically one; but if otherness exists, then so does not-being; for each of the ten categories, if it is different from the others, exists in one way (*monakhôs*), but there are nine ways (*enakhôs*) in which it does not exist; so that it is more 5 non-existent than it is existent, even if you say that it is substance itself. For substance, despite existing as such, is not quality, nor quantity, nor affection, nor activity. Put all this together, then, and you will see the necessity of our doctrine: if beings are many, there is otherness; if there

is otherness, then there is not-being; so if beings are many, there is
not-being. So it is not after all possible to take a stand against the
10   apparent purport of the Parmenidean statement, nor to admit multiplicity, without also introducing not-being. And it is not on this ground,
in truth, that Plato takes issue with Parmenides, but both their accounts are true, yet Plato's is the clearer; for the former was talking
about the intelligible realm alone, and treating it in respect of its unity
15   and the sameness that prevails in it, and Empedoclean Love[428] and so
declared Being to be one; while Plato, recognising first of all that the
sensible realm also exists in a way, while being different from the realm
of true being and for this reason justly describable as non-existent
rather than existent, while the intelligible realm itself is no less a
multiplicity than it is one, introduced the nature of Otherness into the
realm of beings and through this showed that substantial not-being
20   follows along with it, as he has demonstrated through the medium of
many soundly-based arguments in the *Sophist*.

1089a15-20 Further, what kind of not-being and being do existing
things come from? 'Not-being' too has many senses, since 'being'
has: not being a man means not being a 'this'; not being straight
means not being 'such'; not being three cubits long means not
being 'so much'. So from what kind of being and not-being do
existing things come to be many?

Not, certainly, from form and privation;[429] for in general privation
contributes nothing of itself to existent things. But since there are on
25   their theory five genera,[430] one of these is Otherness, and its job is to
make each thing non-identical with other things, it is arising from
non-being in the sense of otherness and from substance that beings are
many; for substance bestows existence on all things, not through being,
as some would have it, their substrate, but rather a principle and fount
of existence, and bestowing this on all things without diminishing itself;
30   Otherness divides beings, not spatially, but in essence, and multiplies
them and makes different things not to be the same as things other than
them, but sees to it that each of them preserves the purity and the
unmixed and unsullied state of their own individuality. And if we,
employing a sense of 'being' unusual for us, were to denominate sense-
objects as such, and were to enquire from what kind of being and what
35   kind of not-being these things derive their existence, these divine men
will once again designate both the other genera of Being and the ones
afore-mentioned, Substance and Otherness; for their activity and generative power extends to all beings of whatever level. This is not, of
172,1 course, to deny that since the lowest level of beings are also subject to
a number of other causes and experience a more variegated degree of
composition, they are composed of being in the shape of Form, and
not-being in the shape of Matter. And that this is all that they are

saying Aristotle himself quite understands; for he writes next as follows:

1089a20-6 He [sc. Plato] means by the not-being which together
with being makes existing things a plurality falsity and that kind
of thing; and for this reason also it used to be said that we must
assume something that is false, like geometers when they assume
a line to be a foot long when it is not a foot long. But this cannot
be right; for geometers do not make any false assumptions (since
the status of the proposition is not involved in the logical inference); and existing things are not generated from or resolved into
not-being in this sense.

Whereas those thinkers declare that not-being has a place even in the   5
intelligible world, in the form of Otherness, and that it exists in the
sense-world precisely in the role of matter, and they call matter not only
'not-being' but also 'falsity' (*pseudos*), because it seems to be everything,
but is deceptive and neither is nor becomes any existent thing, this
wondrous fellow Aristotle, having first enquired of them from what sort
of being and what sort of not-being they generate the multiplicity of   10
substances, then postulates that they maintain that it is <the sort of
not-being>[431] that comes under the heading of matter; and then, taking
them as saying that they termed 'falsity' the matter that they postulated as underlying the Forms,[432] he asserts that they postulate falsity
as the basis for true beings, constructing a syllogism as follows: beings
derive from not-being; not-being is falsity; therefore beings derive from
falsity. To this conclusion he has then added, very cleverly, that they
are perhaps trying to imitate the geometers, but they are not in fact   15
imitating them (for these latter do not claim that they are constructing
a square on the basis of a line drawn as being a foot long, but which
actually is not). Now he is quite right in saying that the geometer does
not in his demonstrations employ falsity, but he sidesteps the whole
issue of not-being in their system, which extends also to incorporeal
substance, and in what sense falsity is by them applied to matter; for it   20
is not in the sense that we use 'false' to apply to a statement or a belief
that does not correspond to the facts that matter is described by them
as 'falsity', but for the reason stated above.[433]

1089a26-31 But not only has 'not-being' in its various cases as
many meanings as there are categories; it is also used to mean
what is false and what is potential; and it is from this last that
coming into being takes place. A man comes into being from what
is not man but is potentially man, and white comes into being from
what is not white but is potentially white, no matter whether one
thing is generated or many.

25   Those men, he says, made multiplicity out of not-being as the false, but
I make from not-being not just multiplicity but each individual thing, it
not being anything in actuality, but only potentially – for which reason
it enjoys a false level of existence. Now if he said this by way of
explaining their position, he would be acting reasonably; but since he is
taking an adversative stance, let him listen to us when we tell him that
'you are expounding their doctrine of not-being in the realm of generation, but you are leaving aside not-being in general'.

30   **1089a31-b2** Clearly the issue is how 'being' in the sense of substances is many; for the things that are generated are numbers
and lines and bodies. It is absurd to enquire how Being as substance is many, and not how qualities or quantities are many.
Surely the Indefinite Dyad or the Great and the Small is no reason
why there should be two whites or many colours or flavours or
shapes; for then these too would be numbers and units.

In enquiring, he says, how Being is many, they were seeking nothing
else but to explain how there are many substances <in the sense of
numbers and lines and bodies>,[434] all of which are substances according
to them. But they should also, he says, have enquired how there are
many colours and how there are many flavours; for they would no longer
be able to attribute these to the Great and the Small.

173,1   We must say to him in reply that in all cases the Dyad is the cause
of multiplicity (for what draws things forth from the One with all their
particular characteristics is just this principle), and there exists at the
level of each order of beings a monad peculiar to that order, and the
dyad that naturally arises along with this and generates the number

5   appropriate to itself. But if they are speaking of a multiplicity of items
in connection with substances rather than accidents, and of intelligible
rather than sensible instances, there is nothing strange in that; for
pretty well the whole concern of those men was with what is clear and
knowable and always in the same state and intelligible, whereas they
very rarely lowered their attention to the realm of shadows and the
lowest manifestations of true beings.

1089b2-7 But if they [sc. the Platonists] had pursued this enquiry,
they would have perceived the cause [sc. of multiplicity] in the
former case too; for the cause is the same, or analogous. This
aberration of theirs was the reason why, in seeking the opposite of
being and unity, from which, in combination with being and unity,
existing things are derived, they posited the relative and the unequal,
which is neither contrary to nor the negation of these ...[435]

10   They took into consideration attributes as well, and saw that the same
first principles are operative analogously in their case, to wit, their

appropriate monad and dyad, the one the cause for them of self-identity, the other of distinctness and multiplicity, and it was not through any 'aberration' from the true cause nor from any other <inadequacy?>[436] that they ranked the dyadic causal principle alongside being and unity. The principle that you favour, of course, by way of negation, is the 15 material; for 'not-man' may be regarded as the matter of man. Now those men recognised this principle as being a necessary component of the lowest rank of beings; nonetheless, they called it, not a cause, but an accessory cause (*sunaition*),[437] while they placed the efficient causes among the demiurgic reason-principles in nature. There is, then, in nature one reason-principle that is generative of all colours, and another which receives its initial inspiration from this, and which gener- 20 ates along with it the multitudes and different types of colours; and these serve as the monad and dyad of colours; and an analogous account may be given in the case of all other attributes, such as are brought to fruition through natural reason-principles.

1089b7-15 ... but is a single characteristic of existing things, just like substance or quality. They should have investigated this question also: how is it that relatives are many, and not one. As it is, they enquire how it is that there are many units beside the primary One, but not how there are many unequal things besides the Unequal. Yet they employ in their arguments and speak of the Great-and-Small, Many-and-Few (from which comes numbers), the Long-and-Short (from which comes length), Broad-and-Narrow (from which comes the plane), Deep-and-Shallow (from which comes solids); and they make mention of even more types of relative. Now what is the cause of these things being many?

One natural class of beings is that of relatives, through which order and sympathy and all harmony and concordance exists in the world; those 25 men certainly did not neglect to study the first principles of this natural realm, but they also sought to explicate both its unitary formal principle[438] and its multiplicity. Now it seems to him astonishing that they, while making use of a multiplicity of unequal things as well as of a multiplicity of units, did not say whence these many unequals had arisen, as well as the many units. To me on the other hand it occurs to 30 wonder that, when he has presented to him, as celebrated by them, both the Forms and the first principles of the Forms, he should feel the further need of other causes of the multiplicity of unequals; for, even as the cause of the many like and unlike things is Likeness Itself <and Unlikeness Itself>,[439] even so of the many equals and unequals the cause is Equality Itself and Inequality Itself. And on these questions something has been said in the *Phaedo*,[440] and there has been a more 35 extensive discussion in the *Parmenides*.[441] But if you were to ascend to the first principles of the Forms, you would discover as even more senior 174,1 causes the Monad and the Essential Dyad, of which the one has as more akin to it Sameness, Equality, and Likeness, while the Dyad has Otherness, Inequality and Unlikeness.

1089b15-20 We must, then, as I say, presuppose in the case of each thing something that is potentially that thing. The author of this theory further explained what it is that is potentially a particular thing or substance, but is not as such existent – that it is the relative (he might as well have said 'quality'); which is neither potentially unity or being, nor yet the negation of unity or being, but just a particular kind of being.

5   That in the case of the lowest grade of things you should select that which is potentially each thing and its material cause is thoroughly commendable and in accordance with nature; however, you are not yet grasping the intention of the Pythagoreans and of Plato himself if you think that their doctrine of the Great-and-Small or the Unequal or in general the Indefinite Dyad involves a 'relative'; for in truth relatives
10 are neither negations nor potentialities of substances. But surely the fact is that mostly they identify the causal principle that generates things along with the Monad as the Dyad; if on occasion they were also to bestow on Matter, as bearing the image of that principle, the title of either Great-and-Small, or Unequal, or Indefinite Dyad, that does not mean that they are assimilating this to a relative, but merely that they are indicating the splitting up of the Forms that takes place in it, and
15 its irregularity and disruptive force;[442] for not only does it separate one thing from another, but – what is most astonishing both to conceive of and to utter – Form[443] both separates and divides itself from itself and becomes something else when it consorts with Matter. Why, then, did he feel it necessary to disregard the intention of these men, and weave cat's cradles of words,[444] and mock them for making the second of their principles, which they rank with the One, a relative, and declaring that
20 one of the categories is the matter of substances?

1089b20-4 And it was still more necessary, as we have said, that, if he was enquiring how it is that things are many, he should not confine his enquiry to things in the same category, and ask how it is that substances or qualities are many, but that he should ask how things in general are many; for some things are substances, some affections, and others relations.

You are not acting as a reliable guide, focusing as you habitually do on the things of this realm, whereas those men, while they do say something also about these, as being projected into the lowest level of reality, nonetheless, as they devote their chief attention to the realm of true
25 beings and the intelligibles, quite naturally, in investigating the first

principles of those substances, provide a stimulus also for those who are enthusiasts for the study of the lowest level of being to investigate also the principles of things in this realm, bearing as they do an analogy to those principles. But one should consider this point also, that it is not difficult to describe in what way sensible things are many (for these are distinct spatially and possess different substrata, and have so much differentiation between them that some of them are actually at war 30 with each other); to describe, on the other hand, how intelligible things are many, things which are not spatially distinct, not dominated by a substratum, exhibiting no relation or inclination towards what is secondary to them – that is a task for someone who is not totally idle and shiftless in wit. And when Parmenides, to whose doctrine they are reacting, declared in quite a different mode that Being was one, and not Quality or Relation or Quantity or in general any relative entity, but 35 rather what really is and is intelligible, they judged it proper not to launch any sort of cheap jibes at the man, but rather to prove that there was multiplicity in the intelligible realm also; but before they proved that, they necessarily sought the principle of multiplicity in that realm, 175,1 and they discovered that, among the genera of Being, it was Otherness, and the not-being proper to that, that was the cause of multiplicity, while among the very first causes it was the Indefinite Dyad, which Pythagoras in his *Sacred Discourse* called Chaos, linking it to Proteus;[445] for it is this title which he bestows upon the Monad in that work. 5 They were correct, therefore, to initiate this enquiry, and communicate to us the cause of multiplicity in the realm of true Being, and neither did they make the second of the principles a relative, nor did they entirely neglect to provide an account of the sensible realm, as is demonstrated by the work of Ocellus *On the Nature of the Universe*,[446] from which the treatise *On Generation and Corruption* is more or less 10 entirely taken, and the bulk of the *Timaeus*,[447] in accord with which the Peripatetic tradition propounds most of its physical doctrine.

1089b24-32 Now in the case of the other categories there is the additional difficulty in discovering how they are many. For it may be said that since they are not separable, it is because the substrate becomes or is many that qualities and quantities are many; yet there must be some matter for each class of entities, only it cannot be separable from substances. In the case of particular substances, however, it is inexplicable how the particular thing can be many, if we do not regard a thing both as a particular substance and as a nature of a certain type. The real difficulty which arises from these considerations is how substances are in actuality many and not one.

In the case of accidents, he says, one might raise this difficulty also, how, while not being separable from their substrata, they are nonethe-

15 less many. In the case of substances it may be granted that multiplicity derives from not-being; but how does colour arise from non-colour? Then, by way of meeting this difficulty, he says that 'it is necessary that accidents also possess matter, but not matter separable from bodies'. And he declares this to be the most troublesome problem, how substances can be many in actuality.[448]

Well now, that we may begin from the last issue, he seems to be
20 asking just the same question as is posed by those men; for they also raised a problem about multiplicity at the intelligible level, where potentiality is totally excluded. He, however, gets bogged down at the stage of raising the problem, since he does not accept the existence of Forms nor of causal first principles, nor in general the concept of a creative first principle among eternal entities (for why the intellects should be just so many according to him, and neither more nor less, we
25 have no basis for saying;[449] for their number is not conditioned by the number of spheres that are moved by them, but, if anything, the other way around. And then, even if one tried to explain it in this back-to-front way (*ex huptias*),[450] we will be confronted in turn by the problem as to how and why the number of spheres is what it is). Those, on the other hand, who attribute the measure of all things in the cosmos to the demiurgic Intellect can deal with these and all other problems with the greatest of both ease and truth.
30   But again, the theorem that he advances in the middle of the passage, that sensible substances derive from things that are not such, makes appeal, even as do those men, to the material cause, but neglects the efficient and the paradigmatic.[451] The difficulty about accidents is actually solved by himself; for the accidents, even if not many in respect of substratum, are at least many in definition (*logôi*); but it is a more sophisticated solution to lay the blame with the visible creation and the
35 distinction between the powers in nature and the distribution of forms-in-matter about their substrata.

176,1   **1089b32-1090a2** But again, if a particular thing and a quantity are not actually the same, an explanation is given, not of how and for what reason beings are many, but of how quantities are many. For all number signifies a certain quantity, including the unit, unless it is measure in the sense of the indivisible in quantity. If therefore how great a thing is and what it is are different, no explanation is given of the reason why and how particular things are many. But if they are the same, many contradictions remain for him who says this.

Formerly Aristotle had criticised those who had investigated only the question as to whence the multiplicity of beings had come to be. Yet now he seems not even to allow them this, but since they are discussing for the most part numbers and magnitudes, he said that they examined

multiplicity in one category alone, not that of substance, but that of 5
quantity. For 'all number', he says, 'is a quantity, including the unit'.[452]
Then, introducing a qualification, he says: 'unless the unit is not a
quantity as being the measure of number and being indivisible.' If
therefore they hold, he says, that quantity differs from substance, then
they only investigated multiplicity as regards quantity. But if they
think that quantity and substance are the same, then they identify
accident with substance, the substrate with what is in it, and find 10
themselves wholly in conflict with what is evident.

Therefore we must give him again the same reply: that these people
called all beings numbers. In investigating, therefore, as to how the
multiplicity in numbers came to be, they were enquiring into all of the
intelligibles and sensibles, finding as responsible for each kind of multiplicity the dyadic cause in everything.

1090a2-15 But one might fasten also upon the question of num- 15
bers, what reason there is to believe that they exist. For numbers
provide the cause of beings for him who posits the Forms, if, that
is, each number is a Form and the Form is the cause of being to
the others in whatever way (let this be their position). But for him
who does not think in this way, since he sees the inherent difficulties as regards the Forms, so that it is not for these reasons that
he posits numbers, why, for him who posits mathematical number,
must there be reason to believe that there is such a number, and
what is its use for other things? For he does not claim that it is the
cause of anything, but he says that it is a nature in itself. Nor does
it seem to be a cause. For all the theorems of arithmeticians will
also apply to sensible things, as has been said.

In these words Aristotle combats him who separates mathematical
number from the sensible and provides it with its proper substance.[453]
But one might be surprised at him thinking that this number is the
cause of nothing. Yet what other number than it[454] is the cause for our
souls of measuring things that are distinct? Where do we see such clear 20
images of the divine as in it? Where would one see figures and the
causes of figures and the principles of all mathematicals as purely as in
these numbers? What is said at the end of the present passage might
therefore also be cause for surprise, to the effect that 'all the theorems
of mathematical numbers also apply to sensible things'. For – a first
point we might make – which are the sensibles which are so ordered in 25
succession that they differ from each other only by a unit and progress
by this difference to completion? Then again: where will one observe a
relation and good order of sensibles such that among multiples in
analogy the third is a square, the fourth a cube, the seventh both a cube
and a square?[455] But even if one were to do violence to reality and order
sensibles in this way, this violence would advance first and foremost 30

only to a certain point in view of the fact that sensibles are not of a nature such as to allow them to preserve such a relation between themselves. Then, it will take this order from mathematical numbers; for the demiurgic process did not place this order in the nature of sensibles. Where is matter able to receive this beauty in theorems? Whence do sensibles have it that there are the even and odd alternately, if it is not that someone, taking also this from numbers, might use it to a minor extent while bringing force to bear on enmattered nature? Were this not so, then, as far as sensibles are concerned, nothing would prevent evens following evens and odds following odds. And if numbers were to admit this order up to a certain point, perhaps one might say that they are ordered in this way in accord with a position and law decreed by our thinking. But since they progress with the same order and the same forms to infinity, and since as far as our reasoning is able to reach, so much of an order does it see in the same variety, thus it is clear to all that numbers have this good order as a concomitant part of the nature proper to them, which Intellect and the paradigmatic cause of prior numbers conferred on them as they were constituted in soul. Therefore let us not, by making number something that comes later (*husterogenê*), thinking of it as an abstraction from sensibles, despise either the beauty, or the order, or the images of separate Forms, or the multiplicity of theorems in mathematical numbers, or the principles of all sciences.

Chapter 3: Forms and numbers as causes (again)[456]

1090a16-30 Those, then, who posit that Forms exist, and that they are numbers, by setting each off from the many, try to take each as one thing and say somehow why each exists. However, since these things are neither necessary nor possible, one must not say either that number exists for these reasons. But the Pythagoreans, seeing that many of the attributes of numbers occur in sensible bodies, made numbers to be beings, not as separate, but as that out of which beings are. But for what reason? Because the attributes of numbers are present in harmony, in the heavens and in many other things. But those who say that there is only mathematical number cannot say this sort of thing, according to their hypotheses, but what they did say was that the sciences would not be concerned with sensible objects. We, however, say that they are, as we have said before. And it is clear that mathematical objects are not separate, for if they were, their attributes would not be present in bodies.

Making mention of three opinions in this passage, one which propounds Form-number, which Aristotle habitually refers to his teacher, one which makes bodies numbers, which he refers to the Pythagoreans, and one which knows only mathematical number, he mostly speaks ill of the third opinion as being more irrational than the others. But we say that he neither gives an adequate account of the first two opinions, the Platonic and the Pythagorean, nor does he say anything sound about the third. For in the first place there was no one who thought that there 25 was only mathematical number, but someone like this perhaps, using mathematical names also for divine numbers, may have caused misunderstanding in some minds. Then, why do they not use an adequate piece of evidence of the existence of mathematicals as separate from sensibles when they say 'if there be arithmetical science, then there is separate number'? But the antecedent holds, so then the consequent. 30 But he says that he has countered the argument before. Yet no adequate refutation of mathematicals is given there, just that the science of universals exists potentially, and the science of particulars in actuality. Neither does what is said here have any force. 'For', he says, 'if numbers were separated, their attributes would not be present in bodies'. He 35 here misuses again the homonymy of numbers and attributes; for such things are ordered in one way with regard to unitary numbers, and proportionately but differently in regard to the products of nature.

1090a30-1090b5 Now the Pythagoreans in this respect are not 178,1 open to criticism. However, in making natural bodies out of numbers, things which have lightness and weight out of what has neither weight nor lightness, they seem to be speaking of another heaven and bodies and not of sensibles. But those who make number separate, because axioms will not be true of sensibles, but what is said (in mathematics) is true and gladdens the soul, they suppose that they exist and are separate, and likewise for mathematical magnitudes. Therefore it is clear that the opposed argument will say the opposite and that the difficulty just raised has to be solved for those who hold this view, why, if (numbers) are in no way present in sensibles, their attributes occur in sensibles.

Basing himself on the assumption that the Pythagoreans do not make number separate, but constitute the sensible world out of numbers, and that certain others, seeing that axioms and universal premises hold 5 true of nothing sensible, make <numbers separate>[457] from magnitudes and sensibles, Aristotle first objects to the Pythagoreans: how can sensible bodies be constituted from numbers which are without weight and magnitude? And to those who separate numbers: how can the attributes of magnitudes and numbers be in sensibles, if numbers are not inseparable from sensibles?

One should say then, on behalf of the Pythagoreans, that they know 10 of other numbers and are not talking simply about the sensible, but teach also about the intellectual, psychic and natural orders, and indeed they constitute the sensible world from immaterial reason-principles

and from productive and prior causes. But those who do not provide
15 nature with reason-principles, lest they double things, wonder at how
weight and magnitude are produced from what has no weight and no
magnitude. However, it has been adequately shown that if a weight or
magnitude is never constituted of *parts* without weight and magnitude,
magnitude is produced from *elements* which are of themselves without
parts, if indeed matter and form are the elements of bodies. And it is
much more so the case as regards all extensions and masses: do they
not receive their coming-to-be, which is in the grip of change, from the
20 truer causes seen in reason-principles and demiurgic forms? For either
bodies are ungenerated and existing from eternity, or one must admit
that what is extended comes from unextended causes, the divided from
the undivided, sensible and resistant bodies from what is invisible and
intangible. And we should agree with those who say in this way that
things which have magnitude come from the undivided.
25   As for those who separate numbers (from sensibles), on their behalf
one should say that there is no cause for surprise that products resemble their causes. Thus, as separate numbers are creative, and they are
imitated by mathematical numbers, it is likely that the sensible world
contains images of the numbers which make it, such that 'all would be
in all, but appropriately in each'.[458] As for the criticism based on axioms
30 and in general on the sciences, we have often said that it is most difficult
to face even for the most disputatious. For either these (axioms) are
false, or they agree and concord with beings. Now if they are false, then
the argument has removed all comprehension (for from these derive
demonstrations), but in removing all comprehension, you end up being
able to assert nothing. But if they are true and concord with some beings,
179,1 since not primarily with sensibles (for sensibles are individuals, and
whatever in them is of the order of the common is mastered by matter), it
remains that they concord with entities at the level of discursive reasoning
(*dianoêta*),[459] as being of equal dignity to them, and with intellectual
entities, as images and imprints in relation to paradigms.

> **1090b5-13** But there are some who think that since the point is
> the limit and extremity of the line, as the line is of the surface, and
> as the surface is of the solid, that there must exist such natures.
> It is necessary, therefore, to consider also this argument, and see
> if it not be excessively weak. For extremities are not substances,
> but rather all such things are limits (since there is also a limit of
> walking and of movement in general, this would therefore be
> something determinate and a substance; but this is absurd). But
> even if they are, then they all will be of particular sensibles (for
> the argument relates to these). For what reason then will they be
> separate?

5 Aristotle says that some of these people take limits as Forms and

substances, and he refutes them because these things are not substances and even less separate substances.[460]

We must respond, then, on behalf of these men that it is not limits as
generally understood that they are making into separate substances,
but rather those in the substantial reason-principles of intellect, of the
soul and of nature, limits which limit in a more proper sense and define
coming-to-be, of which visible limits constitute the lowest level of 10
likeness.

1090b13-32 Furthermore, one who is not too complacent might go
on to raise the issue, as regards all number and mathematicals,
that the prior and the posterior contribute nothing to each other
(for if there were no number, magnitudes will nonetheless exist for
those who say that there are only mathematicals, and if magnitudes did not exist, then at least soul and sensible bodies would
exist; but it does not seem, from what we observe, that nature is
episodic, like a bad tragedy). But this does not affect those who
posit Forms, for they make magnitudes out of matter and a
number, lengths out of the dyad, surfaces perhaps out of a triad,
solids out of the tetrad, or out of other numbers (it doesn't make
any difference). But will these be Forms, or what sort of thing are
they, and what do they contribute to beings? They actually contribute nothing, just as mathematicals contribute nothing. Moreover,
neither is there any theorem that relates to them, unless one
wants to interfere with the principles of mathematics and propound peculiar theories of one's own. But it is not difficult, in fact,
to concoct any hypotheses whatever, and expand and string them
out. These thinkers, then, are quite wrong in thus striving to
connect the objects of mathematics with the Forms.

First of all, against those who advocate mathematical substance only,
<he raises the question>[461] how it is that, while they assert the exist-
ence of numbers and magnitudes and soul and bodies, what comes
second does not come at all events from what is prior, but even if
numbers do not exist, magnitudes exist and come to be, and if one 15
removes the latter also, there is still soul and bodies. Against those, on
the other hand, who admit Form-number, (he asks) whether or not
magnitudes that come immediately from numbers are also themselves
Forms, and if they require a particular form of knowledge, or if one may
apply mathematical knowledge to them.[462]

Now one should first say in response, on behalf of the former group,
that they do not examine mathematical substance only, and in general,
in their assigning of order to objects, they say that prior beings always 20
contribute to the existence of secondary ones. For this is well said, that
there must be a single continuity of natural things, and that nothing
episodic should appear in them. In fact that these men are cognisant

not just of mathematical substance, even if they employ mathematical
25 terms to convey their doctrine concerning intelligible substance, has
been often said earlier, but is also made clear by the raising of the
present difficulty. For if he criticises these men for not making soul out
of magnitudes and numbers, they being prior to it, he clearly testifies
that they postulated the existence of numbers on the intellectual and
divine levels also.

On behalf of the latter group, one should reply that the first magnitudes are Forms, the Circle itself, the Pyramid itself, the Triangle itself,
30 but it is from mathematical reason-principles that the recollection of
these occur in us. For it is not that mathematical knowledge, which is
180,1 discursive and divided and progresses from one point to another and
develops to its conclusions from hypotheses, is adjusted to these Forms,
but rather, as is stated in the *Letters*[463] concerning the Circle itself, that
it is neither the shape, nor the name, nor the definition, nor the science,
that constitutes knowledge of the thing, but there must occur a vision
5 of the thing, and from scientific theorems as if fired by mutual friction
an intellectual light must shine out, through which we will be brought
into conjunction with the Circle itself. Thus mathematical discipline is
a kind of preparation, as exercising the soul with images, for the
immediate grasp (*autoptikê epibolê*) of the paradigm. So these people do
not seek to adjust mathematicals to the Forms, but they strive to lead
up from the former, as from images, to the latter.

10 **1090b32-1091a5** But those people who first made number double,
that of Forms and mathematical number, have not said at all, nor
could they say, how and from what mathematical number will
come. For they put it between Form-number and sensible number.
For if it comes from the Great and Small, this number will be the
same as that of the Forms (from what other Small and Great, after
all, can he produce magnitudes?). But if he names something else,
he will have to name yet more elements. And if some 'one' is the
principle of each, the one will be something common to these, and
we will need to investigate how the One is this multiplicity and at
the same time that number cannot come about, according to him,
otherwise than from the One and the Indefinite Dyad.

He is taking aim now at his own teacher; for it is he who clearly
distinguishes mathematicals from intellectual Forms, even if the other
philosophers know both the one sort and the other. Aristotle says that
Plato does not explain the coming-to-be of mathematical number (this
5 number must come to be, after all, since it is not primal), for this
number ought neither to come from what is the same as Form-number,
lest it appear to be the same as it, nor from anything else, for number
cannot come to be otherwise than from a Monad and the Indefinite
Dyad.[464]

Now why, we will say to Aristotle, not suppose your teacher to be employing that well-worn principle, which you yourself have been accustomed to use in physical discourses, that it is only by analogy that 20 different sorts of number have the same first principles, but not the same principles *tout court*? But in fact you actually hint at something like this, when you say 'from another Great and Small', except not that from which magnitudes come. For the dyad which generates mathematical numbers is different from that which generates magnitudes. For the principles (intellectual, rational, and natural) are recognised specifically in relation to each order of reality. However, to investigate 25 how the One brings forth and generates the many at every level is a properly philosophical question, and one which they investigated in depth.

1091a5-13 Now all this is irrational and contradicts both itself and what is plausible, and indeed it seems to be a case of Simonides' 'long story': for a long story is told, in the case of slaves, when they have nothing sound to say. But it even seems as if the elements themselves, the Great and Small, protest as if being dragged in, for they cannot in any way generate number, unless it be numbers generated by doubling one. But it is also absurd – or rather it belongs to the impossible – to have a generation of things that are eternal.[465]

In these words Aristotle is emulating the perorations of the rhetoricians – indeed he is not even omitting comic buffoonery. So most of this, insofar as it does not have to do with anything substantial, we may 30 either pass over, or at all events abbreviate. What he is referring to is the so-called *Unordered Poems* of Simonides,[466] for they are loosely strung together and show little evidence of planning.

But it even seems ... by doubling one.

Since the Great and Small is a dyad, and the dyad even number only, it 181,1 produces at the most number which is even times even, while Plato says that the other numbers cannot be generated from the Great and Small. But we have explained many times what sort of dyad they call the Great and Small, and that it is that which is generative of all multiplicity.

But it is also absurd ... things that are eternal.

But if by hypothesis they were to do this for instructional purposes, 5 what are they doing wrong? Unless it is your position, Aristotle, that there is no efficient cause of eternal things. These people, however, hold that all things derive their existence from the first principles.

1091a13-22 Therefore there need be no doubt as to whether or not the Pythagoreans held that there was a process of generation. For they clearly say that once the One is constituted, be it from planes, or surfaces, or from a seed, or from something which they cannot specify, immediately that which is nearest of the Unlimited began to be drawn in and limited by Limit. But since they are indulging in cosmogony here and seeking to express themselves in terms of physical philosophy, it is right to examine aspects of their account of nature, but to exempt them from the present inquiry. For we are seeking the first principles of unchanging things, so that what we have to examine is the generation of numbers of this kind.

10 It will not escape the more acute reader with what attitude Aristotle propounds these arguments. But in order that we may unfold the reasoning of the Pythagoreans on the basis of what he sets out here, let us say that in their view the Whole, constructed from Matter and Form, is one. They say that the constitution of this Whole comes to be thus: when the reason-principle proceeding from Nature completely engenders surface, figure and the causal principle, body without quality first comes
15 to be (this is 'that which is nearest of the Unlimited'), then what is ordered, when Limit and the natural reason-principle completely takes hold of the substrate. That it is separable numbers that the thinkers concerned, and most of all these particular men [sc. the Pythagoreans], are talking about here, we have specified also before this.

Chapter 4: First principles and the Good

1091a23-4 They declare that there is no generation of odd number, clearly implying that there is generation of even number.

20 You might find that this is stated by them in a symbolic mode (*sumbolikôs*). For since they assimilate odd number to the gods, they reasonably say that it is ungenerated, while taking even number as being analogous to enmattered things they call it generated and assimilate it to the Dyad; but (there is no problem here), since, as we have often specified previously, they generate the co-ordinate columns of numbers, even and odd, from the same principles, even if they say that the one
25 set resemble the Monad, the other the Dyad.[467]

1091a24-9 But some produce even number first from unequals –
the Great and Small, when equalised. Therefore it follows necessarily for them that inequality applies to them before they are equalised. If they were always equalised, after all, they would not have been unequal before (for nothing is prior to what is eternal), so that it is manifest that it is not as a theoretical analysis that they have postulated a generation of numbers.

Their position is that since even number possesses Matter and Form, by way of Matter it has the Great and Small as proceeding from the Dyad, but in respect of Form it is mastered by Equality – this not to be taken as a temporal process, but as being eternally the case. So if they declare, for instructional purposes, that what is not ordered is prior to 30 what is ordered, this is a common mode of expression for us all. And indeed you yourself say that Matter is prior and the principle of body, although Matter is always ordered.

1091a29-1091b3 But there is a difficulty here – and a reproach to him who sees a solution to the difficulty – as to how the elements and principles are to be related to the Good and the Beautiful. The difficulty is this: whether there is any among them which we would wish to say is the Good Itself and the best of all, or not, these arising later? Among the theologians there are those, apparently in agreement with some contemporary thinkers, who deny this, saying that the good and the beautiful appear only as the nature of things progresses. This they do as a precaution against a real difficulty which besets those who say, as some do, that the One is a first principle. The difficulty lies, however, not in the fact of granting goodness as pertaining to the principle, but in saying that the One is the first principle, and a principle in the sense of element, and that number derives from the One.

Aristotle is right in assigning what is good to the more fundamental of causal principles. However, it was not right to start off his argument in 182,1 this way. It would have been more reasonable to say: 'But there is a difficulty here – and a cause of wonder even for him who sees a solution to the difficulty'. Nor is he[468] right to suppose that the theologians would say anything else. But what is most absurd is to think, either that the Good is co-ordinate with the One in this way, or that the primal One is to be described as a principle in the sense of an element from which, as 5 an inherent component, number is constituted. All this is a distortion of their doctrine; for the One and the Good are the same in Plato, and transcend all being, intellect and life.[469]

1091b4-6 The poets of old agree with this view, in that they say that it is not the first entities, such as Night and Heaven or Chaos or Ocean, which reign and rule, but Zeus.

Nor do these words give an accurate account of the views of the theologians. For they say that Night and Heaven reign and before them 10 their supremely great father:

Taking it, then, he allotted to gods and to mortals an ordered world, over which world there first reigned glorious Erikepaios[470] and after him Night:

15   Who held in her hands the <shining>[471] sceptre of Erikepaios and
after her Heaven:
Who first reigned over the gods after his mother Night.

But Chaos is above the relation of reigning; and as for Zeus, he is clearly
20 named, not as the first, but as the fifth king, by the oracles given to him
by Night:

Of the immortal gods you became the fifth king.

Thus the very first principle, according to them also, is the One and the
Good, after which comes the dyad which is above the function of
reigning, Aither and Chaos, <as the theologians would have it, Proteus
and Chaos>[472] according to Pythagoras. Then come the most primary
and hidden classes of the gods, over which there comes to reign the first
25 manifest father and king of all, whom they addressed for this reason
as Phanes. Therefore, neither do the best of the philosophers distance themselves from the theologians, nor do the theologians say
that secondary principles are more powerful and better than those
which are more fundamental, but there is one and the same truth
maintained by them all.[473]

> **1091b6-16** However, they are led to speak in this way on account
> of the fact that their world rulers change, since those among them
> who compromise in that they do not say everything in a mythical
> way, such as Pherecydes and some others, posit what first gener-
> ates as the best, as also do the Magi, and some of the later sages,
> such as Empedocles and Anaxagoras, the one making Friendship
> an element, the other Intellect his first principle. But of those who
> say that there exist unchanging substances, some say that the One
> Itself is the Good Itself, but they thought that its reality lay
> primarily in its being one. This, then, is the problem: which of
> these two views we should hold.[474]

30 He does well to accept those who say that the first cause is the best.
However, it is not the case that the theologians posit changes in the
reigns of the gods, even if this may seem to emerge from mythical
accounts, but they say that secondary gods come to be while the more
senior ones always remain in their appropriate dispositions.[475]

But of those ...in its being one.

183,1 The One and the Good is supra-essential (*huperousion*) for Plato, for
Brotinus the Pythagorean, and, in a word, for all of those who have come
from the school of the Pythagoreans. Nonetheless, let the One be the

substance of the very first principle, which they called the Good as being the cause for all of unity and good, and let us see if any absurd consequence follows for them.

This then ... should hold.

Let him raise difficulties if he wants; but for these men it is the case, prior to all objection and demonstration, that the very first is the best.

> **1091b16-27** It would be surprising if what is primal and eternal and supremely self-sufficient did not possess this very thing – self-sufficiency and self-maintenance – in a primary degree and as a good. In fact, it cannot be indestructible and self-sufficient for any other reason than that it is in a good state; so that to say that the first principle is such as this is very probably true. But to say that this principle is the One, or if not this, an element, the element of numbers, is impossible. For this involves a serious difficulty, to avoid which some have rejected the theory – those who agree that the One is the first principle and element, but only of mathematical number. For on this view all units come to be precisely the essential good, and there ensues a superfluity of goods. Besides, if the Forms are numbers, all Forms are essentially good.

For the very first and most self-sufficient entity it is this very thing that 10
is good, self-sufficiency; but this is present in it by reason of the simplicity and unity of its existence. For it is not the good and another thing, but it is itself the Good; so that it is one, since its nature is not composed of good and of something else. For then we would require another principle in which the good would be unmixed in relation to every other thing and unblended. Now Aristotle rails at the concepts of 15
'one' and 'element', since he understands these terms in a vulgar rather than in a theological sense; but if certain persons, in positing 'one' as the principle of mathematical numbers, remove the good from it, then they are talking about, not the principle of all things, but the cause of unitary numbers. And it is clear that this is indeed the good of what is generated from it, but it is not the Good *simpliciter*. For if it were, as he 20
says, all the units would come to be precisely a good[476] – not material units, mind you, but those which are viewed as serving as the Forms of numbers, such as are the good of this number or that, the Pentad of the number five and the Decad of the number ten – not, however, as the Good itself taken simply, like the monads or henads which proceed from the primal cause; for the latter are not only gods, but unifying principles 25
(*sunokhai*) of gods. And there is nothing surprising in there being a plethora of goods in the universe. For the divine is free from jealousy and ungraspable by human reasoning, and the Forms and numbers are

divine and good-like, since they are the offspring of the very first cause. And these matters should not be presented as absurd, matters which these men (the Pythagoreans) accept as self-evident.

30   **1091b27-32** But let us assume that there are Forms of whatever we please: if there are Forms only of goods, then Forms will not be substances; but if there are also Forms of substances, then all animals and plants and whatever participates in Form will be goods. So these absurdities follow, and also that the contrary element, whether it be Multiplicity, or the Unequal, or the Great and Small, will be essentially evil.

If the One, Aristotle says, is good, the Forms also will be good-like. But if this is agreed to, it seems to him that there is a difficulty as to of what things Forms should be posited. For if Forms are posited only of goods here below, such as the virtues, then the Forms will not be of substances, nor substances themselves. But if there are Forms of substances, then all substances here below will be good, since they have
35   been generated in accordance with the Forms which are good.[477]
In addition to all this, he says that if the One is good, then what is not one, which one must call the Dyad, or Unequal, or Multiplicity, will
184,1   be evil, so that the generation of things may be from contraries. One might reply to him that, even if there were Forms only of the virtues, this would not have prevented them from being substances. For it is not the case that the image must in every respect be like its paradigm, but even as the partless are the causes of the divided, and intellectual entities causes of the non-intellectual, and divine entities causes of
5   things mortal, so also are substances causes of qualities – not just of any qualities, but of those which are perfective of substances. And even if there are Forms of all substances, as indeed there are, it is not necessary that the things here below all be beautiful and good. For things here below do not always keep the measure that they receive from above, but in the process of deviation they decline towards a lack of measure.
And in any case, what necessity is there that, even though the One
10   be good, the other principle be evil? First of all, they[478] say that that One is the Good which transcends all co-ordination with anything else, and is also beyond the two principles that come after it. And if the prior and more divine of the two principles, which they call the Monad, is said by them to be the Good, it does not follow for them to say that the Dyad, even if it may be opposed to the Monad in other respects, is evil. For it is not from an opposition of that sort that the divine are generated and
15   proceed, but from a principle which is supremely excellent and possesses the good in an unmixed way. Thus the impossibilities that he assembles in what follows as consequences of the hypothesis have no relevance to these men: for them, evil is totally excluded from the

principles, as the divine Plato clearly stated in the *Theaetetus*:[479] 'it
cannot be established among the gods, but it necessarily circulates in 20
this mortal nature and this place.'

1091b32-5 This is why one of them shrank from connecting goodness to the One, on the ground that since generation proceeds from
contraries, the nature of Multiplicity would then necessarily be
bad; while others say that it is the unequal that is the nature of
the bad.

Who is it who shrinks thus? Why does Aristotle vainly upbraid the
golden Speusippus?[480] How could it follow that from such opposites
there could arise the existence of divine things?

While others say ... the bad.

God forbid! For the Unequal which they took as relating to the cause
of beings, being prior even to Difference in the genera of being, they 25
say is not only supremely excellent but also the most generative of
the supremely excellent. But if there is some unequal which they
hold to be bad, something proper to the lowest level of material
things, in no respect is this to be related to the cause that is generative of multiplicity, unless in the sense that it too somehow derives
from this cause.

1091b35-1092a5 It follows that all beings will partake of evil 30
except one thing, namely the One itself, and numbers will participate in it in a more undiluted form than magnitudes, and evil will
be the place of the good, and it participates in and desires what is
destructive of it – for what is destructive of something is its
opposite. And if, as we were saying, matter is potentially each
thing, as for instance of fire in actuality it is fire in potentiality,
evil will be just the potentially good. All this follows partly because
they make every principle an element, partly because they make
contraries principles, partly because they make the One a principle, and partly because they make numbers the primary
substances, and separable, and Forms.[481]

If, then, it is impossible both not to include the Good among the
first principles, and to include it in this way, it is clear that the
first principles are not being rightly represented, nor are the
primary substances.

All this follows for those who hold that there are two principles of the
whole, and distinguish them in terms of good and evil; for all things will
participate in evil apart from one of the two principles, as in Empedocles
all things may seem to participate in Strife, apart from Friendship

35　itself, and primary entities will have evil more undilutedly than secondary ones, and the good will achieve its actualisation through evil, and
185,1　evil will love the good, although it is the occasion of its mutilation and destruction. But if this were of the nature of a material principle, then evil will potentially be the supremely good.

　　Now one has, admittedly, to hand it to Aristotle here once again, for his observation of what absurdities follow from this hypothesis and for the succinctness of his explanation of them. But one must not imagine,
5　for all that, that he is scoring any points against the Pythagoreans, for they nowhere accepted evil as being among the principles.

　　All this follows ... the primary substances.

　　One of the absurdities, Aristotle says, follows from their making every principle an element. What absurdity does he think follows from this? That all things are good, if the good is principle in the sense of an element. Then, that evil also is a principle, if contraries are principles;
10　then, 'that they make one a principle'; for it will no longer be good, he says, if it is one; then, that because they make numbers the primary substances, numbers will participate in undiluted evil. Four absurdities thus follow from his four hypotheses; for all things will be both good and evil, apart from the One, evil will be a principle, a principle is not a good, and numbers will participate in pure evil.
15　　One must therefore reply to him as follows: these men do not make every principle an element in the sense in which you, Aristotle, conceive of an element, nor do they make their principles contraries in such a way that the one is good and the other evil, nor do you understand the One as they conceive it, nor does it follow from numbers being separate that they participate in evil either pure or mixed, since evil has long
20　been banished, not just from intelligible substance, but also from the whole aetherial realm, and it wanders around here in the realm of mortal nature, a side-effect of more partial goods in consequence of falling away from them (*kata tên ex autôn apoptôsin*).[482] Therefore, they actually gave a very good account of the principles, and it is better to say that the Good is One rather Intellect.[483] For he who calls it 'one' keeps the Good as pure and only good. For the One does not allow itself
25　to be coupled with anything; but he who calls the Good intellect makes it not solely good; and if he also calls it a living being, and being, and intelligible, he clearly takes it from the good towards the good-like, and failing to attain the truly one, assigns it to the 'one many'.[484]

Chapter 5: More difficulties with first principles

1092a11-17 Nor is someone correct in his supposition if he likens the principles of the whole to that of animals and plants, because the more perfect always come from what is undefined and imperfect, and is led by this to assert that it is also true in the case of the primary entities, so that the One itself would not be an existent thing. For even in this realm, the principles out of which these things arise are complete, for man begets man, and it is not the seed that comes first.

There were some people, perhaps, who actually supposed that the principles of the whole were less perfect than that which came out of 30 them, thinking all things are disposed like generated things.[485] Against them Aristotle says that not even does generation lead simply from the imperfect to the perfect, as from a seed to the animal, but the imperfect too comes to existence from the perfect. For man is prior to seed and the cause of seed, and in general what is actual is prior to what is in potentiality.[486]

Aristotle's argument is effective in both respects: for he does well to 35 object to those who say that the One is both principle of beings and insubstantial in the sense of being inferior to substance, and he is quite 186,1 sound as regards generated things, in putting the perfect always before the imperfect. Yet, in not admitting the reason-principles in the universe, how he will be able to maintain this doctrine I do not know. For what will he say about animals which come from putrefaction?[487] And about trees or bushes or herbs which grow spontaneously? For we will assume that, in these cases also, there pre-exists in the nature of the 5 universe the reason-principles productive of these things. But since he does not admit these reason-principles, how will he take it that in the universe the perfect is prior to the imperfect? Or how will he bring each thing to exist from what is univocal with it? For to say that the sun and the zodiac, being perfect as they are, bring these things to existence and perfect them is to speak especially of the cause common to all generated things and not particular to each. Then again, how does he attribute 10 organic existence to (*organopoiei*) the gnat, the wasp and the other things that come from putrefaction,[488] if he himself neither has the reason-principles of these things, nor may move what has? Unless by entrusting the coming-to-be and organisation of these things in every case to the spontaneous. Yet the spontaneous does not occur in the same way in every case, but it is seen in things which happen comparatively rarely.[489]

1092a17-21 But it is also absurd to generate place simultaneously 15 with mathematical solids (for place is proper to each particular, which is why they are separable spatially, but mathematicals have no position) and to say that they must be somewhere, but not to say what their place is.

Alexander says that this is a shot at Plato.[490] If then he correctly divines Aristotle's intention here, we might not, in our turn, be beside the mark concerning the divine Plato, if we said that he made our imagination

the place of mathematical bodies, even as matter is the place for
20 enmattered forms, with this much difference, that the matter which
receives from nature the enmattered form neither knows what it receives nor is able to possess it throughout, whereas the imagination
which receives mathematical body from the higher soul both knows it
and is able to preserve it to the extent that it is <in> it.[491] Therefore the
place of natural bodies is one thing, that of enmattered forms another, that
of mathematical bodies another, and that of immaterial reason-principles
25 yet another. And in saying this, we are not saying anything new, but even
Aristotle himself has called the discursive soul the 'place' of the forms.[492]
And those who have examined the *Timaeus* any more than superficially
know that Plato has spoken there about the place of natural bodies.

> **1092a21-b8** But those who say that beings derive from elements
> and that numbers are the first of beings should have distinguished
> the ways in which each different thing comes from something else,
> by telling us in what way number comes from the principles. Is it
> by mixture? But not everything admits of mixture; and what
> comes to be [sc. from mixture] is different, and the original unity will
> not separate out and become another nature; but this is what they
> want to be the case. Then is it by combination, as in the case of a
> syllable? But for this there must be position, and, in thinking, one
> will think of the one and multiplicity as separate. This then is what
> number will be, a unit and multiplicity, or the one and the unequal.
>   And since that which derives from other things derives from
> them either as being inherent in it or as not being inherent in it,
> in which way is it the case for number? Derivation from inherent
> components is not possible except for things which come to be. Is
> it then perhaps derived as from a seed? But it is not possible for
> something to be emitted from what is indivisible. Or as from a
> contrary, which does not persist? But all such things which are
> thus derived come also from something else which does persist.
> Since then one of these people posits the One as contrary to
> Multiplicity, and another posits it as contrary to the Unequal,
> treating of the One as being the Equal, number would come from
> contraries. So there is something else from which number is or
> comes, which persists along with one or the other (of the contraries).
> Furthermore, why is it that all other things which come from contrar-
> ies or which have a contrary are subject to destruction – even if all of
> the contrary is used up (in producing them) – but number is not? No
> explanation is given for this. Yet the contrary tends to destroy,
> whether it be inherent or not, even as Strife destroys the mixture (yet
> it need not have, for it is not a contrary to it).

30 The account of the derivation of mathematical numbers is not the same
as that of Form-numbers. For to the former we grant, if not such matter

as is present in the natural world, yet at least mathematical matter, as the quantitative element (*posotês*) which underlies them; as regards the latter, Form-numbers, we hold them to be entirely without parts and intellectual, active and demiurgic, possessing their existence in forms which are simple, immaterial and tending in no way towards the lowest 35 level of reality. This being so, Aristotle should have clearly discriminated as to what kind of numbers he is inquring into.

Even so, since his questions seem to concern more Form-numbers (for 187,1 these men did not say that mathematical numbers were the first of beings, but rather Form-numbers), let us explain to him again that neither mixture, nor combination, nor a substrate, nor any element which admits of privation or destruction, nor any other such thing should be taken as constituting divine numbers, for all these things 5 relate to enmattered nature which is disposed sometimes in one way and sometimes in another way. But all divine things, since their principles remain always in their proper state, proceed out of themselves in a mode of self-generation (*autogonôs*), both through the superabundance of generative power of their primary generative causes, and through their own distinctive self-revealing (*autophanês*) and self-generative property. They remain always the same in the same state, established, on the one 10 hand, far from coming-to-be and destruction, combination and division, far from all change, while, on the other hand, they lead and correct nature as a whole and the soul which bestrides nature, preparing them to act in accordance with their own directions, lest the realm of generation suffer deficiency or the irregularity associated with matter prevail, and so that 15 all be ordered by the natural and creative rule[493] of the Forms and of numbers. So if they were talking about such numbers as these, how could these men have made any mention of destruction? For how could these numbers, which maintain and renew those things which by virtue of their own nature are in flux, mortal and perishable, be supposed, by people who have correctly grasped their nature, to be subject to destruction?

And neither is Empedocles being justly criticised here, nor for that matter elsewhere, as postulating the destruction of the mixture 20 through the agency of Strife. For neither is Strife destructive (it is actually itself creative of the cosmos), nor is the Sphere ever dissolved in his system, unless one were, by holding to the literal text which veils his whole theology, to deviate from his thought.[494] In fact, his Strife is generative of multiplicity and difference, and Friendship of sameness and unity. Thus Friendship prevails in the intelligible realm, which he 25 called the Sphere, and Strife in the sensible realm. In both realms, indeed, there is both One and Multiplicity, but in the former the One dominates, and in the latter Multiplicity.

1092b8-16 Nor is it in any way defined in what way numbers are causes of substances and of being, whether as limits (such as

points are of magnitudes, even as Eurytus arranged what number
is of what, such as this one of man, that one of horse; like those
who fit numbers into figures, such as the triangle and the square, so
he imitates with pebbles the shapes of living things), or as concord is
a ratio of numbers, so also is man and each of the others? And as for
attributes, how are they numbers – white, sweet and hot?

Aristotle here presents two opinions as to how substances derive their
30 existence from numbers, accepting neither of them. For, he says, neither are numbers the limits of substances, as points are of lines (for this
was the assumption made by the Pythagorean Eurytus, when he asserted that this number is the limit of this plant, that number of that
animal,[495] as 6 is of the triangle, 9 of the square, 8 of the cube), nor is it
35 as others say, that substances are produced through proportions (*lo-*
188,1 *goi*),[496] proportions are concords, and concords are harmonious relations
of numbers. For, he says, on neither of these assumptions is it possible
to say how accidents arise out of numbers.

But one should say in reply to this that Eurytus and his associates,
seeing images of things in mathematical numbers, plausibly assigned
certain images to certain things according to what was appropriate, for
example the number 210 as a 'little altar' (*bômiskos*)[497] to body, the
5 number 216 as an equal-angled[498] cube to soul.[499] As for the second
group, their teaching seems to have related to physical numbers; for
these really are what produce concord in the substrate. For how would
it be possible for the substrate to become one through mastery by any
single given Form, if the contraries within it had not been rendered
concordant and harmonious? And what else but nature could harmonise
10 these? But just as the musician harmonises the lyre through the
mathematical numbers present in him, so nature harmonises its products through its physical numbers.

1092b16-23 But it is clear that numbers are not the substance of
a thing, nor the causes of its shape. For the ratio is substance, and
number is matter. The number, for example, of flesh or bone is
substance only in the sense that it is three parts fire and two parts
earth. And number, whatever it be, is always such as to be of
certain things, for instance of particles of fire or earth, or of units;
but substance is to be 'so much' in relation to 'so much' in the
mixture. This, however, is no longer number, but the ratio of the
mix of bodily numbers or suchlike.

Wishing to show that Form is neither number nor obtained from
numbers, but that if indeed number contributes anything at all to
15 things, it is the quantity of matter, Aristotle borrows inappropriately
the words of Empedocles about the composition of bones:

Two parts of the glitter of Nestis out of eight
And four of Hephaestus, and they became white bones.[500]

But Aristotle says that all number occurs in a substrate, be it in units,
or in dry or in wet bodies, whereas the cause of the mixture is ratio 20
(*logos*) and not number. Now it is ridiculous to take as being relevant to
those men the idea that all number is of some things and needs a
substrate, and again that the ratio that is cause of the mixture is not a
number, since they posit immaterial numbers and affirm that the
numbers in nature are the causes of all harmonic mixture in sensibles. 25
It is therefore not easy to say who else it might be who, rather than
postulating what is [said] in the beginning (1092b19-20), would rashly
assume[501] it.

1092b23-5 Number, therefore, is not a cause by reason of creating
anything, neither number in general nor unitary number, nor is it
the matter, nor the ratio and the form of things. But nor again is
it a final cause.

There being four causes, Aristotle says that number is none of these.
For it does not have efficient power, like a seed, nor is it like a Form in
sensibles, nor like matter, nor like a final cause.[502]   30
Now you speak <the truth, in saying>[503] that all causes are numbers,
with the exception of matter, which is not properly a cause at all, but is
mastered by the causes for the purposes of generation. And indeed the
divine and daemonic numbers produce and bestow other numbers, i.e.
enmattered forms, upon substrates, and create for their own sakes.   189,1

Chapter 6: What is the point of number?

1092b26-1093a3 But one might raise the question as to what is
the good to be derived from numbers, by reason of the fact that
their mixture can be expressed as a number, either an easily
calculable number or an odd number? For honey-water is no
healthier if mixed three times three, but would be more useful if
mixed in no proportion, but were watery, than if it were unmixed
in an arithmetical proportion. Furthermore, the proportions in
mixtures consist in the addition of numbers, not in numbers, such
as three to two, but not three times two. For there must be the
same genus in multiplications, such that 1 must measure the
multiplication series of 1 x 2 x 3 by the factor 1, and that of 4 x 5
x 7 by the factor 4, so that all are measured by the same. So it will
not be the case that the number of fire is 2 x 5 x 3 x 7 if the number
of water is 2 x 3. But if all things must have number in common,
many things must be the same, and there will be the same number
for this and for another.

Since these men everywhere praise what is numbered and since that
5 which does not have a proportion to another, such as number has to
number, is said to be irrational and incommensurable, Aristotle says
that he does not see how honey-water, if it is mixed according to odd or
even numbers (even number he has called here 'easily calculable'),[504]
becomes more beneficial, especially if it is mixed perfectly and uniformly (if, for example, it becomes three times three), than if it is[505] more
10 watery, [thus becoming] less healthy. For he thinks the reverse is
true.[506]

But one should first say in response to this little pleasantry (*skôm-
mation*) that the more beneficial mixture is that which correlates better
and accords better with the nature of the user. But what accords better
is what is harmonious and commensurable: this comes about through
physical arithmetic.[507] Thus also might one object to those who watch
15 out for the opportune moments for each action, by saying that it is better
to act with practical wisdom (*phronêsis*) than in relation to the opportune moment – not of course that they, in looking to the situation as a
whole and using calculation combined with sense-perception, recom-
mend neglecting practical wisdom and having confidence only in the
opportune moment, calculating that this is the first task of wisdom, to
comprehend what are the moments appropriate to each action and then
20 in this way to know the other things which contribute to achieving the
goal. Thus do these men [the Pythagoreans] say, not that bare numbers
and mathematical numbers are preferred both in nature and by wise
men, but that the good comes to each thing through the most beautiful
and harmonious numbers, not mathematical, but natural and productive numbers (for god and nature produce all things according to
25 number); and that[508] wise men <should> endeavour to indicate, by
means of mathematical numbers, the beauty of demiurgic numbers, not
having any other way of teaching about them to those who have not
attended closely to the whole order of beings. We will not therefore
neglect the beneficial, neither selecting opportune moments, nor ap-
pealing to the gods, nor preferring the best and most beautiful numbers
30 to those which are not thus. But we will try everywhere through these
numbers to reach the goal, imitating God as far as possible, who assigns
to each the incumbent good according to the opportune moment and
according to certain appropriate numbers. So much for this, then.

Next he says that numbers are composed in proportions rather than
35 multiplied. For in general in multiplications one factor measures the
whole number, such as 3 for 9, and 3 and 4 for 12. Thus if the product
were a man's body, the sum of 1 x 2 x 3, it would need to be measured
by 1, but if the body of a horse, which is the sum of 4 x 5 x 7, it would
190,1 need to be measured by 4. But this is impossible. For it is necessary to
take fire, water, and the other elements for the constitution of these
bodies, but these cannot be measured by one and the same element.[509]

Here also, the man's false reasoning is evident, for he takes mathe-

matical multiplications as obtaining in natural things, whereas the
philosophers who are his elders called the processes of the reason- 5
principles of nature multiplications, but those <powers>[510] which master substrates harmonic and concordant <numbers>.

What Aristotle says at the very end of the passage has no force, when
he says that if all things have number in common and all number is in
things, then many things must avail of the same number and many 10
numbers be of the same thing. For just as in the case of all words and
expressions constituted from letters, all letters appearing as they do in
expressions, it is not necessary either that different expressions use the
same letters (but in some cases they do and in others not), or that the
different letters be present in the same word (the letters, say, of the
word Plato in that of Socrates), so also, as regards natural reason- 15
principles and numbers, all are active and all natural things are constituted according to them, yet not in such a way that different things will
be ordered by the same numbers without distinction; but we may take
it that what is said about how numbers produce is like what some of
Aristotle's followers are accustomed to say in speaking of individual
substances: that it is not possible that what is present in each one of 20
these all comes together in any other;[511] for neither enmattered
forms, nor their essential properties, nor accidents derive their
proper existence from any other source than from natural reason-
principles and numbers.

1093a3-13 Is then this [sc. number] a cause, in such a way that it
is because of this that the thing exists, or is this unclear? There is
for example a certain number of movements of the sun, and again
of the moon, and of the life and maturity of each animal: what
prevents some of these being squares, some cubes, some equal,
some double? Indeed nothing! But it is necessary that all things be
involved in these, if number is common to them all, and it could
happen that different things come under the same number. Hence,
if the same number is proper to certain things, they would be the
same as each other, since they would have the same form of
number – for instance, the sun and moon would be the same.

It is clear, they say, even to a blind man, that there is a number of the 25
sun, another one of the moon, and a number proper to each of the bodies
moving in the heavens; for the periodic cycles of heavenly movements
would not always be the same and proceed in the same way, were it not
that one and the same number was in control in each case. But all of
these numbers contribute to the cycle of the divine which is generated,
and are included in the perfect number of this cycle. And indeed, after 30
all, there is also in every case a natural number of each animal; for
otherwise animals of the same kind would not possess the same organic
structure, nor would they reach maturity and decline in the same

period, nor generate, nourish, and bring up their progeny, were they not
35 constrained by the same measure of nature.[512] And indeed we have
heard from the greatest of Pythagoreans, Plato, that this number is the
cause 'of better and worse births'.[513] Why therefore must he confuse the
issue by making mathematical numbers into the same thing as natural
and demiurgic numbers? For even if we speak sometimes of some of the
191,1 natural numbers as square or cube, we are not thereby making them
unitary, like the number 9 and the number 27,[514] but we signify with
these names their progression by reason of similarity and the dominance of the Same in generating them. Similarly, if we call numbers
5 equal or double, we show the mastery of forms and concords in them.
Thus it does not follow from this, either that different things will avail
of the same number in differing from one another, or that the same
things will use various different numbers, inasmuch as they are the
same. For these absurdities would not even follow for him who understands numbers in their mathematical aspect, since it is possible to
conceive of many squares and infinite cubes and equals and doubles,
10 and that much less would it present an obstacle to those who pursue the
question on the level of nature, in accord with the intentions of those
who propound this theory.[515]

> **1093a13-26** For what reason, then, are numbers causes? There
> are seven vowels, after all, seven strings in the scale, seven
> Pleiads, teeth are lost at seven (in some animals, not in others),
> and there were seven against Thebes. Is it therefore because the
> number is of such a nature that they are seven, or that the Pleiad
> consists of seven stars? Or were they seven because of the gates,
> or for some other reason, and we number the Pleiad as seven and
> the Bear twelve, but others count more of them? Since they also
> say that [the double consonants] KS, PS, and ZD are concords and
> that they are three because the concords are three. But that there
> might be thousands of such things doesn't seem to matter (for one
> sign might be for G and R). If it is because each [consonant] is the
> double of the others, but no other is, the reason is that there are
> three places in the mouth, one [consonant] is added to the S in
> each: this is the reason why there are only three, not because
> concords are three, since concords are more numerous; but in this
> case there cannot be more.

It is as if he were saying: let us see the arguments on the basis of which
they say that these [sc. numbers] are causes of things. Thus, when they
15 want to praise the number Seven, they say that the vowels, through which
coherent speech is brought to actualisation, are seven; and likewise the
notes of the octave, and also the Pleiades, are seven; animals lose their
teeth in seven years (to which he adds, in a comic and contentious tone, 'in
some cases, in others not'); and there were Seven who marched against

Thebes. Then he shows that none of these things come to be the case on account of the number seven, but by reason of some other cause.[516]

And in truth it is ridiculous to hold the number seven to account for the Argive generals or for the Pleiad; for not even regarding the latter can one with confidence say that it is constituted thus by the Demiurge, but rather that the whole placing of the stars involves much supposition (on our part). Thus it is that the fixed stars are arranged in one way according to the Egyptians, but according to the Chaldaeans or the Greeks in another way. Again, concerning double consonants, he says that they are not three in number because there are just three concords. And here he makes a good point, for it is not possible to relate each of them to each of the concords, as for instance ZD to the quart, or KS to the quint, or PS to the octave; but rather, as he says, since there are three places for vocalisation, for this reason one is produced in each. This account was also given by Archinus, as Theophrastus reports.[517] Archinus said that either something exterior is vocalised by the closing of the lips, like the P, and thus is PS produced near the tip of the tongue as being composed from P and S; or by the flat of the tongue beside the teeth, like D, and thus is Z produced in this place;[518] or by the roof [of the mouth] being pressed from the end, like K, whence comes X. Now everyone would agree that these are, as accounts, nearer to nature than the three concords.

However, just because some of the more recent authorities have indulged in unsound theorising,[519] that does not mean that one should dismiss the account of nature based on numbers. Now if one were to find something of this sort in the divine Plato or in one of the illustrious Pythagoreans, then this would indeed discredit the discipline; but, since Prorus the Pythagorean, in saying many noble things about the number Seven,[520] things appropriate to the divine, uses no such argument, showing with intelligence how nature completes or changes most things of this sort over periods of seven years, or months, or days, and since others,[521] discussing the Decad, have demonstrated its domination throughout the entire divinely-generated realm and its mastery over particular works of nature, and since Pythagoras himself, in instructing us about all numbers from the Monad up to the Decad,[522] uses both a theological and a physical approach, without recourse to cheap and silly argument – why then should the authentic treatises bequeathed by these men, on account of certain texts which masquerade as their philosophy, serve to cast greater discredit on these divine men? Unless we should make the point also that, in those places where he is not being contentious, the ingenious (*daimonios*)[523] Aristotle himself manifests both his admiration for the natural power of numbers and his indebtedness to the knowledge of the Pythagoreans. And to all it is well-known what he says about the triad in the prologue of his treatise *On the Heaven*, calling into evidence the teachings of the Pythagorean school, and finally declaring: 'having taken this number from nature as if her

20

25

30

35
192,1

5

10

15

20

law, we use it in worshipping the gods'.[524] And how would one not find striking what is to be found in *Sense and Sensibilia*? For having worked out that the most general flavours are eight (astringent, harsh, bitter,
25   saline, pungent, sharp, sweet, rich), and eight again the simplest colours (white, yellow, crimson, violet, green, grey, blue, black), he makes each of them seven, supposing that this number is appropriate to the making of the world and compressing into one bitter and saline, black and grey.[525] Therefore let us not permit the rubbishing, in Aristotle's controversial works, of what is approved in his more expository treatises.

30   **1093a26-1093b4** These people are like the ancient Homeric scholars, who see small similarities but overlook large ones. Some of them say that there are many more patterns of this sort, such as that the middle notes are 9 or 8, that epic verse has 17 syllables, which equals the sum of these two, being scanned with 9 syllables on the right and with 8 on the left, and that the distance in letters from Alpha to Omega is equal to that from the lowest to the highest notes in flutes, which number is equal to the whole system of the heavens.

One must agree that some of those who explain Homer do not remain self-consistent, and that some of those who attempt to imitate the Pythagoreans fall short of attaining their true knowledge, being carried away into miserable and ridiculous suppositions. But none of this has
193,1 anything to do with either Homer or Pythagoras, or with those competent to attain their truest doctrines. Those people are, then, certainly ridiculous who assert that because there are two middle notes between 12 and 6, 9 and 8, that epic verse has 17 syllables, or that the two middle
5   syllables are the causes of the line. For, as the saying goes, 'it is quite a different story with the Mysians'.[526] For even if metrical systems make use of numbers, as indeed they do, they are not constructed according to this method. And it is ridiculous to argue that the holes of the flute are as many as they are because of the letters of the alphabet, or to fit the twenty-four letters to the totality of the world. For if there is some single cause of these things, as indeed there is, then this is the subject of a different kind of study. But one ought not have recourse to the
10   failures of those who illegitimately claim to be Pythagoreans in order to discredit the whole philosophy.[527]

        1093b5-6 But one should see that nobody need have difficulty in saying such things, or discovering them, in the eternal realm, since they exist also among perishable things.

Since eternal things are ordered and are always the same, there is no difficulty, Aristotle says, in relation to them, in using the theorems of numbers, seeing that it is possible to conceive many such things even in relation to things whose states vary in time.[528]   15

But this should have been adequate testimony that eternal things are ordered according to certain divine numbers, and mortal things <according to>[529] psychic (?) and natural ones. For if eternal things are always in this state, they are like this according to nature. If therefore we speak the truth about them in grasping them in an arithmetical way, then, just as divine nature gave them existence, so do those who do genuine philosophy attempt to know them. Take one case: the sun   20 completes a cycle in a given time, and this always, so this is according to nature. But this time is a number of this sort, so nature has established it in existence in accordance with such a number, and the moon with such another number, and each of the heavenly beings likewise (not however in accordance with a mathematical number, but with a demiurgic and divine number, even if we can observe certain images of   25 it in mathematical numbers, on account of the fact that these secondary numbers are always dependent on the prior ones, proceeding according to the latter's distinctive property, by virtue of the latter manifesting themselves at the lowest orders of being). And as for mortal animals, to the extent that nature controls them (controlling them as it does for the most part and not always), to this extent are they organised in accord-   30 ance with appropriate numbers.

1093b7-21 But the vaunted characteristics of numbers, and the contraries of these, and in general the properties of mathematics, in the way that some people speak of them, making them causes of nature, all seem in this way to fade away, when one examines them from this perspective; for in none of the ways that we distinguished with respect to first principles is any of them a cause. As they posit things, however, it is clear that goodness is predicable of numbers, and that to the column of the fine belong the odd, the straight, equal times equal, and the powers of certain numbers; for the seasons are connected with a certain sort of number, and the other examples which they derive from mathematical theorems all have this same force. Thus they seem like coincidences; for they are accidental, but all the examples are appropriate to each other, and are united by analogy. For in each category of being there is analogy: as the straight is in length, so the level is in surfaces, and perhaps the odd in numbers, and white in colours.

He agrees that in numbers, figures, colours and in each class of thing are to be found the good and the opposite to the good, and likewise in nature. Yet still he does not account for what is better in nature by the   35 better column of number, but rather as in the case of the seasons of the year, he wants these to be prior and causes to a greater extent than number, and not numbers [causes] of the seasons.[530]   194,1

And it is quite reasonable that he should allow this, since he is thinking of 'later-born' numbers. Nevertheless one must ask him whence it is that the seasons are always the way they are. For it is either due to Zeus, or to the sun, or to some other demiurgic force. Surely it is thence that they are measured and ordered, according to the

5 productive power of numbers. But in general, for what reason should we not make a practice of welcoming what belongs to itself, prior to what is in another? Since to see the good inherent in each thing, and not to trace it back to its cause[531] and relate all things back to one principle [sc. the Good], from which comes what maintains for all things both their being in a certain way and their having proceeded according to the same proportion, is the attitude of one who disintegrates beings and forgets the saying that 'many rulers is not good'.[532] However, who would

10 not agree that there must be the one proportion (*logos*)[533] presupposed by things in analogy? But he denies this, thus involving himself in a situation that he gets into also in his discussions of physics,[534] where he posits that chance is not one cause uniting differing principles, but says that things happening by chance are coincidences and chance is a 'causeless cause'.[535] For which reason it comes about that there is much that is arbitrary and irrational in his thought, which indeed, by insinu-

15 ating itself, sunders the domination of all things by Intellect.[536]

1093b21-4 Furthermore, it is not the Form-numbers that are the causes of harmonic relations and of suchlike (for these, even when they are equal to each other, differ from each other in form, as do their units), so that for these reasons at least there is no call to posit forms.

This is said in rejection only of Form-numbers, which they say have uncombinable units,[537] and for this reason these exhibit a difference even in relation to equals, as for example the Three in that realm is not

20 the third part of the essential Nine, nor is it the half of the essential Six. If therefore, Aristotle says, Form-numbers are like this, they would not be the causes of harmonies, for in concords sounds that sound the same are equal, the top chord (*nêtê*) is double the lowest in tension, and in general 4 is half of 8 and 1 and 1/3[538] of 3, which assumes that the units in these are undifferentiated. His syllogism, then, is as follows: Form-

25 numbers have differing units; but the numbers which constitute harmonies do not have differing units; therefore Form-numbers do not constitute harmonies. So if anyone maintains that these numbers exist for this reason, he is wrong.[539]

But here again one must make the point in reply that Form-numbers are not unitary (*monadikoi*), unless someone wants to call their Forms

30 'monads' or 'henads', nor is it of harmonies in lyres that they are, immediately and without intermediaries, constitutive, but rather, perhaps, of the harmonies in divine souls and of those in the world as a

whole. And in general they say that it is from Form-numbers that there comes about the existence of the harmony of those things which the one and holistic Demiurge[540] is said to bring to existence in a unitary way, and to order and make concordant with himself and with each other.

1093b24-9 These then are the consequences of this theory, and perhaps yet more could be adduced. But it seems to be an indication of the fact that mathematicals are not separable from sensibles, as certain people claim, nor that these are principles, that many difficulties are experienced in explaining their generation, and that they have no way of connecting the various parts of their theory.   195,1

But I would take as an indication of the fact that these divine men have done philosophy in the finest, best and most irrefutable way that you, Aristotle, the most ingenious and productive of those on record, should experience such difficulties in controversy with them, having said nothing that might even be persuasive, not to say conclusive, or indeed anything relevant to them at all, but in most of what you say employing alien hypotheses, in no way appropriate to the doctrines of your elders, while in a number of instances, when proposing to make some point against their true doctrine, you fail to come to grips with them at all.[541]   5

*

These, then, are the criticisms that Aristotle brings in these books against the theories of the Pythagoreans and the Platonists, criticisms contained also in what is said in Book A, as indeed the commentator Alexander has pointed out. For this reason, in dealing with the former, we consider that we have not neglected also the latter, nor even the criticisms levelled against these men in his two books *On the Forms*.[542] For there also, Aristotle runs through almost the same arguments, so that we can take it that these also might be countered by the same means. We therefore will end our discourse by praying to the gods who are the guardians of philosophy. Of the many arguments that have been presented on either side, let there prevail in the readers' mind those that are more true and more pleasing to the gods.   10

    15

Notes

1. That is to say, the *Metaphysics*.

2. A reference to *Gorg.* 473B (Socrates to Polus): 'For truth can never be refuted.'

3. cf. *Tim.* 29B7-8.

4. *agônes* here may well refer literally to the attacks that Syrianus is about to launch on Aristotle, but it also has a technical sense in rhetorical theory, as Syrianus is well aware; cf. *in Herm.* 2,111 and 170 (Rabe). In rhetoric, *agônes* refer to the body of a controversial discourse, following upon the *prooimion*. In general, one may compare Syrianus' portrayal of his position here with the remarks of Simplicius near the beginning of his *Commentary on the Categories* (7,26-8,4 Kalbfleisch), though Simplicius adopts a less adversative attitude.

5. This whole passage, from the beginning of the book, has been well translated and commented upon by Saffrey, 1987.

6. *philengklêmôn*, quite a rare adjective, found first in Philo of Alexandria.

7. cf. Iambl. *DCMS* 10,8-11,7; 95,5-28.

8. That is to say, the level of Soul.

9. Or, 'discursively intellectual'.

10. This appears to be a reference to *Physics* 2.7, 198a24ff. (he is discussing the four causes): 'But in many cases three of these causes coincide; for the essential nature of a thing (*to ti esti*) and the purpose for which it is produced (*to hou heneka*) are often identical (so that the final cause coincides with the formal), and moreover the efficient cause must bear a resemblance in species to these.'

11. An apparent reference to *Tim.* 29E: 'Let us now state the cause for which he who established it established Becoming and this whole universe. He was good, and in him that is good no envy arises concerning anything.'

12. This seems to require some slight over-translation, and some exegesis. In Syrianus' elaborate metaphysical scheme, which he bequeaths to Proclus, the demiurgic function in the universe is proper to the lowest aspect of the realm of Intellect, the intellective hebdomad.

13. A reference here to *Phaedrus* 248B.

14. Syrianus here, rather oddly, uses a neuter singular (*to hêmeteron*); it seems most likely that something like *dianoêton* is to be understood.

15. A reference to *Phdr.* 246C, reading *meteôropolei* for *meteôroporei* – as does Iamblichus (*De Myst.* 2,15,219) and Proclus (*in Tim.* 2,240,5), but not Plotinus (*Enn.* 4.3.7,17; 4.8.2,20; 5.8.7,34).

16. Here he slightly amplifies the Platonic original (*sundioikei tois theois*, in place of the simple *dioikei* of *Phdr.* 246C2), an amplification repeated often by Proclus.

17. A reference here to the whole description of the Demiurge's fabrication of the soul in *Tim.* 34C-37C.

18. *Rep.* 6, 509C-511E.

19. Interestingly, Plato does not in this passage explicitly describe the objects of the third segment of the Line as *eikones* of the fourth, nor yet those of the third as *paradeigmata* for the second, though both of those relations are implied; rather, he uses the term *eikôn* to describe how the sciences make use of sense-objects (e.g. 510B3-4; E3).

20. e.g. 511A2; 511D4.

21. *Phd.* 72E: 'our learning is nothing else than recollection'. Plato does not, of course, specify that the forms concerned are of the 'discursive' variety.

22. This is a favoured Neoplatonic term for Aristotelian universals, as being concepts derivative from our sense-perceptions (cf. e.g. Procl. *in Parm.* 4,892-4 Cousin, a particularly enlightening passage, probably owing a lot to Syrianus; also 971,35ff.). It is used once by Aristotle himself, at *Met.* 14.4, 1091a33, in the course of a critique of the Platonists, but never to describe his own concept of universals.

23. This rare adverb occurs in Procl. *in Tim.* 3,243,10, in conjunction with *heniaia* (*teleiotês*).

24. Homer, *Iliad* 18.400-2. We have inserted the preceding line, which Syrianus does not quote, in order to provide an intelligible context. What we have here is an allegorical exegesis of the passage in which Hephaistos reminisces to Thetis about the time when his mother Hera tossed him out of Olympos, and he fell to earth and was taken in by Eurynome, daughter of Ocean, and Thetis herself, both sea-goddesses, and he made for them many fine ornaments. This symbolises his infusing of *logoi* into the material realm. Proclus also makes use of the allegory at *in Remp.* 1,141,4ff., a passage probably inspired by Syrianus.

25. This is a reference to the beginning of *Metaphysics* 13 (1076a16-19), where Aristotle distinguishes between those who make mathematical entities the primary substances (*ousiai*), and those who favour the Forms for this role. Syrianus now proceeds, for the rest of the introductory section, to engage in a critique of ch. 1 of Book 13, beginning his detailed commentary only with ch. 2.

26. This seems to be a reference to 13.1, 1076a17-19 ('Some say that mathematical entities, such as numbers and lines and things akin to these, are substances'), in which case it would seem to be Syrianus' strategy here to distance Aristotle himself from these views, by attributing them to *hoi polloi*. Aristotle's reference here is primarily to Speusippus.

27. sc. Plato and Pythagoras. The delinquent referred to here (and at 1076a21-2) is primarily Xenocrates.

28. That is to say, all levels of Form being termed in common 'the Form of *x*'.

29. That is to say, at 1076a19-20: 'some recognise these as two classes, the Forms and the mathematical numbers.'

30. This is our rendering of Syrianus' curious use of the third person imperative in this and the next sentence: 'let us grant that he ...' would be more literal.

31. Syrianus' quotation of this passage is interestingly inaccurate, as though he were quoting from memory, which he may very well be doing. It is notable, for one thing, that he uses *mathêmata* instead of *mathêmatika* for 'objects of mathematics'.

32. *skindapsos* and *blituri* were favourite examples among Hellenistic and later logicians for meaningless terms. cf. e.g. Sextus Empiricus, *AM* 8.133. We may note that the term occurs also in Hermeias, *in Phdr.* 180A, the contents of which are substantially Syrianic.

33. As mentioned in the Introduction (p. 21), it is the custom of Kroll, no doubt for reasons of space, to abbreviate lemmata of any length, but we follow the practice of the Coislianus, and presumably of Syrianus himself, in giving them in full, for the convenience of the reader.

34. The reference is back to Book 3, 998a7ff.

35. On Severus, see Dillon, *Middle Platonists*, 262-4. The 'illegitimate use' may perhaps refer to Severus' 'geometrical' interpretation of the soul's composition, for which see Iamblichus, *De Anima*, §4, 364,2-4 (Finamore-Dillon); but this does not in itself involve mathematical entities being immanent in physical objects. As to who Aristotle's real target was in this passage there is no consensus, but it is possible that such a man as Eudoxus might fit, since he seems to have held that Forms were immanent in physical things (cf. *Met.* 1.9, 991a16ff.)

36. The whole passage from 84,27 to 86,7 has been translated and discussed by Sambursky, 1982, 57-61, and Sorabji, 1988, 112-13.

37. As Julia Annas, 1976, 137-8 aptly remarks; 'The reference to B (998a7ff.) is not as straightforward as it appears, since the passage there argues against people who hold that the *intermediates* exist, but in physical objects. Aristotle is assuming without argument that an objection against one type of mathematical object will hold against all types that might be recognised by a Platonist.'

38. On the Stoic doctrine of total mixture, see e.g. *SVF* II, 473 (from Alexander of Aphrodisias, *On Mixture*).

39. Who these people might be is obscure, but Kroll acutely connects the theory with one put forward by Porphyry, as reported by Proclus in *in Remp.* 2,196,22ff., that the pillar of light described in *Rep.* 10, 616E may be identified with the pneumatic vehicle (*okhêma*) of the World Soul, which pervades the whole body of the cosmos, interpenetrating everything. See Sambursky's discussion ad loc.

40. This is a rather rough rendering of the force of *logos* here: the meaning is more like 'projected concept', i.e. Form projected onto a lower level of consciousness than intellect.

41. We apologise for the proliferation of transliterations here, but we are dealing with technicalities of doctrine. On the connection between *phantasia*, *pneuma*, and *dianoia* in the doctrine of the Athenian School from Plutarchus on, see H.J. Blumenthal, 'Plutarch's Exposition of the *De Anima* and the Psychology of Proclus', in *De Jamblique à Proclus, Entretiens sur l'Antiquité Classique*, 21, ed. H. Dörrie, Vandoeuvres-Genève: Fondation Hardt, 1975, 123-47, esp. 133ff.

42. sc. the Pythagoreans and Platonists. For the Neoplatonic tradition on this point, see also J. Finamore, 'Iamblichus on Light and the Transparent', pp. 55-65 in H.J. Blumenthal and E.G. Clark (eds), *The Divine Iamblichus*, London, 1993.

43. That is to say, 'solid' (*sterea*) in the mathematical sense.

44. This is presumably a reference to the pneumatic vehicles which serve to connect the soul to the body. The adducing of light as an example of an immaterial essence is interesting, and recalls the doctrine of Plotinus and of Iamblichus: cf. Finamore, 1993.

45. That is to say, at the beginning of the lemma, 84,20ff. above.

46. This is an interesting Neoplatonic concept. As constituting a bridge between the immaterial soul and the material body, it must be taken as being itself 'half-material', composed of the finest form of fire, and so notionally three-dimensionally extended, to at least some extent.

47. The sense of *daimonios* (as opposed to *theios*), when applied to Aristotle by Neoplatonic authors, usually expresses qualified respect, but here seems more than a little ironic.

48. Accepting here Usener's suggestion, *dianoêtois*, for filling a small lacuna.

49. That is, at 998a12-14; though, as Julia Annas points out, ad loc., Aristotle's arguments there are in fact slightly different.

50. i.e. mathematical points.

51. If that is the sense of *diairetikos* here.

52. *apeira* is found after *genê* in many, though not all, MSS of Aristotle, but not in the text of Syrianus. However, *genê* seems incomplete without an epithet of some sort.

53. A reference to pp. 12,28ff. and 50,4ff. above.

54. sc. at the level of Soul.

55. This seems to be sense of *skômma,* lit. 'mockery', here.

56. That is to say, in Book 3, 997b12-39.

57. A particular application of the originally Numenian principle (fr. 41 Des Places), but adopted by all Neoplatonists, 'all things in all things, but in each in a manner appropriate to each'.

58. Adopting Usener's suggestion *prostithemenos* for *tithemenos* of the MSS, since *tais ideais* is in the dative.

59. This is presumably the sense of *pragma* here, in opposition to *sumperasma.*

60. The most senior follower of Plotinus (*c.* 220-290 AD). Cf. Plotinus, *Enn.* 5.1.1, 1, which Amelius would seem to be summarising here.

61. The lemma in the MSS here only includes the first sentence, but the comment concerns the whole passage, and the next lemma continues from the end of it, so it seems best to include it.

62. sc. of the *Timaeus,* 30C.

63. That is to say, the Chaldaean Oracles, fr. 8 Des Places.

64. Actually the reference should be to *Lambda,* 1072b29 – a strange error for Syrianus to make! 'K' may, of course, be a scribal error.

65. The reference is probably to Book 10.7 (1177a12ff.), where Syrianus could draw the conclusion that man in the truest sense is to be identified with his *nous.*

66. Literally, 'drawn', in the case of geometrical proofs. The first six lines of this comment are actually taken from the commentary of Alexander of Aphrodisias (cf. ps.-Alex. 729,21-7).

67. Diels plausibly reads *katôtera* for the *koilotera* of the MSS, which would mean 'more hollow'. But one might cite several places where Proclus, at least, appears to use *koilotera* in an idiomatic way to mean 'inferior', for instance *in Alc.* 167,12 and *in Parm.* 874,18. I am indebted to Michael Griffin for these parallels.

68. The reference is to *An. Post.* 1.4, 73b39.

69. Presumably on both seeing a figure in the distance.

70. cf. *DA* 3.5, 430a19-20.

71. Or reason-principle?

72. That is to say, the Sun, in the simile of *Rep.* 6, 507Aff.

73. Syrianus here employs an interesting triadic division of reality, with Intellect in the middle, reminiscent of that of Julian in his *Hymn to King Helios,* with Helios-Mithras in the middle position between the Good and the physical sun (cf. esp. 137C-140D). The phrase *polytimêtos nous* is distinctive; used by Syrianus earlier, at 25,4, and frequently by Proclus (e.g. *in Alc.* 247,9; *in Tim.* 1,404,6 (Diehl); *PT* 1.19, 93,13 S-W). It seems to be originally an epithet of divinities, but its immediate provenance is obscure.

74. Syrianus, like many modern commentators, is plainly somewhat confused (and excusably so) as to what Aristotle means by this argument.

75. Who are 'we' here, and in the following lines? In the context, it seems more probable that Syrianus is not referring to 'we Platonists/Pythagoreans', but rather speaking rhetorically, in the person of Aristotle.

76. This is a good Aristotelian principle, cf. *Top.* 6.4, 1412b8ff.; *Met.* 11.1, 1059b30ff.

77. *husterogenes,* lit. 'later-born', a term originating with Aristotle (e.g. *Met.* 14, 1091a33, but commonly used in later Platonism as a term for Aristotelian universals. Syrianus uses the term fully nineteen times in this commentary.

78. In the context, this may refer either to Plato or to Pythagoras.

79. That is to say, presumably, geometry.

80. This verb, and its corresponding noun *parhupostasis,* refers to the occurrence of a secondary or accidental quality or feature of a given entity. Cf. 105,3, 107,8 and 185,21 below.

81. This seems to be more or less the sense of *logoi* here.

82. A board spread with sand, on which geometrical calculations could be made.

83. It is not clear what Syrianus is referring to here; perhaps 1076b11ff.?

84. Accepting here Usener's tentative filling of a small lacuna.

85. This also seems to be a reference to 1076b11ff.

86. Presumably Syrianus is referring to the 'pneumatic vehicle'.

87. *homose khôrôn*: Syrianus here borrows a poetical phrase made use of by Plato in various contexts, but specifically at *Tht.* 165E, where Socrates is envisaging a sophistic attack by Protagoras.

88. cf. Plato, *Tim.* 34C.

89. Kroll refers this to ch. 10, 1034b20-1036a26, but chs 4-5 (1030a17-1031a14) seem relevant also.

90. i.e. a geometrical one, such as a triangle or square.

91. For the concept of mathematical, or intelligible, matter in Aristotle, cf. *Met.* 7.10, 1036a9-12: 'Some matter is sensible and some intelligible; sensible, such as bronze and wood and all movable matter; intelligible, that which is present in sensible things not *qua* sensible, e.g. the objects of mathematics'.

92. *touto proharpasas*: once again, Syrianus borrows a significant phrase from Plato to make his point. Plato employed this verb in the *Gorgias* (454C2) to characterise the sort of disorderly argumentation that is distinctive of sophists.

93. Adopting a suggestion of Kroll for sorting out a corruption here. An anacoluthon, however, still remains.

94. It is plain that Syrianus would make a break here, rather than at 1177b18 (corresponding to the modern ch. 3), since he runs the next lemma through to 1178a14.

95. It is probably necessary, for the sake of Syrianus' argument, to translate *logoi* here as something like 'reason-principles', regardless of the fact that Aristotle is talking simply about definitions.

96. Reading *prolêpsin* for *perilêpsin*, with Usener.

97. Syrianus actually includes here what in modern editions are the last few lines of the previous chapter (1107b15-18), but they can in fact just as well introduce the next one.

98. Reading *prôtôs* for *prôtôi*, in accordance with the suggestion of Kroll (though there is little difference in meaning, after all).

99. Syrianus is, of course, indulging in irony here.

100. Rendering here the Platonic phrase *mê oude themiton êi*.

101. Presumably the sense of *polupragmôn* here.

102. This last phrase is composed from an amalgam of *Rep.* 7, 527E with 533D.

103. A nice rhetorical flourish here: Syrianus echoes in reverse the passages from *Rep.* 7 just quoted, to point up the difference between the Platonic theory of Forms and the Aristotelian theory of abstraction.

104. This corresponds to nothing in the commentary of ps.-Alex.

105. Since Syrianus chooses to talk of *ideai* here, rather than *eidê*, it seems best to follow him in making a distinction.

106. cf. Nicomachus, *Intro. Arith.* 1,3,6.

107. The use of this rare compound, *huposulaô*, is something of a rhetorical flourish.

108. In the technical sense of the form's projection at the level of soul.

109. *anelittein*, lit. 'unroll', being the technical term for what the soul does with the *logoi* or forms within it.

110. Usener is suspicious of the use of *philosophia* here to describe a particular science (instead of *epistêmê*), and we agree. It is best viewed as a slightly inept gloss.

111. This is presumably the meaning of *kat' auton*, 'on its own'.

112. Presumably the meaning of *phusikoi logoi* here.

113. cf. *Rep*. 6, 508E.

114. A reference to 993b30ff., where Aristotle says; 'Therefore in every case the first principles of things must necessarily be true above everything else – since they are not merely *sometimes* true, nor is anything the cause of their existence, but they are the cause of the existence of other things – and so as each thing is in respect of existence, so it is in respect of truth'. This constitutes a nice polemical use of Aristotle against himself.

115. That is to say, ratios.

116. This entity is presumably the same as the *augoeides okhêma* mentioned above, at 86,3. It is held by Syrianus and his successors to be the proper seat of *phantasia*.

117. The reference seems to be, not to *An. Post*. 1.7, 75b15ff., as suggested by Kroll, where Aristotle simply says that the propositions of optics are subordinate to those of geometry, but rather to *Phys*. 2.2, 194a8ff., where he says: 'The point is further illustrated by those sciences which are rather physical than mathematical, though combining both disciplines, such as optics, harmonics, and astronomy; for the relations between them and geometry are, so to speak, reciprocal; since geometry deals with physical lines, but not *qua* physical, whereas optics deals with mathematical lines, but *qua* physical, not *qua* mathematical'. In this passage, we may note, Aristotle is also criticising 'those who posit the Forms' (194a1). The problem with this reference, however, is that Aristotle is precisely saying that optics, in contrast to geometry, treats mathematical lines as physical, which is the opposite of what Syrianus attributes to him here. He may be quoting from memory. It must be said, though, that elsewhere (at *An. Post*. 1.13-14, 78b32-79a24), Aristotle confuses matters, and gives some support to Syrianus here, by using *optikos* to mean the 'mathematical optician', i.e. someone doing optics as a branch of geometry; indeed he confesses (78b39-79a6) that the terminology is ambiguous.

118. That is to say, the structure (*skhêma*) inherent in a given substratum, and one not thus inherent.

119. That is to say, Alexander. This would seem to refer to a lost comment of his on this part of the *Metaphysics*. Alexander is here taking a position on the meaning of Aristotle's enigmatic remark in the last sentence of this lemma, that things exist in one of two senses, 'either in actuality or as matter'. The contrast that Aristotle is seeking to make is by no means clear, but from the context it would seem that he means by 'as matter' (*hulikôs*), 'as raw material for study, sc. by the mathematical sciences'. In this case, Alexander would be correct, as against his teacher Aristoteles, just below; but it is interesting to observe this difference of opinion, from which Syrianus profits.

120. This is a reference to the Peripatetic Aristoteles of Mytilene, one of the teachers of Alexander (cf. Simpl. *in Cael*. 153,16-18), on whom see P. Moraux, *Der Aristotelismus bei den Griechen*, II, 399-425.

121. The insertion of an *ê* seems required before *hôs* here, since it is the interpretation of Aristoteles of Mytilene that Syrianus is commending, albeit ironically.

122. This whole passage corresponds to pp. 739,21-740,1 of the commentary of ps.-Alexander, which seems to suggest that Syrianus is using Alexander here. But cf. also Iambl. *DCMS* 47,1-6 and 55,22-6, which Syrianus probably also has in mind.

123. This sentence is normally included by modern editors as the opening of the following chapter, but it can just as well be seen as a conclusion to chapter 3, which is how Syrianus seems to have taken it, so we follow him in that.

124. The whole passage following, down to 102,35, appears in the Greek as one vast, unwieldy sentence, which I have ventured to break up somewhat, but it is still pretty dreadful. It constitutes a kind of prospectus for Pythagorean mathematics, closely following Iamblichus in *DCMS* 3,6-8,6, as Syrianus acknowledges in a general way at the end of the section (though he claims also to be relying on Nicomachus).

125. Reading *holôn* here, to accord with Iambl. *DCMS*, 3,11, instead of the MSS *hoion*, which does not make much sense in the circumstances.

126. This does not seem to relate to any fragment of 'Archytas' preserved elsewhere, but it sounds as if what we have here is a document purporting to be the original from which Plato took his image of the Divided Line. cf. Iambl. *DCMS* 35,27ff. Syrianus refers to Archytas also at 151,19 and 165,13, but not in such a way as to throw any light on this passage.

127. This being a reference to *Timaeus* 35Aff., and Timaeus Locrus, 96Aff., respectively. It is the latter place that 'mathematical *logoi*' are explicitly referred to.

128. That is to say, etymologising *mathematikê* as 'having to do with learning'.

129. I would accept here Usener's suggested reading *poiêtikais* for *noêtikais*. It makes little sense to talk of 'intelligible' *tekhnai*, as distinct from theoretical ones, while the distinction between 'productive' and 'practical' is common and important.

130. Syrianus here employs a verbatim quotation of *Rep.* 7, 527D-E, which refers to the 'preliminary sciences' as a whole. cf. Iambl. *DCMS* 22,20-3.

131. That is, Nicomachus of Gerasa (fl. *c.* 150 AD) on whom see Dillon, *Middle Platonists*, 352-61. His *Introduction to Arithmetic* and *Manual of Harmonics* are still extant.

132. Not absolutely obvious to a modern reader, I think; but the mention of 'more intellectual theorisings' (*noerôterai epibolai*) certainly seems to point to Iamblichus being the latter.

133. This heading actually occurs in the manuscripts.

134. A quotation from the Orphic poems, popular in the Pythagorean tradition, cf. Iambl. *VP* 162,118,13 (Nauck). Syrianus quotes it again later at 122,33-4.

135. A quotation of Homer, *Odyssey* 20.45.

136. A quotation of Apollonius Rhodius, *Argonautica* 2.755.

137. Syrianus is essaying an etymology on the basis of a stem *ar-*, 'to fit together' – which may in fact not be altogether groundless, unlike most ancient Greek etymologies.

138. The reference here is presumably to the dialogue rather than the person – though the reference to the *Cratylus* is expressed somewhat differently.

139. A reference to *Tht.* 151Eff.

140. Accepting Usener's suggested filling of a small lacuna here – <*hên eristikên*>.

141. The reference is, necessarily, to 597Aff., where the Form of Bed is presented as inhering in the mind of God – the fact that it is a Form of *bed* does not bother Syrianus in the present context.

142. This of course is the Parmenides of Plato, not the Parmenides of real life. The reference is to *Parm* 135B.

143. If this is the meaning of the obscure phase *pros tên khrêsin tês tôn onomatôn sunêtheias*. Presumably what is being referred to is the Stoic theory of what is denoted by a name, i.e. a *lekton*, or 'sayable', defined as 'what subsists in accordance with a rational impression' (*SVF* II, 187).

144. Archedemus of Tarsus, a post-Chrysippan Stoic, often linked in the sources with Chrysippus, as having written on the same topics. Cf. *SVF* III, 262-4.

145. cf. n. 77 on 91,30 above.

146. The reference here seems necessarily to be to the individual intellect, rather than to the hypostasis, but it is true *a fortiori* of the latter.

147. Head of the Academy in Athens in the mid-third century. On this (for a Platonist) remarkable theory of his, cf. L. Brisson and M. Patillon, 'Longinus Platonicus Philosophus et Philologus', *ANRW* II, 36, 7 (1994), 5214-99.

148. The implication here being that what is *noêton* is necessarily prior to what intelligises it.

149. An obscure but interesting figure, a disciple of Ammonius Saccas, who is also reported by Proclus (*in Tim.* 2,154,4-9 Diehl) as postulating a pair of Intellects prior to Soul, one containing the Forms of universals, the other of particulars, and situating the Soul as median between these two, as drawing its substance from both of them. Proclus derives his information on him from Porphyry, who related that Antoninus attributed this doctrine to the Persians. How that doctrine accords with this one, however, is not easy to see.

150. If this is the meaning of *kata tas ennoêtikas ideas*. The terminology is most opaque. Could it simply mean 'in the form of conceptual ideas'?

151. This last is an obscure third-century Platonist, mentioned also by Porphyry (*V. Plot.* 20), Iamblichus, *De Anima* §13, and Damascius, *in Phd.* p. 193,30 Norvin. Iamblichus credits him with attributing the irrational faculties to the essence of the soul, in contradistinction to Plotinus.

152. This presumably refers to the *phantasia;* cf. 110,32-3 below, where it is equated with the *pathêtikos nous*.

153. A reference to *Phdr.* 249BC.

154. Boethus of Sidon, a pupil of Andronicus of Rhodes, flourished in the late first century BC. He commented on Aristotle's *Categories*, in which context this judgement could have been uttered. On him see Moraux, *Der Aristotelismus bei den Griechen*, I, 143-96.

155. L. Annaeus Cornutus, Stoic philosopher, a freedman of Seneca, flourished in the mid-first century AD. He is also attested by Simplicius to have commented on the *Categories*, e.g. *in Cat.* 18,28; 62,27; 129,1.

156. That is to say, as the Pythagorean Tetraktys, which develops into the Decad at its lower manifestation.

157. There follows a quotation from the Orphic Hymn to Number (fr. 315 Kern). The passage is quoted also at Procl. *in Remp.* 2,169,24ff. (Kroll), *in Tim.* 2,53,2ff., 3,107,12ff., and 3,301,30ff. (Diehl) (where it is described as a *Pythagorean* hymn).

158. With this catalogue of things of which there are *not* Forms, cf. the exposition of Proclus, in *in Parm.* 3,815-33 (Cousin), a passage which doubtless owes much to Syrianus.

159. Accepting, provisionally, Diels' conjecture *mataioumenês* for the meaningless *meteuomenês*. The only problem with this verb is that its usage seems virtually confined to the LXX.

160. If that is what is meant by *psukhikê prohairesis*.

161. It would be odd, I think, if this were a disapproving reference to Plotinus' alleged theory of Forms of individuals, but it hard to see to whom else Syrianus can be referring.

162. This is, presumably, the distinction between the *numerus numerans* and the *numerus numeratus*, which corresponds to the distinction between 'monadic' and 'physical' number.

163. A verb would seem to have fallen out here. Kroll proposes *anereunêsai*, which gives the required text, and which we translate here. Usener suggested altering *melloimen* to *metioimen*, which would give more or less the same meaning.

164. This meaning of the adjective *asuntaktos*, as 'not ranked on the same level as', seems to go back no further than Iamblichus, who is credited by Damascius (*De Princ.* §43, 1,86,3ff. Ruelle) with characterising his second One as *asuntaktos pros tên triada*, 'unconnected with the triad' (sc. of limit, unlimitedness, and their product). Syrianus employs the word also at p. 11,29 above.

165. A detail: for the *kath' hekaston* ('corresponding to each') of the MSS, Syrianus reads *par' hekaston*. If anything, this slightly emphasises the transcendence of the Forms, though Aristotle uses *para* just below, in *para tas ousias*.

166. This point is made by Alexander much earlier, at *in Met.* 77,12, but that does not exclude the possibility that he made it again in connexion with this passage (no corresponding passage in ps.-Alex., however).

167. Presumably this refers to non-substantial particulars, such as instances of a quality.

168. That is to say, presumably, what is their *essence*, and what is their *quality*. For this quartet of questions, cf. Arist. *An. Post.* 2.1.

169. A small lacuna here, plausibly filled by Usener from a parallel passage in Proclus, *in Tim.* 3,33,16ff. (Iambl. *in Tim.* fr. 64 Dillon) – a passage which probably itself owes much to Syrianus. The lacuna was doubtless caused by haplology between *aisthêta* and *aisthêta*.

170. All this is, of course, a formalised version of the argument in the *Timaeus*, 29-31.

171. A necessary supplement by Bonitz.

172. Primarily the mathematical sciences. It may seem strange, at first sight, to deny *proper* scientific status to medicine, but after all, one cannot become involved in granting real existence to such 'universals' as gout, or diphtheria.

173. sc. in *De Anima* 3.3-4.

174. Following a suggestion of Usener that *geitonos*, 'neighbouring', which is standing on its own in the MSS, needs some opposite.

175. *periekhon*, lit. 'containing', but a logical term for what is more universal.

176. Again, there is no parallel passage in ps.-Alexander.

177. Or 'species'? It is not clear what the significance of the variation between *idea* and *eidos* is here.

178. If this is the sense of *suneispheromenon* here.

179. Accepting Usener's suggestion of *eidopepoiêmena* for the *pepoiêmena* of the MSS. The latter makes sense, but is not really what Syrianus wants to say here, which is that the Monad grants unity and coherence to all things which possess *form*.

180. e.g. *Enn.* 2.6.3,1-6; 4.7.9,19-21; 6.6.5,18-20.

181. A reference to 1.10, 1059a2ff., where Aristotle declares that such attributes as 'perishable' and 'imperishable' cannot be accidental (*kata sumbebêkos*); 'for that which is accidental may not be applicable to its subject, but perishability is an attribute which applies necessarily when it is applicable at all'.

182. A reference to *Ep.* 7, 342B-D.

183. This characterisation of Aristotle as *daimonios*, as opposed to Plato, who is *theios*, is entirely in accord with later Neoplatonic practice. The reference is to Book 8.3, 1043b25-32, where Aristotle states that there cannot be a definition of the primary constituents of a compound, since they are simple substances. Syrianus is giving a somewhat tendentious interpretation of this here.

184. *Eidos* is used here not in the sense of Platonic Form, but simply of 'shape' or 'appearance'.

185. Reading *hapasi* for *hapasês*, as suggested by Kroll.

186. That is to say, the heavenly bodies.

187. The reference is to *Parm*. 135B-C, though he does not there use the expression '*eye* of the mind'. That is borrowed from *Rep*. 7, 533D.

188. Presumably a reference to 100Bff.

189. In fact, the position of Eudoxus is of considerable interest, since he tried to counter objections (perhaps from Aristotle) against the causal efficacy of transcendent Forms by arguing for their inherence in particulars.

190. Reading *têi epistêmêi*, as suggested by Kroll, for *tês epistêmês* of the MSS.

191. This seems to be the meaning of *phantastôs kai morphôtikôs* here, sc. 'assuming them to have shape'.

192. *Tim*. 39E. We may note here, by the way, a nice example of 'mirror quotation' by Syrianus: he reverses the *hoiai kai hosai*, and *toiautas kai tosautas* of Plato's text.

193. Here once again I am tempted to accept Usener's (albeit palaeographically rather bold) emendation of the MSS *kat' autôn* (which means little, if anything) to *kai tou aidiou*, on the analogy of a parallel triad of attributes listed just below, at 118,13.

194. At *Phaedr*. 245E. However, Plato here, of course, is referring to Soul, not to the Forms.

195. This seems to involve a creative interpretation of *Met*. 12.8, 1073b2ff.: 'Thus it is clear that the movers are substances, and that one of them is first and another second and so on in the same order as the spatial motions of the heavenly bodies'.

196. On this problem, see Theophrastus, *Met*. 5a15-21; Plotinus, *Enn*. 5.1.9,7-27.

197. Here I would agree that *tôn ontôn* of the MSS is rather feeble, just following *tois teleutaiois tôn ontôn* in the first half of the sentence, and would consequently prefer either Usener's *tôn ontôs ontôn*, or Kroll's *tôn holôn*, 'of the universe'.

198. This is a valuable testimony to the doctrine of Amelius on the mode of participation by sensible individuals in the Forms, if only one could decide what exactly the doctrine is. It seems as if three levels of influence are being described, of progressive degrees of remoteness, but this depends on our taking *mallon homoiousthai* in the third clause, in respect of the intelligibles, as describing a remoter relation than *emphasis*.

199. A reference, presumably, to 100D in particular, and 96A-105B in general.

200. Syrianus plainly takes the sentence with what follows, and so as the beginning of the next chapter, rather than as the end of the previous chapter, as do modern editors.

201. Syrianus' use here of the diminutive *epikheirêmatia* (absent from LSJ!) is notable, as giving an edge to his sarcasm.

202. sc. at the beginning of ch. 2 above.

203. The text is certainly defective here, since *ei estin autoarithmos kai mê phusis allê hôn arithmeitai* gives quite the wrong sense. Kroll's proposal, *kainê* for *kai mê*, however, is pretty desperate. Syrianus is plainly closely paraphrasing Aristotle's text here, which runs: *eiper estin ho arithmos phusis tis kai mê allê tis estin autou hê ousia alla tout' auto*, so the solution must lie somewhere in there. We have contented ourselves, however, with translating more or less what the sense must be.

204. cf. Nicomachus' definition of number, *Intro. Ar.* 1,7,1.

205. Accepting Kroll's suggestion of the addition of *pasi* here.

206. Accepting Kroll's suggestion of *aulous* for MSS *autous*.

207. cf. ps.-Alex. *in Met.* 745,23-35. This is a significant passage for indicating the relation between Syrianus and ps.-Alexander, and their common dependence on Alexander. See Introduction, pp. 8-11.

208. Alexander is using the *hoi peri X* formula to refer to Xenocrates here, but it is unlikely that he means more than simply 'Xenocrates'.

209. Syrianus says here *kata tous arithmous,* but the Pythagoreans asserted that they were made *out of* numbers.

210. Quoted also at p. 103,21 above. See note ad loc.

211. 164,27-32 (Thesleff).

212. cf. Thesleff, 150, n. 1. It is not quite clear how far this is intended as a verbatim quotation. Only *kratisteuoisan* ('dominant') is presented in Doric, and accordingly Kroll confines the 'quotation' to that, but the whole phrase plainly presents at least the substance of what 'Philolaus' said. The definition appears previously in Iambl. *in Nic.* 10 (Pistelli). On the whole issue of Plato's dependence on the Pythagorean tradition, Saffrey and Westerink have a useful note to Proclus, *PT* 1.5 (n. 3 on I pp. 138-9).

213. Here Kroll (following Bagnoli), with plausibility, brackets a sentence, 'This is the only sort (sc. of number) and it is absolutely transcendent, and mathematical number is the same as this', as being a gloss on what follows.

214. That is to say, in *Tim.* 35Bff.

215. There is plainly some corruption in the MSS here, signalled by Kroll. We have adopted Usener's rather speculative substitution of *prohuparkhein* for *pros sumpatheian,* but are by no means certain of having extracted the correct meaning.

216. The reference here is to Xenocrates and his theory of indivisible lines, cf. fr. 46 (Heinze)/ 146-7 (Isnardi Parente).

217. The phrase *matên spathatai* is remarkable, and sounds very like a quotation, either from comedy or from oratory. We may note that Aristophanes uses the verb at *Clouds* 55, and Demosthenes at *De Fals. Leg.* 43. Either may have influenced Syrianus, but the latter is more likely.

218. That is to say, made up of units.

219. The additional assumption for Aristotle, we may note, is that 'every number is unitary', and for the Pythagoreans it is 'there is such a thing as a Form-number'.

220. A *dia triôn logos* is an argument with three conditionals; it takes the form 'If *p* then *q*; if *q, r*; therefore, if *p, r*'. (We are indebted to Robert Sharples for this specification.)

221. We require a third clause here by way of conclusion, which may have dropped out of the text, or may simply have been omitted by Syrianus as being obvious – or rather, by Alexander before him, since the parallel passage of ps.-Alex (748,20-2) omits it also.

222. Syrianus here uses *sustoikhiai* in the plural, but the reference is to the Pythagorean Table of Opposites.

223. There appears to be something missing here.

224. Presumably a reference to the second hypothesis of the *Parmenides* (142Bff.), where Syrianus, followed by Proclus, discerns an initial triad comprised of One, Being and their Otherness from one another. Cf. Proclus' discussion in *Theol. Plat.* IV 31, and Damascius, *De Princ.* §48, p. 17, 1-17 W-C.

225. The *megista genê* of the *Sophist*, which the Neoplatonists, ever since Plotinus (*Enn.* 6.6), ranked at the summit of the intelligible world.

226. This sounds Chaldaean in origin (in particular the verb *proethrôskon*). It is not, however, recognised by Des Places. We have translated *ikhnê sômatos ousai* as 'bearing the marks of body', but a more literal translation would be simply 'being traces of body', which makes little sense, unless one takes *ikhnê* rather in the sense of 'foreshadowings'.

227. Added, correctly, by Usener.

228. As Kroll notes, one would expect here *eis tên monada* instead of the MSS *ek tês monados,* and we translate that. The MS reading is very probably a scribal error, influenced by the previous phrase.

229. We take *par' autois* to refer to the higher sort of numbers.

230. This lemma corresponds, apart from the final comment, to ps.-Alex. 750,27-34.

231. We take it that we are talking about the Form of Two, rather than the archetypal Dyad, so that we refrain from using the term 'dyad'.

232. This section corresponds to ps.-Alex. 752,5-14.

233. The rare verb *athurô* is normally poetical, but occurs occasionally in late prose. It turns up, notably, in a similar context in Proclus, *in Parm.* 1106,21, where the influence of Syrianus may be discerned. See also Proclus, *Plat. Theol.* 5,128,25-7 with *in Parm.* 982,16; 1040,32; and 1106,21.

234. I adopt here ps.-Alex's version of the text (with *autois* for *heautois*), as that of Syrianus (omitting *heautois* and changing *ginomenôn* into *diagignomenôn*) is less clear. We seem to have here a nice example of ps.-Alex. (as we should expect) staying closer than Syrianus to the text of Alexander. Any alternative, such as ps.-Alex. altering either Alexander or Syrianus, seems considerably less plausible.

235. This section of the comment is paralleled by ps.-Alex. 752,19-21.

236. Syrianus is plainly interpreting this 'one' and 'two' spoken of by Aristotle as the Monad and Dyad following upon the primal One in his own system.

237. The whole section of commentary down to here is paralleled in ps.-Alex. 752,33-753,8.

238. Or, 'the Dyad which is a principle'.

239. That is to say, the Indefinite Dyad.

240. Usener feels that this should refer, not to Aristotle himself, but rather to Alexander of Aphrodisias (cf. ps.-Alex. 753,17), and thus proposes to read *Alexandros* before *men*. This is a persuasive suggestion; certainly something would seem to be needed before *men*, whether a proper noun or a pronoun (*autos*). On the other hand, the sentence does refer to Aristotle's following remarks.

241. This whole comment corresponds to ps.-Alex. 753,11-17, but, again, with an indication (if Usener is right), that Syrianus is using Alexander.

242. This whole comment, apart from the last sentence, is paralleled in ps.-Alex. 753,21-754,1, though Syrianus' version is somewhat compressed.

243. That is to say, 216, which the Pythagoreans also identified as the period of years elapsing between incarnations. Cf. the fragments of Iamblichus in O'Meara, *Pythagoras Revived*, p. 220 (ll. 48ff.).

244. The text is undoubtedly somewhat corrupt here. We would accept Usener's suggestion of *hôs hupokeimenon ... noeitai* (with a small lacuna), for *the hôs apokeimenon noei de* of the MSS. We would suggest also a *gar* after *noeitai*. The general sense is clear enough, however.

245. Primarily, the Pythagoreans.

246. On these examples, cf. ps.-Alex. 757,14-16.

247. cf. 101C, where Socrates argues that there is no other cause of becoming two than participation in Twoness.

248. cf. Iambl. *in Nic.* 77,21-25; 86,27.

249. A reference both to the cosmogonies of Hesiod and 'Orpheus', and to the myth of demiurgic creation in the *Timaeus*.

250. It is not quite clear what S. means by *oikeiois eidesi tou merismou*; we presume his meaning to be that, even if you mentally divide something up, you must envisage it being divided into *something else* (which has a form of its own), not into something indefinite and formless.

251. If this is the meaning of the unique compound *prometron*.

252. Reading *dekada* here for *duada*, as suggested by Kroll.

253. That is to say, the Peripatetics.

254. There should not strictly be such a thing as a Form of Inequality (*eidos anisotêtos*), but Syrianus refers to such an entity again just below, so we must assume that he means to postulate it.

255. The two previous sentences are borrowed from Alexander, cf. ps.-Alex. 762,3-11. In fact, the Alexander passage probably runs from the beginning of the lemma.

256. This presumably the meaning of the phrase *kata meridas*; see Ross's note ad loc. (p. 440).

257. Reading *ousian* for *auto* with Usener, on the basis of the parallel passage in ps.-Alex., since *auto* really makes no sense.

258. All the foregoing is taken from Alexander, cf. ps.-Alex. 762,17-763,3.

259. The correct MS reading here is *posopoion,* but Syrianus appears to have read *poson poion,* which causes some slight confusion in his exegesis below.

260. Presumably One and Two.

261. We take this to be the meaning of *sunegnôsmenos* in the context.

262. This remark is a consequence of Syrianus' false reading *poson poion,* as mentioned above.

263. For all this passage, cf. Iambl. *in Nic.* 11,1-16.

264. This would seem, on the basis of a comparison with *in Metaph.* 45,20 above, to be a term for Nature. Iamblichus, at *in Nic.* 11,8-9, attributes the formulation to 'the Chrysippeans'.

265. From the Orphic (or Pythagorean) *Hymn to Number* (fr. 315 Kern). Cf. 106,16ff. above.

266. This is one of the lost books of Iamblichus' *Compendium of Pythagorean Doctrine, On Arithmetic in Theological Matters*, the content of which is partially preserved in Michael Psellus' *On Numbers*. See O'Meara, *Pythagoras Revived*, 30-101 (text on p. 226, ll. 70-80).

267. This is generally agreed by modern scholars to be an attack on Speusippus. Syrianus, however, is not prepared to recognise it as being directed against any real opponent.

268. Modern scholars feel that this refers exclusively to Xenocrates, Speusippus having been dealt with above, at 1083a20-7. Syrianus, however, does not feel that anyone fills that bill.

269. The text seems to be confused here. We read: *ton te eidêtikon arithmon <kai ton mathêmatikon ton> ekhonta ....* Some haplography has plainly taken place, imperfectly corrected by inserting the meaningless *hekton ton mathêmatikon* after *poiei* in l. 31.

270. This might not at first sight seem particularly implausible, but Syrianus presumably means that, while the Demiurge *imposes* number, in the form of the basic triangles, on Matter, he does not himself have a mathematical *hexis*.

271. Accepting the suggestion of Usener to read *hê autê* before *theôria*.

272. Reading *heterou* here for *hekaterou,* as suggested by Kroll.

273. We find this definition, and the following one, preserved in Iamblichus' *Commentary on Nicomachus' Introduction to Arithmetic*, 10,12ff. Pistelli – as correctly discerned by the scholiast ad loc.

274. We would be inclined to read *kata* before *taxin aluton*. The bare accusative is difficult to construe. However, Iamblichus (loc. cit.) has the same construction, though with the verb *diêrithmêmena* for Syrianus' *diêrthrômena*.

275. These definitions also are taken from Iamblichus, *in Nic.* loc. cit.

276. That is to say, numbers as operative in nature.

277. *Gorg.* 473B, quoted also above, 81,3; and cf. 131,8.

278. The *bômiskos,* or 'little altar', was a solid number with all its dimensions unequal, bounded by rectangles and trapezia. The *bômiskos* of 210 is made up of 2 x 3 x 5 x 7. This does not, however, correspond to the numbers given by Syrianus here. The total of 210 could only be arrived at from these numbers if one first added the one to the nine, and then multiplied. The correct numbers, 5 x 6 x 7, are found in Iamblichus, ap. Psellus, see O'Meara, *Pythagoras Revived,* p. 220, ll. 49-58.

279. We are inclined to accept here Kroll's suggestion of *esti sustaseôs* for *episustaseôs,* which does not provide the required meaning – and a verb is needed.

280. In this sentence, we would accept Usener's proposal to change the first person plurals *hupethemetha, ênegkamen,* and *edoxamen* to third person singulars, as the reference must be to Aristotle, not to 'us'. Radical as the change may seem, it could be explained by an 'intelligent' scribe initially misreading *enegkamenos* as *enegkamen,* and then altering everything else to fit that.

281. There is a small lacuna here, which can be filled with help from the parallel passage of ps.-Alex.: *ê ex amphoin tôn.*

282. This process of 'equalisation', referred to above by Aristotle in the lemma, seems to involve having limit imposed on the 'great-and-small', or indeterminate, nature of the dyad. Aristotle is, of course, being thoroughly satirical and misleading here, and Alexander is going along with his terminology.

283. It is a considerable problem to know how best to render the terms *monas* and *dyas* in this context. Syrianus may well understand them as 'monad' and 'dyad', with ontological connotations, but he is copying from Alexander, who probably did not.

284. This whole passage is paralleled in ps.-Alex., 767,33-768,26.

285. We translate the *ameres* of the MSS, but we are much attracted by Usener's conjecture of *plêres*, 'fullness', despite the palaeographical difficulties, as making much better sense. It is possible, however, that Syrianus saw partlessness as something that might be conferred by the Dyad rather than the One.

286. There is a serious gap here in Syrianus' text, caused by homoeoteleuton, but it can be filled from the parallel text of ps.-Alex., 768,28-34.

287. Here we would accept Usener's emendation *autois* for *heautois*; the reflexive form is hardly appropriate. It is not quite clear whether the dyad being referred to here is the Indefinite Dyad itself or some projection of it in the mathematical realm, but we accord it a capital letter in any case.

288. sc. the Forms, viewed as divine intellects.

289. A quotation of *Iliad* 8.5, and elsewhere – the point being that there are not really gender differences in the normal sense among divine beings.

290. In his critique here, Syrianus may well have in mind Aristotle's own discussion of infinity in *Physics* 3.7-8, where the notion of potential as opposed to actual infinity is introduced.

291. This is valuable evidence of another distinctive position taken up by Amelius in relation to the Forms, along with his assertion that there are Forms of evils (and presumably also opposites, such as cold or ugliness?). Cf. L. Brisson, 'Amélius, sa vie, son oeuvre, sa doctrine, son style', *ANRW* II 36.2 (1987), 793-860. It is interesting that Syrianus uses here the same verb to characterise Amelius (*neanieuontai*) that Iamblichus uses of him in his *De Anima* (§19 Finamore-Dillon).

292. Usener and Kroll find the text here somewhat elliptical, and wish to make additions, but it seems translatable as it stands.

293. Reading *teleutaion* for *teleutaiôn*, and excising *tôn,* with Usener.

294. Philolaus, fr. B3 D-K. Cf. Iambl. *in Nic.* 7,24-5.

295. The imputation of 'will' (*boulêsis*) to the first principles is notable.

296. An extract from the Orphic *Hymn to Number* quoted above, 106,17ff. (fr. 315 Kern).

297. Reading *kosmikôn* for *kosmôn*, with Usener.

298. It is not clear whether we should translate *eidê* as 'species' here, or as 'forms' (with a small 'f'). Syrianus himself, of course, does not have this problem.

299. *kata tên autên hodeuei mousan* – a notable turn of phrase.

300. Presumably 10 and 1.

301. I read *psukhêi* here, for the *tekhnêi* of the MSS, to bring it into accord with Aristotle's own statement at *Metaph.* 1032b2. The MS reading could be explained by (virtual) dittography from *tekhnêta* just before.

302. The reference is to 7.7, 1032a32ff.

303. This term should mean something like 'things done', or 'to be done' ('products of manufacture' should really be *poiêta*), but in the circumstances this seems to be what Syrianus means. Whether there were Forms of manufactured objects was a long-standing subject of debate in the Platonic tradition, the general view being that there were not.

304. I make an attempt to give some sense to this corrupt and lacunose passage, building on some suggestions of Usener's, and reading *tôi eph' hêmin kuriôs <arkhê estin hê boulêsis> tôn praxeôn*. But I am by no means convinced that this solves the problem.

305. cf. Iambl. *in Nic.* 11,16-17.

306. *deuterôidoumena monas.* This term goes back at least to Nicomachus of Gerasa, I 19, p. 54 10; cf. also *Theol. Ar.* 22,10 (though the Doric form of the participle suggests a pseudo-Pythagoric source). Iamblichus notes it at *in Nic.* 88,25, and Proclus at *in Remp.* 2,67,9 (where he connects it with daemonic souls!)

307. Probably the totality of number is meant here, rather than the universe; but one cannot be sure (and in the Pythagorean mind there is not much difference, after all).

308. This is a reference to the lost fifth book of the *Pythagorean Sequence*, which appears to have concerned the properties of the numbers of the Decad (cf. *in Nic.* 118,14-18) – not to be identified with the surviving *Theologoumena Arithmêtikês*. Fragment given in *Pythagoras Revived*, p. 222 (ll. 90-3).

309. What exactly this denotes is obscure (something like a 'matter' of numbers, as opposed to their form?), but it seems more or less synonymous with *hupodokhê*, 'receptacle', cf. p. 150,4 Kroll below, and fragment of Iamblichus mentioned in previous note.

310. We take this to be the sense of *tôi oikeiôi logôi*.

311. Diels suggests that the numbers 1, 2, 3 and 1, 3, 5 may have dropped out here, but that seems hardly necessary.

312. Syrianus is here referring, not to the Monad and the Dyad, but rather to the supreme One and the pair of Monad and Dyad following upon that; cf. 112,14ff. above, and 160,18 below.

313. cf. for this passage (to 150,32) ps.-Alex. 772,22-8.

314. This is an interesting remark of Syrianus. The doctrine of indivisible lines is generally connected with Xenocrates, but here the suggestion seems to be that the point is actually to be regarded as a sort of minimal line, as being a first principle of linearity.

315. This and what follows in brackets are added from the parallel passage of ps.-Alex. Since these additions are necessary, this seems to constitute good evidence that both authors are in fact using Alexander.

316. If that is the meaning of *elaphrotera* (as opposed to *embrithesterôn* below).

317. sc. the Pythagoreans. Note the Doric form of *korupha*.

318. cf. Iambl. *in Nic.* 94,17; 95,20.

319. That is to say, the Dyad manifested as the principle of quantity.

320. That is to say, presumably, the concepts of Form and Matter.

321. i.e. signifying both '(arithmetical) unit' and '(archetypal) Monad'.

322. It is not clear that this is what Aristotle means – more probably he means 'prior' to be understood here – but this is how Syrianus understands it, so we render it thus.

323. Or possibly, 'mathematical unit'.

324. cf. Thesleff, p. 47.

325. In fact, Aristotle seems to be directing a jibe at what he conceives to be the doctrine of Speusippus, whom he accuses of postulating a first principle that is somehow inchoate and a minimum, cf. *Met.* 14, 1092a11-17 (fr. 43 Tarán), commented on below, 185,29-186,14.

326. *Monas* should probably be read before *hekatera* here, as in the text of Aristotle.

327. cf. ps.-Alex. 774,37-775,10.

328. cf. Nicomachus, *Intro. Arith.* 1,7,1.

329. This jibe about the first principle as 'least part' (*elakhiston*) seems, from other evidence, to be directed primarily at Speusippus. Cf. 14, 1092a11-17, and Syrianus' discussion below.

330. If that is the meaning here of *anastrephomenoi*.

331. *anomoios homoiotês* is a concept occurring also in Proclus. Cf. in particular *in Remp.* 2.232,20; *in Alc.* 189,16; *in Parm.* 741,13; 751,19; and 760,7.

332. Adopting a minor emendation of Usener's, which makes the syntax smoother.

333. For this passage cf. ps.-Alex. 776,32-777,3.

334. cf. Nicomachus, *Intro. Arith.* 2,22,3; Iambl. *in Nic.* 12,23-4.

335. This is a reference to *De Anima* 1, 404b16ff., but it is interesting that Syrianus seems to assume that the mysterious reference there to *ta peri philosophias legomena*, which modern commentators tend to take rather as referring to Plato's unwritten doctrines, is a reference to Aristotle's own lost dialogue *On Philosophy*. It should be noted, however, that, just below (at 159,33ff.), he is able to quote a passage from Book 2 of *On Philosophy*, so he may know what he is talking about. On the other hand, Syrianus gets wrong the references to Xenocrates and Plato respectively, as does ps.-Alex., whereas Alexander, elsewhere, gets them right, and this makes this a key passage in the argument as to whether S. is dependent on Ps. Alex., or vice versa. See Introduction, p. 9.

336. The whole comment down to here is paralleled in ps.-Alex. 777,11-21.

337. Reading *legetai* here with Usener, for the *legei* of the MSS, as giving a rather better sense.

338. This passage is paralleled, though more copiously, by ps.-Alex. 777,23-33.

339. If that is the meaning of *autos heautou sunaisthanetai* here; 'be aware of what he is saying' would be the more obvious translation, but it seems less meaningful in the context.

340. These two terms, lit. 'planks' and 'little altars', are used both for numbers made up of unequal components, and for the corresponding geometrical figures, as here. For the *bômiskos*, cf. n. 278 above.

341. This is a slightly curious use of *phuseis*. I am tempted by Usener's suggested emendation <*aitias*> *epiteleitai phusei.*

342. This word, it must be said, is a conjecture of Kroll's for the *suzêtêsin* of the MSS, which admittedly makes no sense in the context. Usener suggests *suzugian*, which is further from the text, but has the advantage of being an existent word.

343. That is to say, *logoi* of Forms in Soul.

344. Once again, we have a lemma broken up into its individual phrases in the MSS, but united by Kroll.

345. Aristotle is referring here to the theory of Speusippus, though Syrianus does not recognise this.

346. This added from the parallel passage of ps.-Alex. (779,29-34). It would seem to have fallen out by homoeoteleuton.

347. Aristotle is referring here to Speusippus and Xenocrates respectively, but Syrianus is not concerned with this.

348. Usener is suspicious of the text here, but what Syrianus seems to be saying is (a) that the Dyad is not a multiplicity in the 'ordinary' sense (which Aristotle is foisting upon his opponents here) of being a congeries of units, and (b) in any case, its product is not such as it is itself.

349. There would seem to be here a lacuna, in the course of which Syrianus turned from dealing with the first question to the second, in which Aristotle alleges that the Dyad becomes just another number.

350. *anomoiôs homoioutai* – a notable expression of the relation between the One and Matter. Cf. 153,5 (Kroll) above, and note 331 ad loc.

351. Presumably at 1083b36ff. above.

352. As, for example, by Speusippus.

353. This term, *hulopoios*, appears to be a *hapax legomenon*; it refers, presumably, to the Dyad.

354. Another case of Kroll's combining a series of short comments into a simple lemma. I have, however, once again given the whole passage together, in the interests of clarity, while indicating the sub-lemmata in abbreviated form.

355. Reading *taxeôn* for *lexeôn* of the MSS, as Kroll suggests.

356. Once again, Kroll has combined a series of short comments into a single lemma, with sub-lemmata. I follow the same procedure.

357. Reading *eiper <ara>*, with Usener.

358. fr. 9 Rose.

359. sc. at 1087a29. We have no idea who these authorities were, or whether they preceded or followed Alexander. In fact, 1086a21-1087a25 can equally well be seen as constituting a sort of preface to Book 14, as Aristotle now turns to discussing a new topic, which will be taken up in 14.

360. Particularly in Book 10, chs 4-6.

361. Such criticism occurs more or less *passim* in this work.

362. Preserving the MS reading *hôs ousias,* secluded by Jaeger (with much justification); Syrianus, however, plainly read it, and strives to make sense of it.

363. sc. 13.4 above, but before that again in 1.6.

364. cf. p.104,6ff. above (commenting on ch. 4, 1078b12-32).

365. If that is indeed what is meant by the phrase *kai ta aorista*. We are not confident of having uncovered Syrianus' meaning here, or indeed of the soundness of the text.

366. A reference to Cebes' intervention at *Phd.* 72E.

367. We would adopt Kroll's suggestion here to read *holikôterôn* for the MSS *oikeiôn*, despite the paleographical problem. *Oikeiôn* would mean 'proper to them', which makes some sense, but not much.

368. Usener suspects this last item, presumably because he feels that 'mortal' is true of every animal – but what about the heavenly bodies, which would count as *zôia*?

369. I am less than clear as to what Syrianus means by this, but I assume that *hê tôn pragmatôn prohodos* refers to the 'procession of realities' from the lower to the higher realm – which, however, would involve an unusual use of *prohodos*.

370. A reference here both to *Metaph.* 12.7, 1072b9ff. (with reference to the Unmoved Mover), and to the beginning of the *Categories* (1a2-6).

371. sc. Book 3 of the *Metaphysics*, termed here *ta diaporêmata,* and specifically the twelfth and final *diaporêma*, 1003a5-17.

372. We here deviate, with regret, from our policy of printing the whole Aristotelian lemma, since Syrianus in this case proposes to comment on the whole of ch. 10, which would be quite unwieldy to print out.

373. Usener proposes here to emend MSS *sômata* to *kai asômata.* We prefer, however, Kroll's suggestion of *mona,* which, while less palaeographically attractive, conveys a better sense.

374. sc. in *Phys.* 3.4, 203b20ff., where the argument (in favour of the existence of the Unlimited) is found that, 'since whatever is limited reaches its limit by coming up against something else, there can be no absolute limit, for nothing can be limited except by something else beyond its limit'. Cf. also, however, *Phys.* 8.10, 267b20-6 and 266a23-b6.

375. There is a small lacuna here, which may be filled on the basis of the Latin version of Hieronymus Bagolinus, the sixteenth-century translator of Syrianus (on whom see Introduction, p. 21); something like <*ouden estai ho*> would seem to have fallen out.

376. Adding *ekhousin* after *toutôn,* as suggested by Kroll.

377. Syrianus here uses the distinctive verb *apotemakhizontai.*

378. Inserting *enhuparkhein* before *têi aisthêtêi ousiâi* with Usener.

379. In this last phrase, it is necessary that the genitive and accusative elements be reversed, as Kroll does not appear to recognise. The error may be that of an 'intelligent' scribe, failing to recognise Syrianus' introduction of a touch of stylistic *variatio* here.

380. sc. the letters of the alphabet.

381. The concept of the Form of a *phônê* is a slightly odd one, even if *phônê* be taken to mean 'word'; it should, however, be rather broader than that. Presumably what Syrianus means is that our *lektikê phantasia* (cf. above) can express the full range of Forms within us in *phônai* (and combinations of *phônai*), using the letters of the alphabet.

382. cf. *Anal. Post.* 1.24, 86a5-10; 1.31. Usener here, it must be said, rightly concerned by an anomalous *te* in the text, conjectures that another reference may have dropped out before this, and proposes, plausibly, *Metaph.* 3.4, 999a24-34. It is in any case a good example of Syrianus quoting Aristotle against himself.

383. e.g. at *Anal. Post.* 1.8.

384. This rather cumbersome over-translation of *tekhnê* seems necessary to convey Syrianus' meaning.

385. cf. Ar. *Metaph.* 1.1, 981a1-18.

386. This term, *protaktikôs,* and its counterpart *hupotaktikôs,* used just below, are technical terms of grammar, presumably used in this sense here.

387. Ar. *Metaph.* 1.1, 981a25-8.

388. *Rhet.* 1.2, 1356b29ff., though he is paraphrasing here rather than quoting verbatim, as he pretends.

389. This sentence in the Greek is distinctly anacolouthic, if not rambling. I try to put a reasonable shape on it.

390. fr. 1D (Huffman). Syrianus would appear to have derived this quotation from Iamblichus, *in Nic. Ar.* (6,20), a work that, as we have seen, he has close at hand while composing this commentary.

391. This is probably the sense of *gonimôtatos* here, rather than, for example, 'prolific'.

392. A quotation from Euripides' *Medea,* 410.

393. sc. Alexander. Cf. above, 160,6ff.

394. Usener feels here that a step in the argument has been omitted (sc. first principles are <substances; substances are> not in a substratum) and wishes to insert it. He is right, of course, but to insert it would surely interfere with the form of the syllogism, so it seems better to understand it. There is, however, the difficulty that just below, at 166,10, Syrianus refers to the second premise as *hai arkhai ousiai,* which would seem to indicate that it occurred in this passage. Perhaps one could read *hai arkhai <ousiai, hôst'> ouk en hupokeimenôi?*

395. cf. 44B1 Diels-Kranz, though there Philolaus does not explicitly speak of God. Cf. Plato, *Phlb.* 23C9-10, as read by Proclus, *PT* 3.8, 34,12-14 (S-W), who associates this with Philolaus (cf. *PT* 1.5, 26,48 S-W). The association between Philolaus and this passage of the *Philebus* probably goes back to Iamblichus, on whom Syrianus will be drawing in this passage.

396. Since 'Archaenetus' is otherwise quite unattested, Boeckh and others have reasonably conjectured that this is as misprint for Archytas, who has been quoted on a number of previous occasions in the work, and with whose doctrine this detail concords pretty well.

397. The use of the Doric form *arkhan* indicates that this is intended as a quotation.

398. 56,1ff. (Thesleff). This is an important testimony, based as it is on *Rep.* 509B, and indicating the Neopythagorean and later Platonist interpretation of that famous and controversial passage.

399. The references are, respectively, to *Ep.* 2, 312E, *Rep.* 503Bff., *Phlb.* 23Cff., and *Parm.* 137Cff.

400. Syrianus takes the reference to be to Pythagoras here, though Aristotle is pretty certainly referring to Speusippus – who, however, may well have attributed his formulation to Pythagoras.

401. A quotation of *Tim.* 37D; but where Plato intended *en heni* to mean simply 'in the one state', Neoplatonist interpreters, including Syrianus, took it to mean 'in the One'.

402. This quibble arises from Aristotle's polemical assumption that the 'Great and Small' is a sort of numerical dyad, which Plato plainly did not intend it to be.

403. cf. ps.-Alex. 797,12-17. This is actually a most significant passage, since it is clear that Alexander read, at 1087b12, *arithmôi, logôi d' ou,* instead of the *logôi, arithmôi d' ou* of the MSS, and this throws him, as well as both Syrianus and ps.-Alex, into some confusion – though Syrianus discerns the true reading.

404. This is merely an attempt to represent what may be behind this thoroughly corrupt sentence. Even Usener's proposal – *hôs eiôthen ekeina* (for *ekei*) *legesthai, kautê* (for *tauto*) *toutois estin axia dêlousthai kai tois onomasin* – is not very helpful.

405. Presumably this refers to the Indefinite Dyad.

406. This seems the best rendering of *oligon* in the circumstances; it hardly makes sense to describe the One as 'few' (although that is the opposite of 'many').

407. The one picked out here, though Syrianus does not specify this, is Speusippus. This passage in Aristotle, indeed, is doubtless the source of the later *canard* that Speusippus made his first principle 'one' in the sense of a minimum.

408. The reference is to ch. 6 of that book, where problems are raised about the opposition of 'many' to the One, since that would make the One 'few', which is absurd. At 1156b33ff., however, Aristotle grants that 'in the sphere of numbers, 'one' is opposed to 'many' as the measure to the measurable, i.e. as relative terms (*ta pros ti*) are opposed which are not of their own nature relative.'

409. Again this interesting idiom *para thuras,* not noted by LSJ (cf. pp. 80,28; 112,28, and 195,9), but which I take to mean something like 'irrelevant' or 'superficial'. Sextus Empiricus, we may note, uses the singular, *para thuran planasthai* (*AM* 1.43).

410. *ho daimonios houtos anêr – daimonios,* the usual Neoplatonic epithet of Aristotle, being used here with a special ironical edge.

411. A rather apt reference to *Iliad* 1.591, where Hephaestus is recalling his being cast forth 'from the heavenly threshold' (*apo bêlou thespesioio*) of Olympus by an enraged Zeus.

412. Reading *diataxeôs*, with Kroll, for the *dialexeôs* of the MSS.

413. 108,24 ff. (Thesleff). His views on number are also mentioned in ps.-Iambl. *Theol. Ar.* 21 (De Falco).

414. This last term is a *hapax legomenon,* not noted by LSJ. It is to be credited to 'Cleinias', presumably, rather than to Syrianus.

415. This is a reference to *Laws* 4, 715E, with 716C (on God as *metron*) – though with 'beginning and end' being, slightly curiously, put into the plural.

416. Inserting <*ê*> here, as suggested by Kroll.

417. This is not a reference to the *Politics,* but rather to a lost dialogue, the *Politikos* (fr. 79 Rose) – of which, one would think, Syrianus could have had no direct knowledge.

418. We take this to be more or less the sense of *logikôteron* here.

419. A quotation of *Iliad* 7.358 (Paris to Antenor) and 12.232 (Hector to Poulydamas) – though, ironically, in each case the person reproached is actually giving good advice!

420. Once again, with regret, we abbreviate the lemma, as being too long for complete reproduction. Syrianus, at this point of his commentary, is dealing with a large chunk of text.

421. This is a reference to *Metaph.* 9.8, 1050b6ff., apparently being regarded as 'another work' (*en allois logois*). Cf. also, however, *De Caelo* 1.11-12.

422. The best MSS of Aristotle read here *energeia*, rather than *energeiâi*, but we choose the latter reading, since Syrianus appears to read the dative in his text, though he accepts that the nominative is a possible reading also.

423. That is to say, *De Caelo* 1.11-12, to which Syrianus feels that Aristotle must be referring, since he has used the expression *en allois logois* (cf. previous note but one).

424. This would seem to be the sense of *kataskeuê* here.

425. Once again, Syrianus resorts to an Iliadic quotation, somewhat more apposite this time – Poseidon referring to Zeus, in Book 15.185.

426. cf. *Soph.* 257Cff., on the nature of not-being. There would seem, at first sight, to be something of a lacuna here, there being no main clause to follow the conditional. However, it is possible that we have here an elliptical use of *ei* (cf. LSJ s.v. *ei*, VII 1), with the apodosis suppressed for rhetorical purposes – a construction, indeed, much favoured by Homer, as Syrianus would be well aware.

427. Syrianus is here ranking the 'genera of Being' (the Five Greatest Genera of the *Sophist*) at the summit of the intelligible realm, just below the Monad and Dyad in the henadic realm.

428. Syrianus here adopts the standard later Platonist interpretation of the Empedoclean Love and Strife, as referring to the intelligible and sensible realms respectively.

429. A dig here at Aristotle's own theory!

430. That is to say, the five genera of Being of the *Sophist.*

431. Following Usener's very plausible suggestion that *ek tou mê ontos* has dropped out before *tou* here.

432. This would be a reference to the Plotinian (and later) doctrine of intelligible matter.

433. sc. that it gives the appearance of being all things, but is none of them.

434. Accepting Usener's filling of a small lacuna.

435. It is not clear why Syrianus has chosen to break off this lemma here, in the middle of a sentence, but one must respect his decision.

436. A tentative filler for a small lacuna here. The MSS read simply *kat' allên*. Usener proposes *kat' alên*, 'through wandering', which is ingenious, but it seems better simply to suppose that some noun has fallen out.

437. A reference here to *Tim.* 46C.

438. I take this to be the sense of *to heniaion autês eidos* here.

439. Added in, reasonably, by Bagolinus in his translation.

440. A reference to *Phd.* 74Cff.

441. A reference to *Parm.* 130Eff.

442. If this be the sense of *ekstasis* in this context.

443. It seems that, for this sentence to make sense (since it must be something else than Matter, in the last part of it, that 'consorts with Matter'), we must have a change of subject here, whether we postulate that *to eidos* has fallen out or not.

444. A slight over-translation, perhaps, of *sumplekesthai tais phônais*, but we think not far from the sense.

445. This, it must be said, is a conjecture of Usener's for the mangled *prôt...* of the MSS, but it is highly plausible.

446. Edited by Richard Harder, *Ocellus Lucanus, de rerum natura*, Berlin, 1926.

447. Presumably Syrianus means the dialogue of Plato, rather than the work of 'Timaeus Locrus', but, especially in this rather 'Pythagorean' context, one cannot be quite sure. In the latter case, one should translate 'the bulk of Timaeus' work'.

448. For this passage, cf. ps.-Alex. 810,7ff.

449. This is a reference to Aristotle's theory of planetary intellects, as set out in *Metaph.* 12.8.

450. The use of *ex huptias* here seems to be a pointed reference to *Phdr.* 264A, where Socrates is engaged in picking apart the sophistic discourse of Lysias.

451. cf. ps.-Alex. p. 811,30-812,2.

452. Syrianus here omits the words *ti sêmainei* from Aristotle's text.

453. This is an attack on the position of Speusippus, though Syrianus does not recognise it.

454. Reading *plên toutou* (19), as suggested by Kroll.

455. cf. Nicomachus, *Intro. Arith.* 1,19,9.

456. This is also in fact the topic of the last section of ch. 2. This chapter and the next in fact go over much of the same ground as was dealt with above in 13.2-3.

457. Usener detects a lacuna in the text here, which we may fill tentatively thus: *<khôris men arithmous, khôris> de ...*

458. cf. above 82,1-2; Proclus, *Elements of Theology* 103 (with Dodds' commentary).

459. That is to say, entities at the level of Soul.

460. This passage corresponds to ps.-Alex. 815,5-9.

461. There is a small lacuna at the beginning of this lemma, which could be filled simply by *aporei* or something such, as suggested by Bonitz. The object of Aristotle's attack here is Speusippus, but Syrianus is oblivious to that.

462. This passage corresponds to ps.-Alex. 815,21-6.

463. Plato, *Ep.* 7, 342B-344C.

464. This passage, apart from the first sentence, is reflected in ps.-Alex. 817,33-6.

465. Once again, this lemma is divided into sub-lemmata. For convenience, we have printed it all together at the outset.

466. fr. 189 (Bergk).

467. Syrianus is here once again referring to the system of a monad and a dyad subordinate to the supreme One, a doctrine derived originally from Eudorus (but in his view from the Pythagoreans, on the authority of 'Archytas', cf. 166,4 above – assuming Archytas to be lurking behind the otherwise unknown Archaenetus).

468. *tis* should be deleted here, as suggested by Kroll. The subject of the verb should be Aristotle. If it were a general statement, an optative would be required.

469. Syrianus once again entirely misses the reference to the distinctive doctrine of Speusippus, which Aristotle is sniping at here.

470. Orphic. frr. 108, 102, 107 (Kern).

471. *ariprepes* added from parallel passage of ps.-Alex. (821,22).

472. Something is missing here in the text, probably by homoeoteleuton involving *khaos*. We accept the very plausible suggestion of Usener for filling the gap (an alternative for 'the theologians' would be 'Orpheus', but Syrianus is not choosing to be specific here.

473. This whole lemma is paralleled in ps.-Alex. 821,11-20, which would imply, on our theory, that Alexander was familiar with the Orphic poetry – an assumption which seems by no means improbable.

474. Once again, a division into sub-lemmata here.

475. cf. Plato, *Timaeus* 42E5-6.

476. Usener would postulate a lacuna here, but the text seems translatable as it stands.

477. This part of the lemma is paralleled in ps.-Alex. 823,4-12.

478. sc. the Pythagoreans and Platonists. Syrianus once again produces his 'Eudoran' system of principles.

479. *Theaetetus* 176A7-8.

480. At last, recognition for Speusippus! Syrianus may have derived this identification from Alexander, but there is no parallel in ps.-Alex. The identity of the 'others' is not revealed, but Aristotle is probably sniping primarily at Xenocrates.

481. Modern editors make a break here, and begin ch. 5. Syrianus, however, plainly feels that the next sentence rounds off the previous section, rather than beginning anything new.

482. Syrianus here may have in mind a passage near the end of ch. 4 of Iamblichus' *De Communi Mathematica Scientia* (18,9-12 Festa), where evil is described as arising only 'at the fourth and fifth levels of reality, put together from the lowest elements, and even then not primarily (*proêgoumenôs*), but as a result of falling away from (*ekpiptein*) and not being able to control their natural state'. The true author of this passage may well be Speusippus, but Syrianus would not be conscious of that.

483. This is, of course, a dig at Aristotle.

484. Plato, *Parmenides* 144E5; 'assigns' translates *kataneimas* (27), which Kroll regards as corrupt, suggesting instead *kataneusas,* 'declines towards'; in which suggestion he may well be right.

485. Again, Syrianus is oblivious to the fact that Speusippus is being referred to here, albeit tendentiously.

486. This passage is paralleled in ps.-Alex. 824,12-24, but no mention is made of Speusippus there either.

487. See Aristotle, *De generatione animalium* 1.1, 715b5-7, 26-30; 16, 721a5-9 and elsewhere.

488. See previous note.

489. Syrianus here uses Aristotle's *Physics* 2.5, 197a34-5 to argue against Aristotle.

490. cf. ps.-Alex. 824,27ff.

491. Reading <*en*> *autêi,* as suggested by Kroll.

492. Aristotle *DA* 3.4, 429a27-8.

493. We adopt Kroll's suggested reading *epistasiais* ('rule') for *epistemais* ('knowledge'), since the latter makes little sense.

494. Syrianus here assumes the general later Platonist interpretation of Empedocles' system, which sees the cosmic cycle as not to be taken literally, but as setting forth the permanent structure of the universe, the Sphere representing the intelligible realm.

495. It is possible, as Ross supposes, that Syrianus (and Alexander before him) read *grammôn* for *megethôn* in 1092b10 above, and *zôiôn kai phutôn* for *phutôn* here, but it is just as likely that both commentators are merely interpreting Aristotle's rather peculiar terminology. We must assume that Aristotle is using *phuton* to mean 'living thing' in general, odd though that is.

496. Or 'reason-principles', in the later Platonist sense.

497. On the *bômiskos*, cf. n. 278 on 143,7 above.

498. We suggest reading here *isogônion* (see next note) for the problematic *agônion* in Kroll's text. Various other suggestions have been made, by Usener and Hultsch, along the same lines.

499. Syrianus appears to be using here Iamblichus' lost work *On Arithmetic in Physical Matters* (Book 7 of his treatise *On Pythagoreanism*), of which fragments are printed in D. O'Meara, *Pythagoras Revived*, 220 (see lines 47-58, where an explanation can be found of what Syrianus says here).

500. Empedocles fr. 96, 2-3 (transl. Kirk-Raven-Schofield).

501. Reading *proharpaseien* with Kroll, for *prosharpaseien*.

502. This much of the comment corresponds to ps.-Alex, 828,31ff.

503. Following Kroll's suggested insertion of *talêthes*.

504. This is Syrianus' solution (following Alexander) to a peculiar formulation of Aristotle's (contrasting *eulogistos* with *perittos*), but it is something of an over-simplification of Aristotle's meaning. See Ross's note ad loc.

505. A phrase may be missing here ('not determined by proportion and is'), which Usener would supply on the basis of a comparison with Alexander, 829,4ff.

506. This part of the lemma is only partially paralleled by ps.-Alex. (829,8-9 = 189,8-9), but is reflected also in Alexander's own commentary on Book 1, 29,4ff.

507. See above, n. 499.

508. Kroll suggests, plausibly, the insertion of *dei* here, while suspecting some worse corruption.

509. This passage, from the beginning of the paragraph, is paralleled in ps.-Alex., 830,26-37.

510. Addition of this and of <numbers> suggested by Usener.

511. This seems to be a reference to a Peripatetic theory of the unique character of individual substances, analogous to the Stoic doctrine of the *idiôs poion*, but it is not easy to find a precise source for it. Perhaps Alexander?

512. See again Iamblichus' *On Arithmetic in Physical Matters* (above n. 499), lines 33-46.

513. Plato *Republic* 8, 546C7, where, however, he is referring to the famous 'nuptial number', which is not a number of any given animal, but rather a formula for ensuring that they breed at the most favourable time.

514. Syrianus here may be thinking of the construction of the soul in the *Timaeus*, 35Bff.

515. sc. the Pythagoreans and Platonists.

516. All this section is taken from Alexander; cf. ps.-Alex. 832,16-27.

517. Theophrastus fr. 681 (*Theophrastus of Eresus. Sources for his Life, Writings, Thought and Influence*, ed. W. Fortenbaugh et al., Part II, Leiden 1992). Archinus was the politician who established the Ionic alphabet as the official alphabet of Athens in 403/2 BC. He must have composed a theoretical tract on the subject.

518. Syrianus is of course taking Z to represent DS, while Aristotle pretty certainly is thinking of it as SD.

519. This can hardly be a criticism of the arithmological speculations of such an authority of Nicomachus of Gerasa in his *Theology of Arithmetic*, since Syrianus is elsewhere most respectful of Nicomachus, but rather of such shadowy figures as the authority behind Philo Judaeus' hyperbolic encomium of the number Seven in his *De Opificio Mundi*, 89-128.

520. For 'Prorus', see H. Thesleff, *The Pythagorean Texts of the Hellenistic Period*, Abo 1965, 155.

521. For example Nicomachus, in his *Theology of Arithmetic*, excerpted in the ps.-Iamblichus, *Theologoumena arithmeticae*.

522. In his *Hieros Logos*. On this work see Syrianus, above 10,4-5; 123,1-6; Thesleff, *Pythagorean Texts*, 164.

523. The translation of this term, as we have seen, is not straightforward. It is a term of distinctly moderate commendation, accorded by later Neoplatonists to Aristotle by contrast with *theios*, 'divine', which is the normal epithet of Plato (and of such distinguished later figures as Plotinus and Iamblichus).

524. *De Caelo* 1.1, 268a13-14.

525. *De Sensu* 4, 442a19-28. Aristotle does indeed here declare it to be *eulogon* that there should be seven flavours and seven colours. The adducing of these passages is good evidence, if such is needed, of Syrianus' extensive knowledge of Aristotle, as well as of his technique of using Aristotle against himself.

526. A proverbial phrase, to the effect that different sorts of things should not to be confused, cf. A. Nauck, *Tragicorum Graecorum Fragmenta*, Leipzig 1889, 950, No. 560. The Mysians were the butt of many derogatory sayings.

527. Usener thinks something like 'of these men' is missing here, but that is hardly necessary.

528. This passage is paralleled in ps.-Alex. 835,11-14.

529. Reading *kata* for *kai,* with Bagolinus. Kroll suspects that 'divine' here needs to be corrected. Certainly there is something wrong. Perhaps read *psukhikous* for *theious*?

530. This section is paralleled in ps.-Alex. 835,35-836,1.

531. Usener suggests reading *tagathon* ('the Good'), after *auto* here, but the same sense can be derived from the text as it stands.

532. A Homeric tag quoted by Aristotle *Metaph.* 12.10, 1076a4, in the course of an attack on Speusippus (another example of Aristotle being used against himself).

533. Or 'reason-principle'. It is not quite clear which Syrianus intends here.

534. See *Physics* 2.8, 199a1; 2.6, 198a1-13.

535. Aristotle never actually employs this phrase, though, as Kroll points out, something not unlike it occurs at *An. Pr.* 2.17, 65b17: *to anaition hôs aition tithenai.*

536. Again a reference to Aristotle's god, the unmoved mover of *Metaph.* 12.6-10, Intellect. This may be an allusion to the later Platonist accusation that Aristotle does not allow for the rule of providence in the sublunary realm.

537. That is to say, uncombinable with units of other Form-numbers.

538. There is a difficulty here, as of course the half of 3 is 1 1/2, not 1 1/3, but *epitritos* is what Syrianus says.

539. This whole passage is paralleled in ps.-Alex. 836,22-33.

540. This entity equates to the Father of the Demiurges in Syrianus' more developed theological scheme, cf. e.g. Procl. *in Tim.* 1,156,5ff.; *in Crat.* 84-7 (Pasquali). He is described as *holos* in virtue of the fact that he presides over the existence of wholes rather than parts; hence the rather technical rendering of this term.

541. Another use here of the idiom *para thuras apantan*, conjuring up the image of getting stuck outside the door.

542. Once again, this would seem to be evidence of Syrianus' direct acquaintance with this work, but he may in fact know it only through Alexander.

Select Bibliography

The following is a list of the principal works cited or utilised in the Introduction and Notes

Primary sources

Alexander Aphrodisiensis, *In Aristotelis Metaphysica commentaria,* ed. M. Hayduck, Berlin: Reimer, 1881 (*Commentaria in Aristotelem Graeca* 1: 1)

Aristotle, *Metaphysics, Books X-XIV, Oeconomica, Magna Moralia,* ed. H. Tredennick & G.C. Armstrong (Aristotle XVIII: Loeb Classical Library), Cambridge MA/ London: Harvard University Press, 1935.

Damascius, *The Philosophical History,* text with trans. and notes by P. Athanassiadi, Athens: Apamea Cultural Association, 1999.

Marinus, *Proclus ou sur le bonheur,* ed. H-D. Saffrey & A. Segonds, Paris: Les Belles Lettres, 2001.

Syriani antiquissimi philosophi interpretis in II, XIII, et XIV libros Aristotelis Metaphysices commentarius, a H. Bagolino latinitate donatus, Venice, 1558.

Syrianus, *In Aristotelis Metaphysica commentaria,* ed. H. Usener, Berlin: Reimer, 1870 (repr. Berlin/New York: De Gruyter, 1961).

Syrianus, *In Metaphysica commentaria,* ed. W. Kroll, Berlin: Reimer, 1902 (*Commentaria in Aristotelem Graeca* 6: 1).

Secondary works

Annas, J., *Aristotle's* Metaphysics, *Books M and N,* trans. with intro. and notes, Oxford: Clarendon Press, 1976.

Cardullo, R.L., 'Syrianus' Lost Commentaries on Aristotle', *Bulletin of the Institute of Classical Studies* XXXIII (1986), 112-24.

Cardullo, R.L., 'Giamblico nel "Commentario alla Metafisica" di Siriano', in *The Divine Iamblichus, Philosopher and Man of Gods,* ed. H.J. Blumenthal & E.G. Clark, London: Bristol Classical Press, 1993, 173-200.

D'Ancona, C., 'Syrianus dans la tradition exégétique de la "Métaphysique" d'Aristote. Deuxième partie: Antécédents et postérité', in *Le commentaire entre tradition et innovation,* ed. M.O. Goulet-Cazé, Paris: Vrin, 2000, 311-27.

Finamore, J., 'Iamblichus on Light and the Transparent,' in H.J. Blumenthal & E.G. Clark, eds, *The Divine Iamblichus,* London: Bristol Classical Press (1993), 55-64.

Hadot, I, *Studies on the Neoplatonist Hierocles,* Philadelphia: American Philosophical Society, 2004.

Longo, A., *Siriano e I principi della scienza,* Napoli: Bibliopolis, 2005.

Luna, C., 'Syrianus dans la tradition exégétique de la Métaphysique d'Aristote. Première partie: Syrianus entre Alexandre d'Aphrodise et Asclépius', in *Le commentaire entre tradition et innovation,* ed. M.O. Goulet-Cazé, Paris: Vrin, 2000, 311-27.

Luna, C., *Trois études sur la traduction des commentaires anciennes à la Métaphysique d'Aristote,* Leiden: Brill, 2001.

Madigan, A., 'Syrianus and Asclepius on Forms and Intermediates in Plato and Aristotle', *Journal of the History of Philosophy* XXIV (1986), 149-71.

Moraux, P., *Der Aristotelismus bei den Griechen,* vol. I, Berlin/New York: De Gruyter, 1973.

Mueller, I., 'Aristotle's Doctrine of Abstraction in the Commentators', in *Aristotle Transformed: The Ancient Commentators and their Influence,* ed. R. Sorabji, London: Duckworth, 1990, 463-80.

Mueller, I., 'Syrianus and the Concept of Mathematical Number', in *La philosophie des mathématiques de l'Antiquité tardive,* ed. G. Bechtle & D. O'Meara, Fribourg: Editions Universitaires Saint Paul, 2000, 71-84.

O'Meara, D., *Pythagoras Revived: Mathematics and Philosophy in Late Antiquity,* Oxford: Clarendon Press, 1989.

Praechter. K., 'Syrianos', in *RE* IVA (1932), cols 1728-1775.

Ross, D., *Aristotle,* Metaphysics, vol. II., Oxford: Clarendon Press, 1924.

Saffrey, H.-D., 'Comment Syrianus, le maître de l'école néoplatonicienne d'Athènes, considérait-il Aristote?', in *Aristoteles Werk und Wirkung, Paul Moraux gewidmet,* Zweiter Band: Kommentierung, Ueberlieferung, Nachleben, hrsg. Jürgen Wippern, Berlin/New York; De Gruyter, 1987, 205-14 (repr. in *Recherches sur le néoplatonisme après Plotin,* Paris: Vrin, 1990, 131-40).

Sambursky, S., *The Concept of Place in Late Neoplatonism*, Jerusalem: The Israel Academy of Sciences and Humanities, 1982.

Sheppard, A.D.H. , *Studies on the 5th and 6th Essays of Proclus' Commentary on the Republic,* Göttingen: Vandenhoeck & Ruprecht, 1980.

Sheppard, A.D.H., 'Monad and Dyad as Cosmic Principles in Syrianus', in *Soul and the Structure of Being in Late Neoplatonism,* ed. H.J. Blumenthal & A.C. Lloyd, Liverpool: Liverpool University Press, 1982, 1-17.

Sorabji, R., *Matter, Space and Motion,* London: Duckworth, 1988.

Tarán, L., 'Syrianus and Pseudo-Alexander's Commentary on *Metaph.* E-N', in *Aristoteles Werk und Wirkung, Paul Moraux gewidmet,* Zweiter Band: Kommentierung, Ueberlieferung, Nachleben, hrsg. Jürgen Wippern, Berlin/New York: De Gruyter, 1987, 215-32.

Thesleff, H., *The Pythagorean Texts of the Hellenistic Period,* Abo: Abo Akademi, 1965.

Wear, S.K., *The Collected Fragments of Syrianus the Platonist on Plato's Parmenides and* Timaeus, unpubl. PhD thesis, Trinity College, Dublin, 2005.

English-Greek Glossary

This glossary lists a selection of the more important words, either from a philosophical or from a philological perspective, occurring in the Greek text. The translations given here may not always correspond to the rendering of them in a particular passage in the English text, since the demands of idiomatic translation may call for variations, but it should always be possible to work out what word is being translated.

a fortiori, into the bargain: *ek peri-ousias*
above nature, supernatural: *huper-phuês*
above substance: *huperousios*
abstraction: *aphairesis*
accessory cause: *sunaition*
accident: *sumbebêkos*
accidentally: *sumbebêkotôs*
active, actualised: *energos*
active, effective: *drastikos*
activity, actuality: *energeia*
actuality, in: *energeiâi*
additional distinction: *prosdiorismos*
admitting in: *pareisdusis*
advance preparation: *proparaskeuê*
all: *pas*
antecedent (log.): *hêgoumenon*
appearance, image, imagination: *phantasia*
apprehend, focus on: *epiballein*
apprehension, focus, intuitive grasp: *epibolê*
appropriate: *epiballôn, oikeioun*
appropriately: *oikeiôs*
appropriateness: *oikeiotês*
argument proper to such a proof: *epi-kheirêmatikos (logos)*
arise as a by-product: *parhuphistas-thai*
arouse beforehand: *proanegeirein*
art, craft, skill: *tekhnê*
articulate, distinguish: *diarthroun*
assimilate: *exomoioun*

assimilate to: *prosomoioun*
assimilate to oneself: *sunexhomoioun*
associate with: *prosoikeioun*
attack (in argument): *apoteinesthai (pros)*
attribute organic existence to: *organopoiein*
axiom: *axiôma*

back to front: *huptios*
be coupled with: *sunduazesthai*
be distinctive: *idiazein*
be dominated, controlled by: *krateisthai*
be interwoven: *sumplekesthai*
be superior, prevail: *kratisteuein*
beam (geometrical figure): *dokis*
being: *to on*
bestow form on, enform: *eidopoiein*
bestowal of form, construction: *eidopoiia*
both together: *sunamphoteros*
bring to perfection/completeness: *teleioun*
bringing together, uniting: *sunagôgos*
buffoonery: *bômolokhia*
by way of departure from: *parekbasis*

capable of being affected/acted upon: *pathêtikos*
capable of laughter (of man): *gelastikos*
capable of perfecting, perfective of: *teleiôtikos*
categorical (of syllogism): *katêgorikos*

cause: *aitia, aition*
celebrate: *exhumnein*
chance: *tukhê*
characteristic, peculiarity: *idiôma*
circumscription: *perigraphê*
coincidence: *sumptôma*
column (in Pythagorean Table of
　Opposites): *sustoikhia*
combinable (of units): *sumblêtos*
come together, agree: *suntrekhein*
coming after, 'later-born': *husterogenês*
coming-to-be: *genesis*
common characteristic, commonality:
　koinotês
complete living being: *panteles zôion*
comprehend: *periekhein*
comprehension, grasping: *perilêpsis*
comprehension: *katalêpsis, periokhê*
comprehensive in advance: *prolêptikos*
comprehensive of: *periektikos, peri-
　lêptikos*
concept: *ennoêma, epinoia*
conception: *ennoia*
conceptual: *ennoêtikos*
concerned with division: *diairetikos*
conclusion (log.): *sunêmmenon*
conclusion: *sumperasma*
concord: *sumphônia*
confer quality on (*pepoiômena,* quali-
　fied): *poioun*
confirmation, support: *sustasis*
connect, link up: *sunaptein*
constitutive of: *sustatikos*
contentious: *philenklêmôn*
contents, sum-total: *plerôma*
contradiction: *antiphasis*
contrariety: *enantiôsis*
controlling: *kratêtikos*
controversial: *antilogikos*
conversion: *periagôgê*
co-ordinate, in the same column: *sus-
　toikhos*
co-ordinate: *suntattein*
co-ordination, ordering: *suntaxis*
corporeal: *sômatoeidês*
correct: *epidiorthousthai*
correction: *epidiorthôsis*
countable: *arithmêtos*
create a cosmos: *kosmopoiein*
create: *demiourgein*
creation of a cosmos: *kosmopoiia*
creation: *dêmiourgia*
creative of matter: *hulopoios*

creatively: *dêmiourgikôs*
creator (god): *dêmiourgos*
creator (of a cosmos): *kosmourgos*

daemon: *daimôn*
daemonic status, marvellous (epithet
　of Aristotle): *daimonios*
decad, the number ten: *dekas*
decadic, belonging to the decad:
　dekadikos
decadically: *dekadikôs*
deficiency: *huphesis*
deficient (to be), to fall short:
　huphienai
define: *horizein, aphorizein*
defined: *hôrismenos*
definition: *horismos*
deliberate, give attention to:
　ephistanai
demiurgic, creative: *dêmiourgikos*
demonstration, proof: *apodeixis*
demonstrative: *apodeiktikos*
demonstratively, convincingly:
　apodeiktikôs
destructible: *phthartos*
dialectical proof: *epikheirêsis*
dialectical, dialectician: *dialektikos*
dialectical, non-syllogistic proof/
　argument: *epikheirêma*
dialectically: *dialektikôs*
difficult to face: *dusantibleptos*
difficult to fathom: *dusphôratos*
difficult to understand: *dusepinoêtos*
dignity, seniority: *presbeia*
discursive reasoning: *dianoia*
discursive reasoning (employing):
　dianoêtikos
discursive reasoning (object of):
　dianoêtos
displacement, disruptive force: *ekstasis*
dissimilar: *anomoios*
distinct: *diôrismenos*
distinctive property: *idiotês*
distinctly: *diakekrimenôs,
　diêrthrômenôs*
distinguish: *diakrinein*
distinguishing, discernment: *diakrisis*
distort: *parhelkein*
divide together with: *sundiairein*
divided, divisible: *meristos*
dividedly: *memerismenôs*
dominant: *kuriôdês*
doubt, objection: *epistasis*

duplicative, productive of duality: *duopoios*
dyadic: *duoeidês*

each: *hekastos*
effectively: *drastikôs*
efficacious: *drastêrios*
efficiaciously: *drastêriôs*
eidetic, Form-(number): *eidêtikos*
eliminate mutually (log.): *sunanairein*
embrace, comprehend: *perilambanein*
engage in shadow-boxing: *skia-makhein*
enmattered: *enulos*
enter in with: *suneisienai*
entirely best: *panaristos*
entirely perfect: *pantelês*
equal speed, at: *isotakhôs*
essential living being: *autozôion*
essential, the Form of: *auto-*
essentially: *kat' ousian*
essentially: *ousiôdôs*
establish: *hidruein*
eternal: *aiônios*
eternal generation: *aeigenesia*
eternally: *aiôniôs*
everlasting: *diaiônios*
everlastingly: *diaiôniôs*
evidence: *enargeia*
exceed: *huperekhein*
exceed in simplicity: *huperhêplôsthai*
exceedingly: *huperphuôs*
exclude: *exhorizein*
exercising providence, providential: *pronoêtikos*
existence: *huparxis, hupostasis*
exposition: *diexodos*
expository: *diexodikos, huphêgêtikos*
expressive of: *exangeltikos*
extend along with: *sumparekteinein*
extended: *diastatos*
extension: *ektasis*

fallacious: *paralogistikos*
fallaciously: *paralogistikôs*
falling short, inferiority: *elleipsis*
false reasoning: *paralogismos*
falsehood: *pseudos*
father of the arguments (Plato): *patêr tôn logon*
father: *patêr*
fictional, far-fetched: *plasmatôdês*
final (*ta teleutaia*): *teleutaios*

final: *telikos*
fire-stick: *pureion*
fit for guarding, protective: *phrourêtikos*
fluid: *rheustos*
Form (Platonic): *idea*
form in matter: *enulon eidos*
Form of Forms: *eidos eidôn*
form, species: *eidos*
form-creating, enforming: *eidopoios*
formless: *aneideos*
fount: *pêgê*
from a more logical point of view: *logikôterôs*
fundamental: *arkhêgikos, arkhoeidês, arkhikos*

genera of being: *genê tou ontos*
general: *katholikos*
generated, subject to generation: *genêtos*
generative: *gennêtikos, gonimos, hupostatikos*
generator: *hupostatês*
generic: *genikos*
genus: *genos*
give shape to: *morphoun, dia-morphoun*
Good, the: *t'agathon*
good-like: *agathoeidês*
goodness: *agathotês*

heavenly, celestial: *ouranios*
heptad, seven: *heptas*
here, in this realm: *têide*
hexad, six: *hexas*
hidden (Chaldaean term for *noêtos*): *kruphios*
highest of three strings, but the lowest in pitch: *hupatê*
homoiomeries: *homoiomerê*
homonymous: *homônumos*
homonymously: *homônumôs*
homonymy: *homônumia*
honey-wine (as example of mixture): *oinomeli*
horizon: *horizon*

illuminate: *ellampein, epilampein*
illumination: *ellampsis*
image: *eidôlon, eikôn, indalma*
imagined, object of imagination: *phantastos*

imitate: *mimeisthai*
imitation, copy: *mimêma*
immaterial: *aülos*
immediate (grasp): *autoptikos (autoptikê epibolê)*
immediate: *prosekhês*
immediately: *prosekhôs*
immediately, self-evident: *autothen*
impose limit, bound: *peratoun*
in a determinate way: *aphôrismenôs*
in a divided mode: *meristôs*
in a hidden mode: *kruphiôs*
in a superior mode: *kreittonôs*
in a symbolic mode: *sumbolikôs*
in a tetradic mode: *tetradikôs*
in accordance with the rules of mathematics: *mathêmatikôs*
in an extended mode: *diastatôs*
in an opposite sense: *antikeimenôs*
in cooperation with: *sundromos*
in general: *katholou*
in many ways: *pollakhôs*
in sympathy (of the cosmos): *sumpathês*
in the mode of shape, literal-minded: *morphôtikôs*
in the proper sense, properly: *kuriôs*
incalculable, ungraspable: *aperilêptos*
inclination: *rhopê*
incline inwards towards: *sunneuein*
incline: *rhepein*
incommensurable: *asummetros*
incorporeal: *asômatos*
individuals: *ta kath' hekasta*
indivisible: *adiairetos, ameristos, atomos*
indivisibly: *adiairetôs, ameristôs*
infinite in power: *apeirodunamos*
inseparable, immanent: *akhôristos*
inseparable, not proceeding forth: *anekphoitêtos*
insinuate itself: *parempiptein*
inspired: *epoptikos*
insubstantially: *anousiôs*
intellect: *nous*
intellectual, intellective: *noeros*
intelligible: *noêtos*
introduce (surreptitiously): *pareiskuklein*
introduce along with: *suneispherein*

last: *hustatos*

letter (of the alphabet), element: *stoikheion*
life: *zôê*
life-giving: *zôiogonos*
like an image: *eidôlikos*
limit, Limit (as principle): *peras*
limitlessness: *apeiria*
little altar (geometrical figure): *bômiskos*
living being: *zôion*
logical, rational: *logikos*
lord: *krantôr*
love, Friendship (Empedoclean principle): *Philia*
loving controversy: *philapekhthêmôn*
lowest of three strings in the musical scale, but highest in pitch: *nêtê*
luminous: *augoeides*

maintain, champion, preside over: *presbeuein*
making odd: *perittopoios*
man, the concept of: *ho kat'epinoian anthrôpos*
manufactured, product of art/craft: *tekhnêtos*
many times: *pollaplous*
masculine: *arrhenôpos*
material: *hulikos*
maternal (principle): *mêtrikê (arkhê)*
mathematical: *mathêmatikos*
matter: *hulê*
measure, to: *metrein*
measure: *metron*
minor premiss: *proslêpsis*
mixture: *krasis*
model, paradigm: *paradeigma*
moon, (the number) proper to: *selêniakos (arithmos)*
moon: *selênê*
moulting, loss of feathers: *pterorrhuêsis*
mount upon: *epibateuein*
multiplication: *pollaplasiasis, pollaplasiasmos*
multiplicity: *plêthos*
multiply (intrans.): *plêthuein*
multiply (trans.): *plêthunein*

natural, proper to nature: *phusikos*
nature, natural order: *phusis,*
necessary conditions: *aneu (ta hôn ouk aneu)*

nine ways: *enakhôs*
non-combinable (of units): *asumblêtos*
non-extended: *adiastatos*
non-extendedly: *adiastatôs*
non-qualitative: *apoios*
non-quantitative: *aposos*
non-substantial: *anousios*
not-being: *mê on*
note, indicate: *episêmainesthai*
number: *arithmos*
number proper to the sun: *hêliakos*
  (*arithmos*)

object of conjecture: *eikastos*
object of creation: *dêmiourgêma*
object of imagination: *phantasma*
object of science: *epistêtos*
objection: *enstasis*
oblong: *heteromêkês*
odd (of number): *artios, perittos*
odd-even (of number): *artioperittos*
of equal value: *isaxios*
of the same genus: *homogenês*
of the same kind, species: *homoeidês*
of unlike species: *anomoiogenês*
on a secondary level: *deuterôs*
on an intellectual level: *noerôs*
on an intelligible level: *noêtôs*
on the level of imagination, impressionistic: *phantastôs*
on the level of imagination: *phan-
  tastikôs*
on the level of nature: *phusikôs*
one: *heis, to hen*
opinion, belief: *doxa*
order, organise: *diakosmein*
order: *taxis*
order, realm: *diakosmos*
ordering, disposition: *diakosmêsis*
organisation: *diorganôsis*
organise: *diorganoun*
otherness: *heterotês*

paradigmatic: *paradeigmatikos*
paradigmatically, as a model:
  paradeigmatikôs
partake of: participate in *metekhein*
partial, individual: *merikos*
participation: *metalêpsis, methexis*
partless: *amerês*
partlessly: *amerôs*
partlessness: *amereia*
paternal: *patrikos*

per accidens: *kata sumbebêkos*
perceptible: *aisthêtos*
perfection, completeness: *teleiotês*
perfection: *teleiôsis*
perfective: *telesiourgos*
permanent: *monimos*
place: *topos* (*eidôn*)
point: *sêmeion*
polygon: *polugônon*
power, potentiality: *dunamis*
predominance, mastery: *epikrateia*
predominate: *epikratein*
premiss: *protasis*
primally: *prôtôs*
primally efficacious: *prôtourgos*
primarily: *proêgoumenôs*
principle: *arkhê*
prior measure: *prometron*
privation (opp. *eidos*): *sterêsis*
prize of seniority: *presbeion, ta
  presbeia*
proceed: *proienai*
procession: *proodos,*
produce: *paragein*
product: *apotelesma*
product of manufacture: *praktos*
productive, creative: *poiêtikos*
proof: *kataskeuê*
proportion: *analogia*
provide, arrange: *khoregein*
providence: *pronoia*
provider: *khorêgos*
pure, unsullied: *akhrantos*
purpose: *prohairesis*
pythagorise: *puthagorizein*

reality: *ta pragmata*
realm, level (of being): *platos*
receptacle: *hupodokhê*
receptive: *khôrêtikos*
reckoning-board: *abakion*
recollection: *anamnêsis*
reduce to order: *tattesthai*
reflection: *emphasis*
relation: *skhesis*
relative: *pros ti*
resistance, solidity: *antitupia*
resistant, solid: *antitupos*
reversion: *epistrophê*
revert: *epistrephein*
rotting, decay: *sêpsis*
ruling, dominant: *hêgemonikos*

same: *tauton*
sameness: *tautotês*
school (Pythagorean): *didaskaleion*
science: *epistêmê*
science: *mathêma*
secondary: *deuteros*
self-generated: *autogenês, autogonos*
self-generatedly: *autogonôs*
self-revealing: *autophanês*
seminal (*logoi*): *spermatikos*
senior: *presbuteros*
separate, distinguish: *khôrizein*
separate, transcendent: *khôristos*
serious, important: *pragmateiôdês*
setting forth, exposition: *ekthesis*
shadow: *skia*
shape, form: *morphê*
shaping: *morphôma*
similarity: *homoiotês*
simple: *monoeides*
singly, in one way: *monakhôs*
skill (non-technical): *empeiria*
so many times removed (in time or
    space): *pollostos*
specific: *eidikos*
speech, discussion, account, argu-
    ment, ratio, reason-principle: *logos*
speech-related: *lektikos*
sphere (Empedoclean): *sphairos*
sphere (heavenly): *sphaira*
spirit: (*augoeides*) *pneuma*
spontaneous, accidental, the: *automa-
    ton, to*
stable: *statheros*
standard of judgement: *kriterion*
state of being: *hexis*
state, situation: *diathesis*
Strife (Empedoclean principle): *Neikos*
striving, appetition: *ephesis*
structure, organise: *kosmein*
subdivide: *hupodiairein*
subject to death: *epikêros*
subsist in advance: *prohuparkhein*
subsist together with: *sunhuphistanai*
substance, essence, being, substantial-
    ity: *ousia,*
substantial, essential, really existent:
    ousiôdês
substrate, what underlies, object: *hu-
    pokeimenon*
such as to fill: *plêrôtikos*
sun: *hêlios*
superabundance: *periousia*

superior: *kreittôn*
superior classes of being, the: *ta kreit-
    tona genê*
superiority: *huperokhê*
supervene upon: *episumbainein*
sympathy (cosmic): *sumpatheia*
synonymously: *sunônumôs*

take on in advance: *prolambanein*
term, boundary, definition: *horos*
tetradic, proper to four: *tetradikos*
tetraktys (Pythag.): *tetraktus*

there (of the intelligible realm): *ekei*
thing: *pragma*
thingummybob (meaningless word):
    skindapsos
thought (object of): *noêma*
thought: *noêsis*
thought-process, (discursive) reason-
    ing: *dianoêsis*
timelessly: *akhronôs*
totality: *holotês*
transcend: *exairein*
transcending: *exêirêmenos*
transitive, discursive: *metabatikos*
true beings, true reality: *ta ontôs onta*
two, Dyad: *duas*

unceasing: *anekleiptos*
unconnected, non-co-ordinate: *asun-
    taktos*
underlie: *hupokeisthai*
understand, comprehend: *para-
    kolouthein*
undifferentiated: *adiaphoros*
ungenerated: *agenêtos*
ungeneratedly: *agenêtôs*
unification, unity: *henôsis*
unify: *henoun*
union, unifying principle: *sunokhê*
unit, Monad (as principle): *monas*
unitary (number): *monadikos (arith-
    mos)*
unitedly: *hênômenôs*
unity: *henotês, to hen*
universe, the: *to pan*
univocal, synonymous: *sunônumos*
unmoved: *aklinês, akinêtos*
unorganised: *akosmêtos*

variegation: *poikilia*

vehicle, luminous (of the soul): *ok-hêma* (*augoeides*)
vital, life-giving: *zôtikos*

weightless: *abarês*
well-known: *sunegnôsmenos*
what pertains to: *ta huparkhonta*
whole: *holos*

within the cosmos, encosmic: *perikos-mios*
without bulk: *amegethês*
womb: *kolpos*
worship: *sebein*

zodiac: *zôidiakos* (*kuklos*)

Greek-English Index

This index lists a selection of the more important words, either from a philosophical or philological perspective, occurring in the Greek text. The translations given here may not always correspond to the rendering of them in a particular passage in the English text, since the demands of idiomatic translation may call for variations; but it should always be possible to work out what word is being translated.

abakion, reckoning-board, 91,35; 92,27

abarês, weightless, 176,6.16

adiairetos, indivisible, 99,24ff.; 124,4; 128,2; 132,28; 133,3; 143,11ff.; 151,15; 152,32; 157,34

adiairetôs, indivisibly, 85,17.21

adiaphoros, undifferentiated, 124,26; 125,10.14; 126,10; 131,10; 134,15; 135,17ff.; 138,2; 140,25; 156,25; 194,23

adiastatos, non-extended, 87,31; 93,2; 178,22

adiastatôs, non-extendedly, 123,28

aeigenesia, eternal generation, 163,23

agathoeidês, good-like, 183,28.31; 185,26

agathon, t', the Good, 90,29; 112,14; 137,11; 182,4.22; 183,1ff.; 185,23; 189,22

agathotês, goodness, 82,10; 107,1

agenêtos, ungenerated, 133,22; 145,31

agenêtôs, ungeneratedly, 146,1

aiônios, eternal, 142,24

aiôniôs, eternally, 166,22

aisthêtos, perceptible, (opp. *noêtos*) 82,1; (opp. *khôristos*) 118,23 ; *to aisthêton*, 92,1ff.; 171,16; *ta aisthêta*, 88,36; 89,1; 93,23ff.; 101,24; 129,12; 136,37; 142,5; 145,21; 171,3

aitia, cause, 106,33; 117,11; 133,26; 162,12; *aitia pro aitias*, 'cause prior to cause', 166,4

aition, cause, 82,4.11; 116,20; 117,28; 118,25; 188,28

akhôristos, inseparable, immanent, 83,5.18; 84,11; 97.20; 104,34; 119,33; 121,26ff.; 142,5.28; 143,24; 155,29ff.; 160,32ff.; 178,8

akhrantos, pure, unsullied, 106,24; 121,30; 142,13; 143,19; 169,5; 171,32

akhronôs, timelessly, 133,15

akinêtos, unmoved, 81,16

aklinês, unmoved, 84,34; 123,5; 169,5

akosmêtos, unorganised, 133,18; 134,19

amegethês, without bulk, 178,6.16

amereia, partlessness, 120,6

amerês, partless, without parts, 119,5.19; 122,21; 184,4

amerôs, partlessly, 156,5

ameristos, without division, indivisible, 128,1; 136,28; 163,13; 164,32; 178,22; (opp. *meristos*) 115,21

ameristôs, indivisibly, 107,6; 109,22

analogia, proportion, 150,4

anamnêsis, recollection, 82,25.26; 83,8; 102,10; 106,3; 161,1; 179,30

aneideos, formless, 120,25; 132,13.18.24; 134,19; 135,6; 144,29; 146,20; 153,3; 158,10; (opp. *eidêtikos*) 133,20

anekleiptos, unceasing, 120,31; 132,19

anekphoitêtos, inseparable, not proceeding forth, 109,25

didaskaleion, (Pythagorean) school, 151,6; 183,3; 192,19

diexodikos, expository, 103,4; 179,31

diexodos, exposition, 80,13; 115,22

diorganôsis, organisation, 186,12

diorganoun, organise, 190,31

diôrismenos, distinct, 81,37; 176,19

dokis, 'beam' (geometrical figure), 155,7

doxa, opinion, belief, 111,4; 161,27

drastêrios, efficacious, 186,33; 189,23

drastêriôs, efficiaciously, 82,31

drastikos, active, effective, 178,13

drastikôs, effectively, 156,5

duas, two, 132,10; 145,16; 170,19; 181,22.24; 182,23; (*aoristos*) Dyad (as principle) 112,16.35; 121,32; 125,26; 129,24.34; 130,15.16; 131,28; 132,19.27; 134,35; 137,29; 139,31; 144,4ff.; 154,6; 155,1; 157,3; 160,19; 166,18; 167,17; 174,8.12; 175,3; 180,17

dunamis, power, potentiality, (*phusikê*) 143,10; (*dunamei*, potentially) 99,22; 139,5; 146,20; 152,3.11; 163,28; (*to dunamei*) 99,32; 175,20; 185,34

duoeidês, dyadic, 113,13.24; 173,14

duopoios, productive of duality, duplicative, 130,3; 131,31; 134,2; 145,16; 158,8

dusantibleptos, difficult to face, 178,30

dusepinoêtos, difficult to understand, 160,24

dusphôratos, difficult to fathom, 151,22

eidêtikos, eidetic, Form-(number), (*arithmos*) 81,21; 103,15; 113,33; 122,13; 123,13ff.; 126,31ff.; 129,15ff.; 134,4; 140,26; 141,4ff.24; 145,8; 153,32; 159,8ff.; 167,18; 186,31; (*aitia*) 104,1; 110,21; 112,20; 133,25; 150,12

eidikos, specific, 95,10.11; 107,5; (opp. *genikos*) 167,15; (*diaphora*) 148,27

eidopoiein, bestow form on, enform, 132,22.24; 133,10.19; 134,32; 150,16; 152,11; 157,22

eidopoiia, bestowal of form, construction, 86,1

eidopoios, form-creating, enforming, 132,27; 157,5; 158,26

eidos, form, species, 82,26; 85,10; 87,16.19; 96,26; 105,16; 119,14.28; 120,4.12; 121,22; 133,21.29; 134,24; 136,15; 139,2; 142,18; 147,12; 157,26; 161,3; 171,23; (*eidos eidôn*, 'Form of Forms', of the Monad), 140,8; 149,18; (*hoi tôn eidôn philoi*, 'the friends of the Forms') 83,34; 105,16; 120,18

eidôlikos, like an image, 101,24

eidôlon, image, 88,36; 89,16; 129,13; 160,28

eikastos, object of conjecture, 101,3

eikôn, image, 116,29; 119,26.31; 143,6; 147,5; 162,4.11; 163,30; 176,19; 180,6; 188,2; 193,25

ekei, 'there' (of the intelligible realm), 118,25; 119,30; 145,30; 173,34

ekkeisthai (*ekkeimena*, topic or words to be discussed, presentation), 147,10; 176,23

ekstasis, displacement, 'disruptive force', 174,14

ektasis, extension, 142,15

ekthesis, 'setting forth', exposition, 162,2

ellampein, illuminate, 85,27

ellampsis, illumination, 107,14

elleipsis, falling short, inferiority, 155,21

empeiria (dist. from *tekhnê*), (nontechnical) skill, 164,26

emphasis, reflection, 119,14

enakhôs, nine ways, 171,4

enantiôsis, contrariety, 144,8

enargeia, evidence, 165,17

energeia, activity, actuality, 99,32; 142,15; (*energeiâi*, in actuality) 99,22ff.; 120,4; 139,2; 146,20; 148,13; 152,4; 163,28; 175,18

energos, active, actualised, 190,16

ennoêma, concept, 105,28

ennoêtikos, conceptual, 105,30

ennoia, conception, 90,9.22.38; 96,10; 101,23

enstasis, objection, 99,17; 130,6; 161,35

enulos, enmattered, 84,30; 85,18.29; 93,8.17; 98,35; 99,20; 117,9; 136,27; 177,5; 181,22; 184,27; 187,6; (*enulon eidos*, form in matter) 80,10;

92,16; 105,31; 119,33; 120,24; 175,35; 186,19

ephesis, striving, appetition, 117,33; 118,12

ephistanai, deliberate, give attention to, 84,30; 86,9; 129,1; 169,33; 175,16; 176,6; 195,13

epiballein, apprehend, focus on, 110,5.31; 187,18; 193,18

epiballôn, appropriate, 189,32

epibateuein, mount upon, 187,11

epibolê, apprehension, focus, intuitive grasp, 81,1; 90,29; 103,9; 109,28; 130,32; 180,7

epidiorthôsis, correction, 167,7

epidiorthousthai, correct, 167,11

epikêros, subject to death, 187,17

epikheirêma, dialectical, non-syllogistic proof/argument, 89,30; 92,13; 95,7; 135,14; 147,2; 170,19; 171,20; 178,30

epikheirêmatikos (*logos*), argument proper to such a proof, 121,5

epikheirêsis, dialectical proof, 159,31; 169,28

epikrateia, predominance, mastery, 122,8.33; 137,13; 188,7; 191,3.4; 192,10; 194,15

epikratein, predominate, 187,27

epilampein, illuminate, 168,4; 169,5

epinoia, concept, 107,7; (*ho kat'epi-noian anthrôpos*, the concept of man) 161,26

episêmainesthai, note, indicate, 138,32; 147,27; 153,33

epistasis, doubt, objection, 170,9; 175,32; 183,7

epistêmê, science, 163,1.2; 164,4.7.31

epistêtos, object of science, 102,3

epistrephein, revert, 82,8; 106,28; 108,4; 115,3; 130,4

epistrophê, reversion, 127,9.10

episumbainein, supervene upon, 112,32; 118,30.37

epoptikos, inspired, 81,11

exangeltikos, expressive of, 164,2

exairein, transcend, 107,26; 115,21; 168,19; 182,7; 184,10

exêirêmenos, transcending, 80,11; 84,35; 104,35; 106,9; 108,17; 114,31; 117,11; 119,20; 124,12; 134,31; 141,4; 163,10; 166,3

exhomoioun, assimilate, 82,9.14; 134,24

exhorizein, exclude, 184,18

exhumnein, celebrate, 173,30

gelastikos, capable of laughter (of man), 131,21; 161,18

genesis, coming-to-be, 83,8; 92,23; 105,13.33; 120,2; 145,10; 169,27; 172,28; 185,31; 187,13; 188,31; (*en genesei*) 169,27

genêtos, generated, subject to generation, *passim*; (*theion genêton*, generated divinity, of the heavens) 190,29; 192,9 (*genêtos topos*, opp. *aithêr*) 109,19

genikos, generic (opp. *eidikos*), 106,7; 152,26; 167,12.14; 199,23

gennêtikos, generative, 108,3; 110,19; 116,8; 127,30; 157,22; 158,20.29; 184,27.28

genos, genus (opp. *eidos*) 132,30; (*genê tou ontos*, genera of being) 81,36; 137,23; 171,25; 175,2; 184,25; (*deka genê*) 170,34ff.

gonimos, generative, 82,7; (*dunamis*, power) 112,35; 131,29; 166,21; 171,36; 187,8

hêgemonikos, ruling, dominant, 141,3

hêgoumenon, (log.) antecedent, 90,3; 125,2; 126,7; 141,18; 177,30

heis, one: *to hen*, the one, unity, 108, 20; 121,32; 124,14; 125,25; 140,34; 141,8; 144,4; 160,18; 166,1; 167,9; 174,18; 182,4.6.22; 183,3; (diff. from *monas*) 151,18; (*hen plêthos*) 140,10; (*hen polla*) 185,27

hekastos, each (individually): *ta kath' hekasta*, individuals, 104,17; 136,7; 164,5.12; 170,7; 177,33

hêliakos (*arithmos*), (number) proper to the sun, 190,25

hêlios, sun, 186,7; 193,21; 194,3

henôsis, unification, unity, 87,16; 92,15; 103,26; 137,12; 141,13; 144,17; 156,20; 168,2; 169,4; 171,14; 183,4; 187,24

henoun, unify, 82,4; 90,30; 100,31; 109,25; 119,27; 134,12; 144,16; 153,18 *hênômenôs*, unitedly, in a mode of unity, 87,13

henotês, unity, 183,11

heptas, heptad, seven, 191,14; (as *kairos*, 'opportunity, critical moment') 104,26; 130,33

heteromêkês, oblong, 145,17; 155,8

heterotês, otherness, 81,36; 122,4.7.8; 147,32; 171,2ff.; 175,2

hexas, hexad, six, (as number of marriage) 104,27; (as number of soul) 130,34

hexis, state of being, 113,18; 133,24; 141,32

hidruein, establish, 106,31; 142,17; 187,10

holos, whole (*ta hola*) 82,12; 140,35; 141,10; 183,26; 185,29

holotês, totality, 193,8

homogenês, of the same genus, 168,7.15

homoeidês, of the same kind, species, 136,7; 155,30; 168,14; 190,31

homoiomerê, (Anaxagorean) homoiomeries, 75,3; 117,3

homoiotês, similarity, (*anomoios*, dissimilar) 153,6

homônumia, homonymy, 151,10; 153,5; 159,7; 177,35

homônumos, homonymous, 108,26.28; 134,33

homônumôs, homonymously, 112,2.32; 115,6

horismos, definition, 80,10; 163,2

horizein, define, 142,12; 149,18; 179,9; (*hôrismenos*, defined) 104,11; 163,32; (**horizôn**, horizon) 82,32

horos, term, boundary, definition, (term, boundary) 84,36; 87,25; 101,7ff.; 102,32; 107,10; 115,35; 187,30; (definition) 126,5

hulê, matter, 90,15; 98,26.29; 120,8; 133,13; 139,10; 143,22; 144,21; 156,3.5; 157,2ff.; 160,28; 161,7; 186,19; (opp. *eidos*) 132,8; 133,4.29; 145,14; 172,2; 178,18; 181,12.27; (comb. with *sterêsis*) 117,8; (comb. with *genesis*) 105,34; (comb. with *ta aisthêta*) 129,13; (*mathêmatikê*) 186,32

hulikos, material, 107,11; 163,11; 172,6; 185,2; (*aitia*) 108,16; (*ai-*

tion) 120,9; 145,11; 166,16; 174,5; 175,31; (*arkhê*) 165,1; (*diairesis*) 128,3; (*monas*) 152,14; 156,24; 157,30.31; 183,21; (*stoikheion*) 169,34.36

hulopoios, creative of matter, 156,26.28

huparxis, existence, 82,2; 84,1; 108,33; 131,7; 141,12

huparkhonta, ta, what pertains to, 97,18.29; 161,15; 166,20; 190,21

hupatê, highest of the three strings on the musical scale, but the lowest in pitch, 194,22

huperekhein, exceed, 167,11

huperhêplôsthai, exceed in simplicity, 168,6

huperousios, above substance, 112,15; 118,21; 140,35; 141,4; 165,33; 166,11; 169,4.26; 183,4

huperokhê, superiority, 108,22; 123,11; 156,7; 167,5.26; 168,6; (opp. *elleipsis*) 155,21

huperphuês, above nature, supernatural, 135,10; 166,9

huperphuôs, exceedingly, 80,7

hupodiairein, subdivide, 121,3; 142,4

hupodokhê, receptacle, 84,36; 101,16; 150,4

hupokeisthai, underlie, 101,35; (*hupokeimenon*, substrate, what underlies, object) 86,27; 93,4.6; 94,23; 95,12; 97,31; 98,23; 99,8.9.24; 114,16; 119,33; 128,22; 133,6.29; 134,9; 139,6.8; 145,11; 151,7.24; 157,8; 158,1; 165,26ff.; 167,2; 168,9; 171,28; 174,29; 176,10; 187,3; 188,7

hupostasis, existence, 81,19.26; 84,13

hupostatês, generator, 141,31

hupostatikos, generative, 129,13; 150,2; 157,3; 165,10

huptios (*ex huptias*, back to front), 175,25

hustatos, last, 153,4

husterogenês, coming after, 'later-born', 82,27; 91,21; 92,9; 101,2; 106,11; 107,29; 110,12.19; 136,37; 161,25; 163,7; 177,16; 194,1

huphêgêtikos, expository, 192,28

huphesis, deficiency (opp. *huperokhê*), 81,35; 129,11

huphienai, be deficient, fall short,

131,32; (*hupheimenos*, deficient) 166,2; 170,24

idea, Form (Platonic), 83,37; 90,1; 96,26; 103,15ff.; 107,7ff.; 119,9.34; 143,7; 179,17.29; 180,8

idiazein, be distinctive, 102,30; 173,3

idiôma, characteristic, peculiarity, 103,22; 153,15; 155,11

idiotês, distinctive property, 82,2; 97,27; 98,7; 117,17; 145,31

indalma, image, 144,30; 158,9.11.26; 174,11

isaxios, of equal value, 129,4; 179,2

isotakhôs, at equal speed, 95,19

katalêpsis, comprehension, 178,32.33

kataskeuê, proof, 103,8; 165,2; 191,13

katêgorikos, categorical (of syllogism), 126,3

katholikos, general, 90,5.28; 100,32; 161,24

katholou, in general, 90,14; 136,4; (*hoi katholou logoi*) 82,27; 88,26.31; 89,31; 97,4; 105,37; (*to katholou*) 92,6; 95,9; 96,11; 97,14; 98,35; 151,14; (opp. *aisthêta*) 91,17; 99,3.4; 104,34; 107,7; 110,10; 156,4; 160,25; 161,5ff.; 177,32

khoregein, provide, arrange, 118,2; 119,7; 141,13; 171,29

khorêgos, provider, 90,39; 118,4.12.26

khôrêtikos, receptive, 85,10

khôrizein, separate, distinguish, 138,13; 154,23; 160,31; 177,28

khôristos, separate, transcendent, 84,2; 89,35; 90,4; 97,19; 99,21; 120,28; 155,26; 160,33; (*aitia*) 99,9; (*aition*) 153,21; (*arithmos*) 89,36; 98,24; 99,18; 121,16; 132,1; 141,17; 142,11; 159,22; 185,18; (*eidos*) 83,6; 103,18; 105,7; 111,23; 116,1; 117,28; 118,10.16.21; 177,14; (*ousia*) 81,18; 83,29

koinotês, common characteristic, commonality, 95,17; 99,13; 105,39

kolpos, 'womb' (Chaldaean term – *kolpoi tês dianoias*), 81,32

kosmein, structure, organise, 109,23; 133,18.24; 134,20; 152,7.10; 178,28; 181,30.32; 187,14; 190,17; 193,16

kosmopoiein, create a cosmos, 187,21

kosmopoiia, creation of a cosmos, 142,22

kosmourgos, creator (of a cosmos), 123,8; 142,23

krantôr (Pythagorean term), 'lord', 123,2

krasis, mixture, 144,14; 157,24

krateisthai, be dominated, controlled by (e.g. *logoi*), 139,8; 153,36; 155,10; 174,31; 179,2; 181,28

kratêtikos, dominant, controlling, 190,6

kratisteuein, be superior, prevail, 123,4.6; 142,25; 161,34

kreittôn, superior, 140,1; 159,11; (*ta kreittona genê*, the superior classes of being, sc. daemons and heroes) 97,26

kreittonôs, in a superior mode, 97,9; 109,25

kriterion, standard of judgement, 102,3

kruphios, 'hidden' (Chaldaean term for *noêtos*), 126,22; 182,24

kruphiôs, in a hidden mode, 147,31

kuriôdês, dominant, 168,22

kuriôs, in the proper sense, properly, 174,24; 188,31

lektikos, speech-related (*lektikê phantasia*), 163,21

lêmma, statement, assumption, 170,10.12

logikos, logical, rational, 89,13; 180,24

logikôterôs, from a more logical point of view, 81,12

logos, speech, discussion, account, argument, ratio, reason-principle, 83,10; 85,4; 88,35; 97,2; 143,12; 155,30; 163,12.27; 168,11; 187,35; 188,20; (opp. *hupokeimenon*) 167,2.4; 175,34; (*logoi tês phuseôs*) 82,28; 107,30; 116,18; 119,13; 154,25; 165,8; 173,18; 181,13; (*phusikoi logoi*) 124,12; 149,6; 181,16; (*logoi tês psukhês*) 83,18; 90,5; 95,16; 101,19; 113,7; 123,24; 160,27; (*aüloi*) 134,11; (*spermatikoi*) 97,23; 142,16

mathêma, science, 81,17; 83,37; 100,16

Index of Concordances with
Ps.-Alexander
(Michael of Ephesus)

References are to page and line numbers of Kroll's edition. Only the most substantial of these have been indicated in the notes, but a full record is helpful in appreciating the extent to which Syrianus is dependent on the real Alexander for the 'non-controversial' aspects of his commentary (for which we are much indebted to the most useful compilation of Concetta Luna, *Trois études sur la traduction des commentaires anciennes à la* Métaphysique *d'Aristote*, Leiden: Brill, 2001, Appendice 1, pp. 191-2).

Book 13 (M)

Syrianus	Ps.-Alexander	Syrianus	Ps.-Alexander
83,37-9	722,9-13	127,4-6	750,19-22
84,13-14	724,11-12	127,19-25	750,27-34
86,12-14	725,20-3	128,11-18	752,5-14
86,18	725,26	128,27-30	752,17-23
86,20-1	726,4-5	129,15-25	752,33-753,8
86,23-4	726,11-13	129,32-130,6	753,9-17
89,30-6	729,21-7	130,8-20	753,21-754,1
90,2	729,30-1	133,31-4	758,3-7
92,12-20	731,2-12	138,6-8	761,19-23
92,30-1	731,36-7	138,11-14	761,32-6
93,1	732,14-15	138,14-19	762,3-11
93,22-4	732,19-26	138,24-30	762,17-763,3
94,31-4	734,5-8	141,7-9	765,34-6
95,2-4	734,19-21	141,17-18	765,31-2
95,19-22	734,36-735,3	141,22-6	766,4-8
97,21-4	737,7-10	142,6-7	766,28-9
99,17-31	738,24-739,12	143,6-10	767,11-13
100,15-24	739,21-740,1	144,5-19	767,33-768,26
103,15-18	740,14-18	145,4-6	768,28-34
115,11-18	742,11-24	145,20	768,37
121,7-8	743,6-7	146,25-8	769,22-770,1
121,11-13	743,13-17	149,15-16	771,12-14
122,13-15	745,23-8	149,25-33	771,15-36
122,18-19	745,31-5	150,7-9	772,10-13
123,17-19	746,13-15	150,14-15	772,18-20
125,9-27	748,8-22	150,28-32	772,22-8
126,32-4	749,3-6	151,26	774,21-2
127,3-4	750,4-5	152,2-12	774,37-775,10

Syrianus	Ps.-Alexander	Syrianus	Ps.-Alexander
152,18-21	775,28-776. 6	155,15-17	778,16-18
152,30-153,1	776,11-17	156,28-32	779,29-34
153,29-32	776,32-777,3	158,14-16	781,20-3
154,5-13	777,11-21	160,15-16	785,12-13
154,17-20	777,23-33	162,2	786,33
154,32-155,4	778,8-14		

Book 14 (N)

Syrianus	Ps.-Alexander	Syrianus	Ps.-Alexander
167,9-11	797,24-8	185,6-14	823,28-824,2
172,13-14	806,22-3	185,29-36	824,12-24
172,31-2	807,20-6	186,36	824,36
172,33-4	808,11-12	187,31-2	826,35-6
175,33-4	812,1-2	188,15-18	828,7-9
176,6-7.10-11	812,22-4	189,8-9	829,8-9
176,16-17	812,28-9	189,34-190,2	830,26-37
179,5-6	815,5-9	190,8-10	831,14-16
179,12-15	815,21-6	191,13-19	832,16-27
179,16-17	816,25-6	191,25	833,40-1
180,16-17	817,34-6	191,29-35	834,5-11
180,32-181,2	818,22-3	191,31-4	834,13-14
182,9-21	821,11-20	193,5-8	835,2-6
183,2	821,34	193,13-15	835,11-14
183,17	822,28	193,32-4	835,35-836,1
183,31-184,1	823,4-12	194,17-27	836,22-33
184,32-185,2	823,14-26		

Index of Aristotelian and Platonic Passages

References, in bold type, are to the page and line numbers of Kroll's edition, which appear in the margins of the Translation.

Subject Index

This index consists primarily of proper names mentioned in the introduction and text. Most major items of philosophical or philological interest are in fact covered in the Greek-English Index, but a few topics have been included here.